The Battle of
HASTINGS

JIM BRADBURY

To my mother, Sarah Helena Bradbury née Joel
in her ninety-first year
and to all the many friends met and made
at Pyke House, Battle

This book was first published in 1998 by
Sutton Publishing Limited · Phoenix Mill
Thrupp · Stroud · Gloucestershire · GL5 2BU

This new paperback edition first published in 2005

British Library Cataloguing in Publication Data
A catalogue record for this book is available from the British
Library.

ISBN 0 7509 3794 7

Typeset in 10.5/12pt Photina.
Typesetting and origination by
Sutton Publishing Limited.
Printed and bound in Great Britain by
J.H. Haynes & Co. Ltd, Sparkford.

Contents

Preface   v

1   Anglo-Saxon England: Alfred to the Confessor   1

2   The Reign of Edward the Confessor   20

3   Normandy before 1066   32

4   Arms and Armies   60

5   The Year 1066   88

6   The Sources for the Battle   110

7   The Battle   121

8   Afterwards   155

Notes   182

Bibliography   203

Index   209

PREFACE

Writing a book on the battle of Hastings for a medieval historian is a bit like reviewing one's life. Among the souvenirs of the past, our home is decorated with such things as Bayeux Tapestry curtains and a Bayeux Tapestry cover on a dressing table. My wife Ann and I have spent many holidays in Normandy, from Bayeux and Rouen to Caen, Falaise, Fécamp, Alençon . . . the Conqueror's footprints tread a wide path.

The project provides an opportunity to thank all those who have contributed to one's education and interests. These are many and various. They include my father who had an interest in history which probably stirred my earliest curiosity. At secondary school my interest in medieval history was first seriously sparked by Mr R.A. Dare, whom I can see now with his eyes closed and arms waving, carried away by some event from that era. At university I received much help and inspiration from Charles Duggan, who was my tutor, and Gerald Hodgett, who also taught me.

Interest turned to something more on the MA course I took as a mature student, married and with children, in London. The tutors on this course I viewed rather as friends, and their assistance was patient and changed my life. They were Christopher Holdsworth, Julian Brown, and above all Allen Brown, who went on to supervise my unfinished MPhil and PhD research. I recall an essay I wrote for Allen Brown in the early days of that course, on the battle of Hastings. I chose to praise the qualities of Harold rather than those of William as a general, for which temerity I suffered a certain amount of criticism.

Allen's help is almost impossible to record, it was so varied, from teaching to advice and especially the various social occasions he supervised. I remember in particular the many evenings spent at the pub, the Marquess of Anglesey, where most – I think all – of my supervisions took place. There I gained much from the friendship of other medievalists, including such lifelong friends as Nick Hooper, Matt Bennett, Chris Harper-Bill and Richard Mortimer. No doubt the scene helps to explain the failure to complete the project (on warfare in Stephen's reign) on which I spent eight years of part-time research, though I think in the end it was not entirely without profit.

Hastings inevitably takes one to Battle. It is impossible in one book to acknowledge all the information, help, discussion, encouragement received there. Battle means Pyke House and the Anglo-Norman Studies conference, and here another debt to Allen Brown, who initiated the conference with help from Gillian Murton and who kept it going through the rest of his life. The friends made and met at Pyke House are myriad. It was the most congenial of all meeting places, thanks to the ministrations of, among others, old Hobby and, more particularly, Peter Birch and his aides, including especially that gourmet's delight, the catering head for many years, Yvonne Harris.

I have been to Pyke House times beyond counting: for the annual conference, to teach East Sussex County Council weekend courses, and to take student groups during the twenty odd years I taught at Borough Road and West London Institute. At the conferences one met virtually every historian who mattered for the Anglo-Norman period, including friends from Holland, Japan, France, Germany and the States. Outstanding among these was Warren Hollister, whose work on warfare I much admired before I met him, and who became a long-standing friend with his wife and companion at Battle, Edith.

Perhaps the first course I participated in at Pyke House was one on medieval warfare in general, which Allen organised. One of the speakers was the great later medievalist whose life came to a tragic end, Charles Ross. Allen always believed in a good lunch-time session in the pub, and as a result a number of speakers and members of the audience were rather drowsy during the afternoon sessions, not least himself. One afternoon Charles Ross was lecturing and noticed that Allen was gently snoozing in the front row. When it came to question time, a difficult point was put to him and, with malicious glee, he retorted, 'ALLEN! [waking him up] what do you think about that?'

The lectures at the main conferences were most valuable and

are of course recorded in the *Anglo-Norman Studies* journal, commencing in 1978 and continuing after Allen's death under the editorships of Marjorie Chibnall and Chris Harper-Bill. But even more valuable, to my mind, have been the social occasions: the sherry parties at the abbey and above all the drinking sessions in The Chequers, the pub next door. Who could forget in that hostelry seeing Allen Brown and Raymonde Foreville replaying the battle of Hastings on the bar billiards table, or Cecily Clark selecting her horses for the day? Numerous interesting day-trips were organised during the conferences, and these too hold many happy memories.

Pyke House was also the venue for various student trips. The attraction, of course, was in the first place its position on 'the battlefield' of Hastings, the back garden being the best surviving slope of the hill. Here I spent many enjoyable weekends, often with students from other institutions, sharing the lecturing with friends such as Ann Williams, Chris Harper-Bill and Brian Golding, of what were then North London Poly and Strawberry Hill, and what is still Southampton University. My companion from West London on these trips was often Nick Kingwell, who would generously submerge his fifteenth-century interests to participate in these eleventh-century celebrations.

A memory that slips unbidden into one's mind is of waking in one of the pleasant bedrooms at Pyke House to open the curtains and watch the sun rising over 'the battlefield', of quietly going out to tramp through the dewy grass. I have always been an early riser and liked to walk into Battle to buy a *Guardian*, an *Observer*, or latterly the *Independent*. On many an early morning I would pass others out for their early morning constitutional, most memorably Brian Golding, the fanatical bar billiards player, whose pace at walking was twice that of any other person I have known. I accompanied him on an hour's walk one morning, but only once. On other occasions one remembers Ann Williams' or Christine Mahany's dogs diving into the muddy pools at the foot of the hill.

A lasting memory of Battle and Pyke House is of my friend Ian Peirce. Ian seems to have been at almost all these events: conferences, student weekends, East Sussex weekends. Sometimes indeed I shared with him the teaching of a course on the Norman Conquest. But always, usually without any recompense beyond a drink in The Chequers, Ian would perform for an audience, bringing his collection of medieval weapons, his own constructions of weapons and armour and his expertise on the subject for the benefit of all and sundry. Many, like myself, must have gained from the experience of being dressed as a Norman warrior, and I have embarrassing photos to prove it in many cases, from Simon Keynes and Marjorie Chibnall to Dominica Legge, who had to be rescued as she tottered down the hill under the weight of the armour.

In short, this for me is a book of many memories, nearly all pleasant. I should like also to thank all those involved at Sutton Publishing, at whose suggestion this book was written, in particular Roger Thorp and Jane Crompton, and for their patience and care in seeing it through; and Clare Bishop for all her hard work in editing and assembling in the final stages. For all the many other friends at Battle and elsewhere whose names I have failed to recall or mention, thanks too, and may we raise another glass in The Chequers one day soon.

Jim Bradbury
Selsey 1997

ONE

ANGLO-SAXON ENGLAND:
ALFRED TO THE CONFESSOR

DEVELOPMENT OF THE KINGDOM

In April 1066 Halley's comet crossed the English heavens. It appeared in the north-west and was visible for a week or two. Many commentators noticed it, and it is represented pictorially in the Bayeux Tapestry, with a tail looking somewhat like a garden rake, 'the long-haired star' according to one who saw it, wondered at in the Tapestry by a group of pointing men. Recently we have been able to watch a comet (Hale-Bopp) crossing the night sky in a similar manner, and have perhaps experienced something of the wonder felt by men in 1066, though Halley's comet appears more regularly than Hale-Bopp, about every seventy-five years. Halley's comet appeared last in 1985–6, but its position in 1066 would have made it a good deal brighter, rather as Hale-Bopp looked in 1997. The slightly blurry object of Hale-Bopp, moving a little in the sky each night and plainly distinct from all the stars, will not appear again in our lifetime. It reminds one of the smallness of man and the shortness of life.

In 1066 most commentators in England felt that the appearance of the comet presaged change and perhaps evil. One chronicler, writing a little later, said that 'learned astrologers who investigate the secrets of science declared that this meant change in the kingdom'. A poet thought that it 'announced to the English fated destruction'. William of Poitiers addressed the dead Harold Godwinson: this comet was 'the presage of your ruin'.[1] Their minds were moulded by a recent history which had seen raids and conquest, changes of dynasty, disorder and instability. No wonder they were resigned to expecting further change, and pessimistic about its nature.[2]

By 1066 it is true that England was one of the most developed political units in western Europe, in an age when the West itself was beginning to flex its muscles with regard to the wider world. The boundaries with neighbouring countries were not quite as they are now but, nevertheless, England was a geographical entity which we can recognise. By 1066 the kings of England had begun to establish some domination over the Scots and the Welsh, though it was far from complete or certain to survive. Scotland was itself developing as a kingdom, and the relationship with England was one of acknowledgement of power but nothing close to English conquest and control. Wales seemed more vulnerable, lacking the political unity which was emerging in Scotland. Ireland had escaped any contact as direct as that in Scotland and Wales so far. However, Scandinavian settlements in Ireland, and raids from there against England, were a constant reminder of the dangers of hostile elements in such a nearby island.

Across the Channel the political units also had a face which is familiar, but with a structure unlike that of the later nation states. The French kingdom, formed from the western section of the old Carolingian Empire, was finding its feet. But the Capetian kings were struggling to maintain power within their own demesne lands, mostly around Paris.

Royal power was not unrecognised in the counties and duchies which we consider to be French, but those principalities were not far from being independent, the dukes and counts often having almost royal power. This was true of the duchy of Normandy, geographically bound to have connections with England. It was also true of the county of Flanders. Flanders was less tightly linked to France than was Normandy, though there were connections. Placed as it was on the borders of France and the German Empire, Flanders looked in both directions. In the eleventh century Flanders seemed potentially greater than Normandy, not least because of its rapidly growing towns. Flanders, like Normandy, was geographically near to England,

and even more than Normandy had economic links with England through the growth of the Flemish cloth industry, which was already in evidence.

The English kings had been more successful by the eleventh century than their Capetian counterparts in establishing authority over the great magnates in the provinces. In the case of England, this meant over the former kingdoms of Northumbria, East Anglia and Mercia. Historically, since the royal dynasty had come from the former kingdom of Wessex, which had in earlier centuries established authority over much of the south, the kings could usually rely on holding that area safely, but the hold over the northern areas was less certain.

The Wessex kings had faced invasion from without as well as opposition from within. The success of Alfred the Great had been only partial, and Scandinavian settlement often provided a fifth column of support for any Scandinavian-based invader. Such invasions brought periods of severe instability. Ironically, although in many ways England was better unified and economically stronger by the eleventh century than it had been, it was also less politically stable.

These two threads, of economic and political advance on the one hand, and invasion and instability on the other, are our main themes in this chapter. The political instability encouraged hopes of success by invaders, while the economic success provided wealth, which gave a motive for making the attempt. The history of England from the ninth century onwards is marked by periods of crisis.

The most consistent cause for this was the threat from Scandinavia. The earliest Viking raids had been mainly by the Norse, but through the ninth century the chief danger came from the Danes. The Scandinavian threat was at the same time the spur towards unity and the threat of destruction to the kingdom of England. From the middle of the ninth century the scale of the raids increased, so that large fleets of several hundred ships came, carrying invaders rather than raiders.

In the ten years from 865, East Anglia, Northumbria and half of Mercia had been overrun. The Vikings attacked and conquered the great northern and midland kingdoms – Northumbria, with its proud past achievements, and Mercia, which under Offa had dominated English affairs through much of the ninth century. As earldoms, these regions would have a continued importance, but after the Danish conquest they would never again be entirely independent and autonomous powers.

The Scandinavian invasion was also a threat to Christianity, by now well established in England. When the Viking attacks began the raiders were pagan and the wealth of the churches and monasteries became a lucrative target. Even by 1012 the Vikings could seize and kill Aelfheah, the Archbishop of Canterbury, when he refused to be ransomed: 'they pelted him with bones, and with ox heads, and one of them struck him on the head with the back of an axe so that he sank down with the blow and his holy blood fell on the ground'.[3] It does not suggest much respect for organised Christianity. Sweyn Forkbeard and Cnut were committed Christians, but many of their followers were still pagan. One notes that in the 1050s an Irish Viking leader made a gift of a 10-foot-high gold cross to Trondheim Church, but it was made from the proceeds looted during raids into Wales.

The Viking conquest pushed the separate kingdoms and regions of the English into a greater degree of mutual alliance. History, race and religion gave a sense of common alienation from these attackers: 'all the Angles and Saxons – those who had formerly been scattered everywhere and were not in captivity to the vikings – turned willingly to King Alfred, and submitted themselves to his lordship'.[4] So the Viking threat played a major role in bringing the unified kingdom of England into being.

The reign of Alfred the Great (871–99) was of fundamental importance in the unification process. After a century of Viking raids, the English kingdoms crumbled before the powerful Scandinavian thrust of the later ninth century. Alfred could not have expected his rise to kingship: he was the last of four sons of Aethelwulf to come to the throne. Though severely pressed, Alfred saved Wessex in a series of battles which culminated in the victory at Edington and the peace treaty at Wedmore.

Wessex was the only surviving Anglo-Saxon kingdom, and the nucleus for a national monarchy. The taking over of London by Alfred in 886 was a significant moment in the history of the nation. Alfred was also instrumental in the designing and implementing of a scheme of national defence through the

Anglo-Saxon England: Alfred to the Confessor

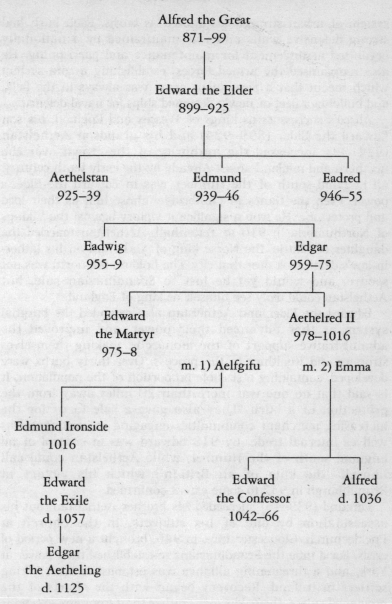

Alfred the Great
871–99

Edward the Elder
899–925

Aethelstan
925–39

Edmund
939–46

Eadred
946–55

Eadwig
955–9

Edgar
959–75

Edward
the Martyr
975–8

Aethelred II
978–1016

m. 1) Aelfgifu

m. 2) Emma

Edmund Ironside
1016

Edward
the Exile
d. 1057

Edward
the Confessor
1042–66

Alfred
d. 1036

Edgar
the Aetheling
d. 1125

Wessex dynasty Kings of England

system of urban strongholds known as burhs. Each burh had strong defensive walls and was maintained by a nationally organised arrangement for maintenance and garrisoning. He also reorganised the armed forces, establishing a rota system which meant that a permanent army was always in the field, and building a fleet of newly designed ships for naval defence.

Alfred's successors as kings of Wessex and England, his son Edward the Elder (899–924) and his grandson Aethelstan (924–39), increased the authority of the crown over the northern and midland areas. Already by the early tenth century, all England south of the Humber was in Edward the Elder's power. Even the Danes in Cambridge 'chose him as their lord and protector'.[5] He won a significant victory against the Vikings of Northumbria in 910 at Tettenhall. Aethelstan married the daughter of Sihtric, the Norse king of York, and on his father-in-law's death took over that city. The hold on the north was not secure, and would yet be lost to Scandinavian rule, but Aethelstan could truly see himself as king of England.

Edward the Elder and Aethelstan also extended the burghal system as they advanced their power, and improved the administrative support of the monarchy, making themselves stronger and wealthier in the process. Over thirty burhs were developed, containing a sizeable proportion of the population. It is said that no one was more than 20 miles away from the protection of a burh. They also gave a safe focus for the increasing merchant communities engaging in continental as well as internal trade. By 918 Edward was in control of all England south of the Humber, while Aethelstan could call himself 'the king of all Britain', which his victory at Brunanburgh in 937 to some extent confirmed.

Edmund (939–46) succeeded his brother Aethelstan, but his assassination by one of his subjects, in the church at Pucklechurch, Gloucestershire, in 946, brought a new period of crisis. For a time the Scandinavians re-established their power at York, and a threatening alliance was established with Viking settlers in Ireland. Recovery began with the efforts of the provincial rulers, the ealdormen, rather than from any exertions by the monarchy, through such men as Aelfhere in Mercia, Aethelwold in East Anglia and Byrhtnoth in Essex. Thus Mercia was recovered in 942, and Northumbria in 944. The expulsion of Eric Bloodaxe from York in 954 finally brought the north under southern influence again.

The monarchy recovered through the efforts of Edgar (959–75). He was 'a man discerning, gentle, humble, kindly, generous, compassionate, strong in arms, warlike, royally defending the rights of his kingdom'; to his enemies 'a fierce and angry lion'.[6] A clearer picture emerges of the government of the land through shires and courts. It was the time of the great church leader Dunstan, who became Archbishop of Canterbury and oversaw important monastic reform and revival. On a famous occasion seven (possibly eight) 'kings' from various parts of the British Isles came to Edgar at Chester and, to symbolise his lordship over them, rowed him in a boat on the River Dee. It was Edgar who made an agreement with the king of Scots, which for the first time established an agreed boundary between their respective kingdoms.

Edgar also reformed the coinage, and by his time there is good evidence for such regular features of government as a writing office, the use of sealed writs, a council known as the witenagemot, and the writing down of laws. Under Aethelstan and Edgar, the ealdormen gained a broader power, often over former kingdoms – Mercia, East Anglia and Northumbria. Their power has been seen as vice-regal. Beneath this was developing the organisation of shires, themselves subdivided into hundreds, probably for military reasons in the first place, but certainly also for the convenience of local administration under the monarchy. Edgar's reign has been called 'the high point in the history of the Anglo-Saxon state'.[7]

Edgar was only thirty-two when he died in 975. His son Edward (the Martyr, 975–8) succeeded him. Although he quickly made himself an unpopular king, his murder at Corfe in 978 was widely condemned and blamed upon his brother Aethelred, who thereby gained the throne. Edward was hurried to his grave, according to the *Anglo-Saxon Chronicle*: 'without any royal honours . . . and no worse deed than this for the English people was committed since first they came to Britain'.[8] Aethelred was very young, and is unlikely to have had any real part in the killing, but it is possible that his mother (Edward's stepmother) had, and men from Aethelred's household were implicated. The irritable and unlikeable Edward ironically has gone down in history as Edward the Martyr, though it is unlikely that he sought death or that piety was in any way involved. It was claimed that 'strife threw the kingdom into turmoil, moved shire against shire, family against family, prince against prince, ealdorman against ealdorman, drove bishop against the people and the folk against the pastors set over them'.[9]

Natural phenomena, like the comet, were always noted and taken as presages of the future. In the year of Aethelred's ascension the Anglo-Saxon chronicler reported that: 'a bloody cloud was often seen in the likeness of fire, and especially it was revealed at midnight, and it was formed in various shafts of light'. It was an inauspicious beginning to the unfortunate rule of Aethelred II (978–1016), though he was 'elegant in his manners, handsome in visage, glorious in appearance', it was to be 'a reign of almost unremitting disaster'. Work on his charters has shown something of how his government worked, but has done little to retrieve his reputation in general.[10] One charter read: 'since in our days we suffer the fires of war and the plundering of our riches, and from the cruel depredations of our enemies . . . we live in perilous times'.

In 986 there was a 'great murrain'; in 1005 a 'great famine throughout England', the worst in living memory; in 1014 there was flooding from the sea which rose 'higher than it had ever done before', submerging whole villages. Of 987 it was said there were two diseases 'unknown to the English people in earlier times', a fever in men and a plague in livestock, called 'scitte' in English, and '*fluxus*' of the bowels in Latin, so that many men and almost all the beasts died. Ravaging and natural disasters seemed to match each other in their destruction.[11]

We know the king, through mistranslation, as Aethelred the Unready. The name Aethelred means noble or good counsel, and he was punningly nicknamed 'unraed', which means not unready but bad, evil or non-existent counsel, making him 'Good Counsel the Badly Counselled'; or perhaps 'Good Counsel who gives bad advice'.[12] The death of Edward immediately set that king's close followers against Aethelred. Aethelred's reign in many ways is representative of the whole dilemma for English kings in the pre-

Conquest period: whether to concentrate most on the fight to maintain stability at home, or to focus on defence.

It was in this period that the Viking threat emerged once more, and on a greater scale than ever previously. When one thinks how close England had come to submission when defended by the great Alfred, it is less surprising that a threat greater than he faced should be too much for the less impressive Aethelred II. The major difference was that leading Scandinavian figures, including ruling monarchs, now became involved in the attacks on England. Conquest rather than raiding became a clear objective.

The new wave of threats opened with the raid of Olaf Tryggvason in 991. Aethelred himself did not take part in the main attempt to deal with this attack, when an army met the Danes at Maldon. A famous poem commemorates the event. The English leader, Ealdorman Byrhtnoth, seems overconfidently to have allowed the Vikings to cross from Northey Island to the mainland, no doubt believing he would be able to defeat them in battle. He had miscalculated: the battle was lost and he was killed. Viking attacks increased in the eleventh century with the invasion of Sweyn Forkbeard, king of Denmark (983–1014), soon aided by his son Cnut. During the eleventh century there were at least five attempts at invasion, three of which succeeded.

Aethelred pursued a policy of attempted appeasement, paying tributes to the attackers. The *Anglo-Saxon Chronicle* records in 991: 'it was determined that tribute should first be paid to the Danish men because of the great terror they were causing along the coast', and it was even recognised as 'appeasement'.[13] Tribute was paid in that year of £10,000, and again, for example, in 994, 1002, 1007 and 1012.

Promises were made not to attack again in return for large sums of money. The promises were sometimes kept and sometimes ignored. In any case the hope of obtaining such easy reward for simply going away was not likely to have a deterrent effect. This was expressed by an Englishman as 'in return for gold we are ready to make a truce'. Over half a century some £250,000 was paid in tribute.[14] One has the vision of Viking leaders scrambling over each other in haste to get at the cash from wealthy but weak England. One tribute paid in order to buy time so that on the next occasion a solid fight might be made would have been one thing; but tribute followed by tribute followed by tribute, in what became virtually an annual ritual, presented little hope of resolving or even lessening the problem. The *Anglo-Saxon Chronicle* thought that these efforts caused 'the oppression of the people, the waste of money, and the encouragement of the enemy'.[15]

England may have been wealthy in comparison to some states, but to Englishmen at the time life did not seem rosy. Taxes had to be imposed: the heregeld or army tax, later known as danegeld, first appearing in 1012. Money was levied both to support armed forces and to pay off the enemy. The heavy taxation which the tributes necessitated was resented, and royal reeves pressed demands which made them unpopular. Wulfstan said of them that 'more have been robbers than righteous men'.[16] Property might be seized without apparent just reason. One Englishman wrote 'the Lord multiplies children, but early sickness takes them away'; and another spoke of the various ways in which death might strike: wolves, hunger, war, accident, hanging, and brawling. There was a desperate desire for more order. The general feeling of malaise in England, of ineffective defence, is reflected in the *Anglo-Saxon Chronicle*.[17]

In the eleventh century the English lacked that unity of purpose which had supported Alfred the Great and others in earlier crises. There were two significant factors. One was the attitude of the descendants of Scandinavian settlers in eastern England, who inevitably tended to feel sympathetic towards new Scandinavian leaders who appeared on the scene.

Such latent hostility to the Wessex kings was worsened by Aethelred's inconsistent conduct. One moment he was paying tribute to raiders, the next he was killing Danes settled in England. In 1002 occurred the famous slaughter of St Brice's Day, when the king ordered 'to be slain all the Danish men who were in England'. This is no doubt an exaggeration, and perhaps he had some cause for action; possibly only recently arrived Danes were the victims, and it was said that he had heard of a plot against himself and his counsellors.[18] But his action did not remove the Danish settlements, and it did not help to remove the ethnic division within the kingdom.

The second factor was the lack of cohesion among the English magnates. The eleventh century is dotted with tales of treachery and rebellion, of disputes between magnates and between magnates and the king. The English monarchy was in many ways an impressive development, but it had failed to ensure a submissive nobility. Under Aethelred one has, for example, the treachery of Eadric Streona in Mercia, described as 'a man of low birth whose tongue had won for him riches and rank, ready of wit, smooth of speech, surpassing all men of that time both in malice and treachery, and in arrogance and cruelty'; and more succinctly as 'perfidious ealdorman'.[19]

There was also the treachery of the ealdorman of Hampshire in 992, whose son was blinded by Aethelred in the following year, and the treachery of Wulfnoth of Sussex, who joined the Viking invaders in 1009. Thorkell the Tall was a double traitor, deserting Cnut for Aethelred, and then in 1015 going back to Cnut. It is true that some of the criticism of treachery comes from hostile partisan sources, and probably such men had a greater degree of accepted independence than we sometimes realise and did not see themselves as acting badly, only as making new alliances and agreements. Even so, such fickle loyalty undermined the stability of government.

One way Aethelred did attempt to solve his problems, which had enormous consequences, was to seek alliance with his neighbours across the Channel. In 991 he concluded a treaty with Richard I (942–96), duke of Normandy, and in 1002 he married as his second wife Emma, Richard I's daughter, who was also the sister of his successor Richard II (996–1026). (His first marriage was to Aelfgifu of Northumbria.) The details of this policy we shall pursue further in the following chapter. Aethelred's efforts were always inadequate, and the most useful thing his Norman alliance brought was a place of refuge as his fortunes plummeted. In 1013 he sent his wife Emma back to her homeland along with their two sons, Edward (the Confessor) and Alfred, and he himself followed shortly.

Sweyn Forkbeard was able to take London and claim the kingdom in 1013. In this year 'all the nation regarded him as full king'.[20] But his triumph was soon followed by his death, in February 1014. He planned for his son Harold to take over the

Danish throne, and for Cnut to have England. Cnut's success did not seem certain, and he was forced to return to Denmark. This brief respite encouraged some of the English magnates to ask Aethelred to return, which he did. They were not overly enthusiastic, inviting him back only 'if he would govern them more justly than he did before'.[21] Aethelred seems by this time to have been a spent force, a tired man. No doubt he thought he could leave things to his progeny: he had some thirteen children from his two marriages. He allowed power to pass to his son by his first marriage, Edmund Ironside.

This position also was not long to endure. In 1015 Cnut was ready to return to England and seek the throne, with support from Thorkell the Tall and Eadric Streona. Edmund Ironside had to abandon London, though he won a victory at Brentford. He was forced to move his base to the north, where he made alliance with Uhtred, earl of Northumbria. Northern support for southern kings was never very reliable throughout the eleventh century; indeed Northumbria could hardly be regarded as under southern rule, while what we would call Yorkshire and Northumberland were not united.[22] Cnut pursued his rival and attacked York. Uhtred was persuaded to submit to the Dane, which gave Cnut the upper hand, but did Uhtred little good for the severe Scandinavian had him killed. Cnut appointed his own man, Eric, who had served Sweyn Forkbeard, to be the new earl.

In April 1016 Aethelred died. The *Anglo-Saxon Chronicle* summed up with some accuracy: 'he had held his kingdom with great toil and difficulties as long as his life lasted', but his death made little change to the situation, possibly if anything strengthening the hand of his more energetic son Edmund.[23] The latter still had friends in the old base of the Wessex kings and in the south. He was accepted as king in both London and Wessex. A bruising and decisive battle was then fought between the rivals at Assandun (possibly Ashingdon in Essex), when Eadric again deserted the English. Both sides suffered heavy losses, but Cnut emerged as the victor.

It is clear that at this point Cnut had doubts about his ability to remove Edmund. He agreed a treaty whereby Edmund would keep Wessex, though Mercia and London would be his. But this settlement too was short-lived in the political maelstrom of the

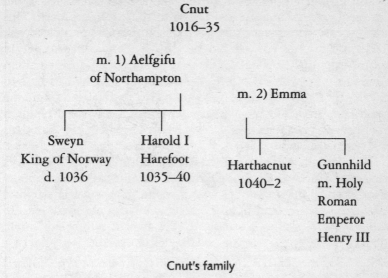

Cnut's family

eleventh century, for Edmund died suddenly in November 1016. His sons for safety were sent abroad, to Sweden, later ending up in Hungary. His son Edmund died there, but Edward the Exile stayed at the Hungarian court and married a noblewoman called Agatha, the niece of the German Emperor, Henry II. We shall hear of him again in due course.

Edmund Ironside's death allowed Cnut (1016–35) to become the sole ruler of England. His father had claimed to be king, but the events of the previous few years show that the claim had never been truly substantiated. Now Cnut became in fact as well as in name the Scandinavian ruler of the English kingdom. An early act to cement his position was the surprising move to marry Aethelred's Norman widow, Emma. This was a wise act, since it gave him an additional claim to the throne, hopes of alliance with Normandy, and it undermined thoughts in Normandy of giving aid to Aethelred and Emma's sons (Edward (the Confessor) and Alfred). These two were brought up at the Norman court, but Duke Richard II seemed content to accept Cnut as king of England. Later Cnut's sister, Estrith, married Robert I, duke of Normandy, which for a time at least nullified

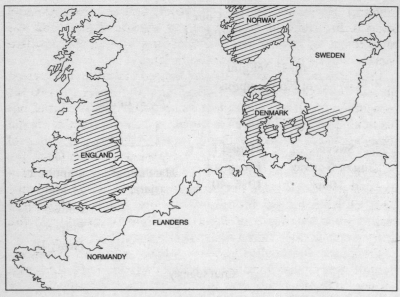

The empire of Cnut. (Map: Mike Komarnyckyj)

the position of the exiled sons of Aethelred; though Robert was to repudiate her before his expedition to the Holy Land.

The initiative for the marriage to Cnut may have come from Emma who, at every turn of fortune, made efforts to keep herself at the centre of power. She had favoured her stepson Edmund Ironside but with his death transferred her ambitions to a match with the conqueror Cnut, whom she married in 1017. There seems to have been a tacit agreement that Cnut's existing wife, Aelfgifu, should not be thrown out, but that children by Emma should have preference as heirs. Although her sons by Aethelred were safely in Normandy, and in the long run her alliance with Cnut helped to bring one of them to the English throne, at the time it appears that Emma did not give priority to their hopes, and indeed rather abandoned them for the sake of retaining some personal status in England.

Cnut is justly known as Cnut the Great. His greatness lies perhaps less in his rule of England than in his European importance, controlling much of Scandinavia as well as

England. He gained Norway by 1028, and also held parts of Sweden. In Britain he became ruler of the Isle of Man, and was recognised as lord of the Scottish king and of the Scottish islands, as well as of Scandinavian Ireland.

Cnut was a tough, even ruthless king in England. On occasion he had hostages mutilated: hands, ears and noses cut off. His recognition of Christianity may have been from genuine belief, but his actions and attitudes were aimed at political benefit. He did though make a journey to Rome in 1027 for the coronation of the German Emperor Conrad II, which seems to have taken the form of a pilgrimage. His political executions do not speak of a merciful or likeable man. But his laws support a wish to be a just king, and his success brought a stability which England had lacked since the death of Edgar. This had its benefits in the development of the Church and in economic growth.

Cnut used the English system of ealdormen over provinces, though with him we begin to call them jarls or earls. An initial act was to appoint earls over the main regions. He was aided by the death in 1016 of Ulfketel of East Anglia, and soon cleared the decks of magnates he distrusted, including, as we have seen, Uhtred of Northumbria and, late in the following year, Eadric Streona (the Acquisitor) of Mercia.[24] Cnut's new earls included the two men who had most aided him in gaining the kingdom: Eric who became earl of Northumbria, and Thorkell who was given East Anglia. England was in effect divided into four regions by 1017: Wessex, which the king kept directly under himself; Northumbria for Eric; Mercia for the soon to be disposed of Eadric; and East Anglia for Thorkell.[25]

Throughout the reign further reorganisation was made, and some of Cnut's earls held sway over smaller districts. Later, an earl, Godwin, was also appointed over Wessex, a choice of great significance for the future. Godwin was probably of English descent, thought to be the son of the Sussex noble Wulfnoth Cild the thegn. Little is known about the family's history in this period, but they had presumably been helpful to Cnut during the period of conquest. Cnut trusted other English nobles, and Mercia in time went to Leofric, probably the son of one of Aethelred's ealdormen. Northumbria passed to Siward, who married the former Earl Uhtred's granddaughter.

Cnut was a harsher and tougher ruler than Aethelred, but he also had problems with his earls, which suggests that they continued to have more power and independence than was good for the kingdom as a whole. When Cnut returned to Denmark in 1019, Thorkell acted for him in England. But when Cnut returned in 1020, he quarrelled with the great earl, and Thorkell went into exile for three years having been outlawed in 1021. Later they were reconciled. Under Cnut at least, the great earls were kept in their place.

The return to some stability under Cnut benefited England's economy. The towns in the south grew, coinage was reformed. We hear of some industrial development, for example in salt, lead and tin. Cnut was often in London, which was increasingly looking like a capital. The period of Scandinavian rule, with the inevitable turn towards the north and east for trade and communications, showed the value of London's position.

Cnut died at Shaftesbury in 1035, and was buried in his acquired English kingdom, at Winchester. It is not certain that had he lived his empire would have survived. It was already breaking up. His Scandinavian lands were reduced, and even Denmark was proving difficult to retain. Cnut's death, and his marital arrangements – seemingly married twice at the same time – left an uncertain succession and a period of renewed trouble in England.

Cnut's first wife, Aelfgifu of Northampton, was to some extent sidelined when he married again, but she was still treated as a wife. She was mother to Sweyn and Harold Harefoot, and assisted in the government of Norway. The failure of the family in Norway gave an increased interest in the English succession. Emma, mother to Edward and Alfred by Aethelred, also gave Cnut a son in Harthacnut. Cnut seemed to have ensured that there would be no problem over having sufficient heirs for his various lands, yet within seven years all his sons were dead.

Cnut's intention was that his son by Emma, Harthacnut, should be his chief heir, and succeed him in both Denmark and England. Harthacnut had already been recognised as king in England during his father's lifetime. This recognition, together with Edmund Ironside's position before his father's death, seems to be following a continental practice in succession which is not normally found in England, but may cast an interesting light on some post-Conquest situations.

In the event, Harthacnut, like all of his half-brothers except Harold, was out of the country. The two in Normandy, the sons of Aethelred and Emma, were given some hope from a recent breach between Cnut and the new Norman duke Robert I (1027–35). But Robert went to the Holy Land and then died in 1035, so that Alfred and Edward were in no position to intervene in England. Meanwhile, Sweyn, the son of Cnut and Aelfgifu, like Harthacnut, was occupied by Scandinavian troubles at the time.

Harthacnut had his father's blessing and the aid of his closest followers, his mother's encouragement, and the support of the two men who mattered most at the time: the Archbishop of Canterbury and Earl Godwin. Sweyn's brother, Harold Harefoot, did have northern support, from the earls of Mercia and Northumbria, perhaps chiefly in order to oppose southern interests; but they would not have had the capacity to displace Harthacnut had he been present.

However, Harthacnut's continued failure to come to England decided the issue. His support did not entirely die out, but it reduced. Most of those concerned realised that there must be a king in position, and Harold Harefoot gradually gained supporters from the south. Emma seems to have toyed with ambitions for her older sons in Normandy and probably wrote to get them to come to England, no doubt in order to seek the succession.[26]

Edward did not come to England, but his younger brother Alfred did, probably buoyed with false hopes from his mother's encouragement. Unfortunately for him, by the time he arrived Earl Godwin had decided that his best bet was to accept Harold Harefoot, who, as Harold I, was established in power. What happened next is not certain, and Godwin's supporters claimed him innocent. The likelihood is that he cooperated with Harold I in the capture and murder of Alfred. Godwin took him to Guildford, where, after a day of feasting, Harold's men attacked at night and captured the young man. He was blinded and taken to Ely where he shortly died.

After all this effort to gain the throne, Harold I (Harefoot, 1035–40) had a brief and miserable reign. Emma had acted

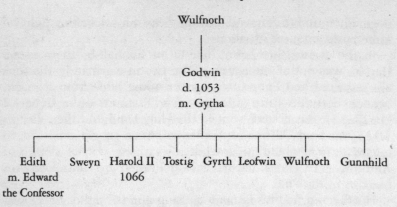

Godwin's family.

deviously over the succession, first favouring Harthacnut and
taking control of the treasure at Winchester, then turning to her
sons in Normandy. She even seems to be responsible for trying
to undermine Harold by disinformation, spreading the tale that
he was really the son of a servant, some said of a cobbler.[27]

When Harold Harefoot's success was certain, Emma chose to
remove herself to the safety of Flanders. But like other political
women of the medieval period, she had tasted too much power to
go away quietly. In Bruges, after the death of Harold Harefoot,
she met both her surviving son by Aethelred, Edward (the
Confessor), in 1038, and then her son by Cnut, Harthacnut. She
seems to have achieved some alliance between them. The latter
had agreed a settlement with Magnus of Norway in 1038, and
belatedly in 1039 began to take action over his rights in England.
He had brought a fleet of ten ships to Flanders, but in the event
did not need any greater force to invade England because of
Harold I's sudden death in March 1040.

Now Harthacnut (1040–2) was able to add England to
Denmark and revive some semblance of his father's empire. He
had raised a fleet of sixty ships, envisaging the need for invasion,
and sailed with it to Sandwich, accompanied by the ever
ambitious Emma. She gave assistance in his attempt to resolve
the Norman threat. Through her Harthacnut had come to terms
with his half-brother Edward, who was also invited to return to

England in 1041. Edward was to have an honoured place at court, and may even have been treated as Harthacnut's co-king or heir.[28] Harthacnut ruled harshly but effectively. In Worcester in 1041 there was opposition to heavy taxation. Two collectors were forced to take refuge in a room at the top of a church tower, but even that refuge failed them and they were murdered. Harthacnut sent a force which ravaged the shire, killing all males who came before it in a four-day orgy of revenge.

The long period of uncertainties with many twists of fortune and several sudden deaths reached a new resolution with Harthacnut himself succumbing to the grim reaper at Lambeth in June 1042, when over-indulging at a wedding feast: 'he was standing at his drink and he suddenly fell to the ground with fearful convulsions, and those who were near caught him, and he spoke no word afterwards'.[29]

TWO

THE REIGN OF EDWARD THE CONFESSOR

Edward the Confessor (1042–66), who had probably been present at his predecessor's death, was to have a lengthy and relatively secure reign. The drawing of him in the manuscript of the *Encomium Emmae*, written by a cleric of St-Omer for Queen Emma, is the best likeness we have. In it he appears with trimmed hair in a fringe and a short, wavy beard with perhaps the hint of a moustache. While in the *Vita*, written for his wife, Edith, he is described as 'a very proper figure of a man – of outstanding height, and distinguished by his milky white hair and beard, full face and rosy cheeks, thin white hands and long translucent fingers . . . Pleasant, but always dignified, he walked with eyes downcast, most graciously affable to one and all'.[1] He could also be thought 'of passionate temper and a man of prompt and vigorous action', but Edward was no soldier. The medieval writer who said 'he defended his kingdom more by diplomacy than by war' had it right; but failure to act as a commander of men was a grave disadvantage in this period.[2]

We should be under no illusion but that the Scandinavian conquest and the frequent switches of dynasty during the first half of the eleventh century had greatly weakened the kingdom. There were no other surviving sons of either Aethelred II or Cnut, but there were too many with claims and interests in England for its good. For example, Sweyn Estrithsson was the grandson of Sweyn Forkbeard; he was to become king of Denmark, and was not keen to see the old Saxon dynasty replacing that of his own line in England. Meanwhile, Magnus of Norway still saw possibilities for his own expansion. Later he was succeeded by the famed adventurer Harold Hardrada, who also dreamed of bringing Scandinavian rule back to England. Nor was Edward's reign free from Viking raids of the old kind.

The northern earls, Leofric and Siward, accepted Edward, but cannot have been enthusiastic about his succession. The north had never been firmly under southern control, and would continue to offer threats to the peace of England under Edward. Nevertheless, given the difficult period before Edward's accession and the long-term weaknesses displayed by the troubles, the Confessor's reign was better than one might have expected. The view of Edward as 'a holy simpleton' is not easy to maintain.[3] At least some historians now are prepared to be more respectful to the Confessor.

He could expect renewed attacks from Scandinavia, hopes of reward from Normandy, which might be difficult to satisfy, and opposition from at least some of the English magnates. His new realm was divided between English and Scandinavian populations, and into politically powerful earldoms. His most powerful earl, Godwin of Wessex, had been implicated in the murder of his own brother, Alfred.

At the same time, Edward possessed an advantage which most had lacked during the century: he was indisputably king and, unlike his immediate predecessors, he came from the old house of Wessex. He was also wealthy. His own possessions were valued at about £5,000, with an additional £900 coming through his wife. This made him wealthier than any of his magnates, including Godwin, though royal landed wealth was unevenly distributed, and in some areas of the realm the king held very little.[4]

Edward's position was helped further by the death of Magnus, king of Norway and Denmark, in 1047. The Confessor's Norman mother and Norman upbringing – he had received an education at the ducal court and it is said was trained as a knight – gave him the probability of a good relationship with that emerging power.[5] His sister, Godgifu, had married from the Norman court into the French nobility, and this gave Edward a number of noble relatives on the continent. But in any case, in the early years of the reign England could expect neither aid nor opposition from Normandy, which was undergoing much internal turmoil during the minority of William the Bastard.

Edward had to rely on his own wits, and had at least learned some tricks of survival and diplomacy from his years as a relatively insignificant figure at a foreign court. The exchange of status from pawn to king was rather sudden, but at least he had some experience of the game. Edward also received the blessing of the Church, and both the archbishops of York and Canterbury were present at his coronation on Easter Day 1043. The recognition of Europe was underlined by the presence at the ceremony of representatives from the German Emperor and the kings of France and Denmark.

As Edward's reign progressed, relations with Normandy did indeed prove generally amicable. Not surprisingly, he had forged bonds with Normans during his youth in the duchy, and a number of Normans were invited to his court. Indeed, several

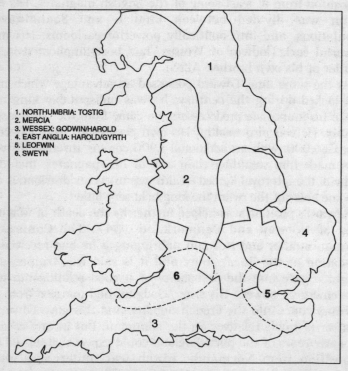

1. NORTHUMBRIA: TOSTIG
2. MERCIA
3. WESSEX: GODWIN/HAROLD
4. EAST ANGLIA: HAROLD/GYRTH
5. LEOFWIN
6. SWEYN

Earldoms of the Godwin family. (Map: Mike Komarnyckyj)

continentals had come to England with Edward in 1041. Among those in his household was the later Archbishop of Canterbury Robert of Jumièges, and Edward's nephew Ralph of Mantes, who was to become earl of Hereford. Some received lands and some received appointments in the Church. It became one of the points of dispute with his English earls, and especially with Godwin of Wessex.

The lands and wealth of the Godwin family made it outstandingly the strongest in England, with about twice the income of any other family in the land. The author of the *Vita* gives a more restrained picture of the great earl than we expect, and it has a ring of truth about it. He thought Godwin 'the most cautious in counsel and the most active in war', with an 'equable temperament' and a penchant for hard work, eloquent, courteous and polite to all, treating inferiors kindly.[6] In 1019 Earl Godwin had married Gytha, sister of a Danish earl and related by marriage to Cnut. In 1045 the Godwin family held four of the six great earldoms in England. They had moved within a couple of generations from obscure if respectable origins to the fringes of royalty. The writer of the *Vita* saw Godwin as 'vice-regal, second to the king'.[7]

To confirm the status of the family, Edward the Confessor took as his wife Edith, the eldest daughter of Earl Godwin and Countess Gytha. He was in his forties and she was about twenty-five. They married in January 1045, and Edith was crowned as queen. Edward's motives for taking her as a wife are not clear. Some have thought that Godwin pressured the match, but Edward had already shown that he could act independently and had been tough with his mother. No one was in a position to make him marry. The liaison was clearly intended to seal an alliance between king and earl, and probably we need to look no further for its reason.

There would be problems with the marriage, but it endured for twenty-one years. That there was some affection in the match seems likely. There is a contemporary description of the couple, with Edith content to sit at his feet. The suggestion that it was never consummated seems unlikely though not impossible. Edward's pious nature, their failure to produce children, and his later alienation from her, all give the story some credibility, but the main evidence for it comes from later attempts to give Edward a saintly character.

It was then claimed that Edward spent 'all the days of his life in the purity of the flesh', and that he treated Edith as a daughter rather than a wife: 'she called him father and herself his child'. The tone of the *Vita*, written for Edith, is affectionate towards Edward and does not suggest a failed marriage, though it does say that in a vision the king was marked out by St Peter for 'a life of chastity', and that he 'lived his whole life dedicated to God in true innocence'.[8]

In 1043 Edward was seriously at odds with his own mother. Her behaviour had always been geared to her own profit rather than to his, and some think that he harboured resentment for her neglect of his interests in the past. The D writer of the *Anglo-Saxon Chronicle* wrote 'she formerly had been very hard to the king her son, in that she did less for him than he wished both before he became king and afterwards as well'.[9]

Now suddenly Emma was accused of treason. The earls Leofric, Siward and Godwin were with the king at the time, and may have been implicated in her fall. Her protégé, Stigand, who was at the time Bishop of East Anglia, was deposed and his possessions seized. The accusation of treason was quietly forgotten, and later Stigand was restored. Possibly Emma had been involved in some conspiracy, possibly Edward simply sought to show her who was now master.

The Godwin family was powerful, but not everything went as it wished. The oldest son, Sweyn, who had been given an earldom in the west midlands, brought about his own downfall by going off the rails in a spectacular manner when he kidnapped and seduced (or possibly raped) Eadgifu the abbess of Leominster. He found little support, even from his family, and fled to Bruges and then on to Denmark. He returned to England in 1049, landing at Bosham. He sought pardon from the king, coming to him at Sandwich. But he received little sympathy even from his brothers or from his cousin Beorn, and Edward banished him again.

When Beorn then changed his mind and agreed to meet Sweyn, he soon had reason to regret his decision. Sweyn made him captive and killed him when they got to Dartmouth, presumably because he would not give the assistance Sweyn desired. Harold Godwinson disowned his brother's action and brought his cousin's body to Winchester for honourable burial. Sweyn was now declared *nithing*; an object of scorn and legally able to be killed by anyone. Even some of his own men and ships deserted him, and two of his ships were captured by the men of Hastings. He fled to Bruges, where Baldwin V (1035–67) demonstrated his hostility to Edward the Confessor by giving shelter to the fugitive. Perhaps through his father's intervention, and with the aid of Bishop Eadred of Worcester, Sweyn was pardoned by the king in 1050. It suggests that at this time Edward was prepared to go to almost any lengths to keep on good terms with the Godwin family.

A test of the powers of the king and Earl Godwin came when the archbishopric of Canterbury fell vacant on the death of Archbishop Eadsige in 1050. Godwin supported a relative, Aelric, for the post, but Edward favoured the Norman, Robert of Jumièges, already appointed Bishop of London with his backing. In 1051 Robert became archbishop and, in the conflicts which followed, was loyal to Edward against the Godwin family. The writer of the *Vita* suggests that English clerics also resented the appointment, and protested against it.[10] Other Normans were given bishoprics, at Dorchester and London, and other continentals won favour.

A second cause of conflict between the Wessex family and the king came over the king's favour to Eustace of Boulogne. Some historians suggest that Edward, now well established, brought on the break with the Godwins deliberately.[11] The political links between the powers in north-west Europe at this time form a vital background to events. Political alliances and hostilities between France, Scandinavia, Flanders, Normandy, Boulogne and England governed much that occurred.

In some ways Edward had reason to fear Flanders more than Normandy in the early period of his reign. He certainly paid heed to links with those who might help to counter the power of Flanders. In the clash between Baldwin V and the German Emperor, Edward sided with the Emperor. Edward kept connections with others who might be useful against Flanders, such as the counts of Ponthieu and Mantes, and not least with Eustace II, count of Boulogne, whose first wife was Edward's widowed sister Godgifu, and who visited Edward in England in 1051.

On his way home Eustace intended to pass through Dover. It may be that Edward meant to make a grant of Dover to Eustace. At any rate, when Eustace came there, apparently looking for somewhere to sleep, he was involved in a brawl with the townsmen. Eustace's men, according to one version of the incident, 'killed a certain man of the town, and another of the townsmen killed their comrades, so that seven of his comrades were struck down. And great damage was done on either side with horses and with weapons.' Another version says that twenty men were killed.[12] Dover lay within the earldom of Godwin, and Edward ordered his earl to punish the town by ravaging. Godwin's sympathies clearly lay with the town and he refused. Edward called a council at Gloucester at which Robert of Jumièges put the case against Godwin and even accused him of plotting to kill the king.

The simmering resentment between earl and king now came to a head. Godwin assembled a force, but found that opposition to a crowned king was not easy. The king, probably encouraged by the archbishop, wanted a trial of Godwin and his sons to be held in London, for the earlier killing of the king's brother Alfred, while the pardoned Sweyn Godwinson was outlawed once more.

Ralph of Mantes and many thegns rallied to the king's cause. A sarcastic message was sent to Godwin that he would be pardoned if he could restore to life Edward's murdered brother Alfred. The *Vita* suggests that it was Archbishop Robert who persuaded the king that Godwin would attack him 'as once upon a time he had attacked his brother'.[13] Godwin's own people hesitated to use force against their monarch, showing that this incident had not been forgotten. The king also got the support of the northern earls, Leofric of Mercia and Siward of Northumbria.

Godwin backed down. When he received the message about Alfred he was dining. He 'pushed away the table in front of him', realising that his position was impossible.[14] He and his family fled that night, riding to his manor at Bosham, and sailing into exile. His sons Harold and Leofwin made for Bristol, and took ship for Ireland. Godwin himself and most of the family left for Flanders, whose count, Baldwin V, as we have seen was generally hostile to King Edward. The Godwin family had close connections with Flanders, and at about this time Godwin's son Tostig married Judith, half-sister to the count.

A royal council declared the whole family outlawed. Some of the Godwin lands were granted out to royal favourites, including Edward's nephew Earl Ralph, known as 'timid', and Archbishop Robert.[15] Godwin's daughter, Queen Edith, was sent to a nunnery. Edward had attempted to throw off the hold of the Godwin family, but as a permanent move it proved more than he could manage.

Edward had shown sufficient strength to force the whole Godwin family into exile, but he lacked the power to keep them there. Within a year, in 1052, Godwin was able to return with a force partly supplied by the count of Flanders. Feeling in England had not been united against Godwin and his family. Some whispered against Godwin, 'the malice of evil men had shut up the merciful ears of the king', but others sympathised, and few were prepared to take arms against him. Harold meanwhile, also with an armed force, had sailed from Ireland and finally joined up with his father on the south coast. The Godwins advanced on London, and two armies faced each other across the Thames. Stigand negotiated on behalf of the Godwins.

Now Godwin had his revenge, and forced the king's hand so that he 'outlawed all the Frenchmen who had promoted injustices and passed unjust judgements and given bad counsel'.[16] The earl was insistent that Archbishop Robert give up Canterbury and leave the country, along with a number of Edward's foreign courtiers. Robert went to Rome to protest, but finally returned to his abbey at Jumièges where he died. The archbishop was replaced at Canterbury by Stigand, bishop of Winchester, at the heart of Godwin's Wessex. One writer thought that Stigand had 'deceived the innocent simplicity of King Edward'.[17] Leofric's son Aelfgar had been given East Anglia but now Harold Godwinson was able to recover it as his earldom.

The Godwins were restored in full: the father to Wessex, the sons to their earldoms, Edith to court, 'brought back to the king's bedchamber'.[18] Only Sweyn was missing, and that was probably a blessing. He had set off for the Holy Land, no doubt seeking the divine pardon he richly needed. He was to die at Constantinople on his return.

At Easter 1053, Earl Godwin suffered a sudden stroke at dinner with the king, and 'suddenly sank towards the foot-stool, bereft of speech and of all his strength'. He was carried by his sons to the royal chamber, dying a few days later 'in wretched pain'. The death of Godwin did not lessen the family's influence. Harold Godwinson 'wielded his father's powers even more actively, and walked in his ways, that is, in patience and mercy and with kindness to men of good will'.[19] Harold succeeded him as earl of Wessex, and a younger brother succeeded Harold. When Siward of Northumbria died in 1055 that earldom also went to the Godwin family, to another of Godwin's sons, Tostig. However, southern insertions in the northern earldoms were not popular, and Tostig found it difficult to establish himself. But it meant that only one earldom, Mercia, was not held by a Godwinson.

Edward the Confessor had some success as a British ruler. The Scottish king, Malcolm Canmore, came to his court and recognised English overlordship. He married Margaret, the daughter of Edward the Exile, who was the son of Edmund Ironside. There were also successful military expeditions against the Welsh, where Harold Godwinson, described as 'strong and warlike', laid the foundations for the later Norman advances with a raid into Wales first in 1055.

There is a story that when Edward met Gruffydd, the Welsh prince carried him on his shoulders as a mark of humility, and like the Scots king recognised his lordship.[20] But later Gruffydd raided into Mercia, and Harold, 'the vigorous earl of the West Saxons', was again sent with an army against him in 1063.[21] On the second invasion Harold and his brother Tostig led separate forces into Wales. Harold burned the Welsh prince's palace and set fire to his ships. The Welsh submitted but Gruffydd escaped by sea. However, his own people murdered him in Snowdonia, and brought his head to Harold, who sent the gory trophy of his triumph on to Edward.

Gruffydd's brothers swore fealty both to King Edward and to Harold. They divided up their brother's lands between them. Harold ordered the construction of 'a large building' at

Portskewet (Monmouthshire) in 1065. It would be interesting to know exactly what sort of structure this was and whether it was fortified in any way. It was used to store food and drink, and as a base for the English. But the precarious position of the invaders was soon demonstrated when the Welsh prince Caradoc attacked the new building, killed the 'labourers' and took the stores. This suggests that it was unfinished.[22]

The unity of the Godwin family did not endure to the end of Edward's reign. There was rebellion in Northumbria against Tostig at the end of 1065, partly caused by his attempts to tax the earldom with 'a large tribute', and for what some saw as his 'iniquitous rule', but it was mainly a chance to demonstrate the latent hostility towards him. It was also claimed that he robbed the church and took land. The comment of the *Vita* blames both earl and subjects: he 'had repressed with the heavy yoke of his rule because of their misdeeds'.[23] In October, with Tostig at the king's court, Northumbrian rebels led by thegns attacked his men in York, killing two hundred, including his Danish housecarls Amund and Ravenswart, and seizing his treasure.[24]

The Northumbrians invited Morcar, the younger son of Aelfgar, whose brother Edwin was earl of Mercia, to be their earl, and virtually everyone bar Tostig was prepared to accept the change.[25] It seems likely that his brother Harold thought that Tostig had brought the rebellion on his own head, and believed that restoration was either not possible or not wise. He gave his brother no support. As a result, Tostig became enraged at his brother and did all in his power to oppose his interests; he even accused Harold of being involved in the rebellion against him. This rift in the Godwinson family probably did as much as anything to undermine Harold's position in the long run. It was the division which gave William of Normandy his chance and made the Norman Conquest possible.

Harold and his brother Tostig were a striking pair, and caught the attention of contemporaries: 'distinctly handsome and graceful persons, similar in strength . . . equally brave'.[26] They were even described as 'the kingdom's sacred oaks, two Hercules'. Harold was depicted as taller, more open, more cheerful, more intelligent; Tostig as quicker to act, more determined, more secretive and more inflexible.[27]

How far Tostig's failure in Northumbria was his own fault is difficult to say. It seems that he did try to introduce southern laws and to impose heavy taxation. Whether he was too harsh is hard to judge. He was accused of three killings, two of men under safe-conduct. However, they might have been involved in a conspiracy against him.[28] It may be simply that the imposition of this representative of the leading southern family was unpalatable to the northerners, however able he might be. He did retain power in Northumbria for a decade.

It is also difficult for us to judge Harold's attitude to his brother. One might have expected more aid than Harold gave. But we cannot know if he believed his brother's fall was his own fault and his brother not worth aiding, or if politically it was unwise to make such a move, or if already there was little brotherly love between them. One source suggests that Edward's advisers believed Tostig to be at fault. There is some evidence that Edward preferred Tostig to his brother and was upset by his downfall, which further fuels the idea that Tostig was at fault, since Edward made no move to reimpose him.[29]

It is not clear that *anyone* had the power to restore Tostig in Northumbria. What is certain is that after Tostig's deposition and his brother's failure to assist him to recover the earldom, he became thoroughly hostile to Harold. It seems likely that Queen Edith, who also favoured Tostig rather than Harold, and who may have influenced her husband's attitude, thought Harold was at fault in the affair and became cool towards him. Her attitude is revealed by the *Vita*, in which it has been suggested that Tostig 'is the real hero of the story'.[30]

The fate of the English kingdom became increasingly open to question in the 1060s. Edward had no heir and seemed now unlikely to produce one. From the several claims made later it would appear that Edward promised the succession to a number of people. It is possible that they invented this later, but it seems more likely that Edward used the succession as elderly modern patriarchs brandish their wills over their heirs. It is likely that he favoured a different heir at different times through the reign. Among those given promises were William of Normandy, Sweyn of Denmark and Harold Godwinson.

Edward also thought about another possible successor, with a better claim by descent than any of those already mentioned, and who might also have been given private assurances about the throne. This was Edward the Exile. The Confessor made contact with Edward the Exile through the German Emperor Henry III, and invited him to come to England: 'for the king had decided that he should be established as his heir and successor to the realm'. The Exile would hardly have made all the effort to come had he not been given some indication of the likely consequence. But having arrived in England in 1057, Edward the Exile died in London. He did not even get to see his relative the king, and was buried at St Paul's.

In 1064 Edward the Confessor seems to have sent Harold Godwinson to Normandy. We shall look at the details of this expedition in the next chapter, but we need to consider its significance briefly. It is uncertain what was the purpose of the visit, and the main evidence for it comes from Norman sources. It is unlikely that Harold carried a promise of the throne to William, but the wily Edward may have seen the humour of the situation as the two potential rivals eyed each other up.

The chief puzzle of the situation is to see Harold's motives for going. One can hardly envisage the Confessor being able to order his premier earl to go on an expedition of this kind, though at this juncture we should not necessarily believe Harold hostile to the duke. It is more likely that Harold saw his status as a kind of ambassador, concerned about the fate of two relatives who were currently held as hostages by the duke. It may indeed have been primarily a goodwill mission to keep warm the friendship between the two powers.

The events of the trip certainly increased its significance and gave William a new lever, albeit through some rather underhanded action to force an oath out of Harold. We may believe that when Harold left Normandy, both he and his rival had their own views about how they would act when the English king died. They each had new cause to respect the abilities of a rival seen close up. Events were to catch up on them, perhaps more quickly than they expected. Edward became ill in 1065 and died at the very beginning of the new year. The future of the English crown seemed uncertain.

THREE

NORMANDY BEFORE 1066

In the first two chapters we have reviewed, along with the earlier history of England, reasons why England might be invaded in 1066: in brief, the attraction of a wealthy land, together with the hope of success against a divided and unstable state. Now we need to consider, along with Normandy's earlier history, how the ruler of that duchy was able to invade in 1066. This is an important consideration, for it is probably true that before 1066 such a venture would not have been viable.

Under the early rulers, from about 911 to 1026, Normandy grew into its recognised boundaries, and the interest of its rulers was inevitably upon this internal growth. Normandy then underwent a period of troubles, under Richard III (1026–7) and Robert I (1027–35), lasting through the minority of William the Conqueror. Only by about 1047 was the Conqueror really safe in his own duchy.

There then followed a period when his main task was to deal with enemies and rivals in France. He could not possibly have invaded England, and left Normandy open to invasion from the Capetian monarch or the count of Anjou. Only with the deaths of his main enemies on the continent, in 1060, was William relatively free to contemplate some broader project.

Even after 1060 for some time those broader projects were still nearer to home, in Maine and Brittany. That the death of Edward the Confessor occurred in 1066 and not earlier was in many ways a stroke of luck for the Conqueror. It came at just the moment when he could truly think about pursuing claims in England, with sufficient stability in the duchy and on its borders to leave it for

Normandy before 1066

Right: England's cross-Channel neighbours in the eleventh century; below: Normandy In the eleventh century. (Maps: Mike Komarnyckyj)

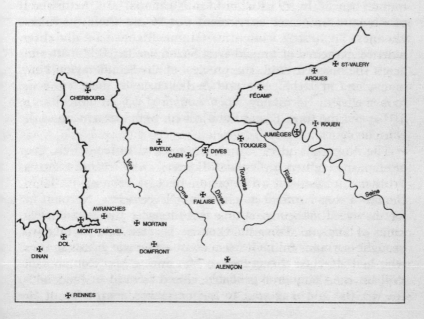

some months, and with a degree of wealth and support which had not been available to him before the 1060s.

We shall note more closely than in the opening chapters the growing links between England and Normandy after AD 1000. The geographical proximity of the two was bound to bring some connection, but in the first half of the eleventh century there were new dimensions to the relationship: economic, social and political.

Both areas had strong Scandinavian settlements, and common interests from them. According to Dudo of St-Quentin, a clerk from Picardy who came to the Norman court, the links went back as far as Rollo or Rolf, the Viking leader and first ruler of Normandy. Dudo's work, especially for the early years of Norman history, is now widely questioned. One historian has seen the *Customs and Acts of the First Dukes of Normandy* as 'a mere farrago of distorted and altered fragments from the old annalists'.[1] Dudo was a chaplain at the court of Duke Richard II, and becomes more trustworthy when dealing with his own lifetime, though never exactly reliable.[2]

The English kings, after a period of hostility, began to seek better relations with Normandy, and to make agreements for mutual benefit. In 991 Richard I of Normandy and Aethelred II of England made an agreement not to aid their respective enemies. Stemming from this, Emma, Richard I's daughter, married Aethelred of the old West Saxon line in 1002. (After his death she married Cnut, the greatest of the Scandinavian kings of England in 1017.) She and Aethelred, with their two sons, took shelter in Normandy when Aethelred was in difficulties in 1013; and the sons, Edward and Alfred, were brought up at the Norman court.

The Normans gave Emma's sons assistance when they attempted to return to England. Robert I, who treated them 'as brothers', organised an invasion fleet at Fécamp in 1033, though a storm ruined its chances.[3] Nevertheless, Norman aid for the exiled aethelings was a real threat to the Scandinavian kings of England. Edward, when he became king of England, brought Normans to the English court and made grants to those who had attached themselves to him during his Norman exile. William the Conqueror probably visited Edward in England in the 1050s, and was said to have received a promise of the

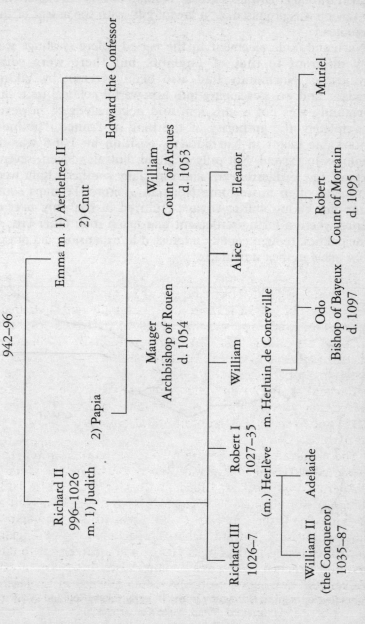

The comital family of Normandy from 942. (Notes: William the Conqueror was William I, King of England, but William II, duke of Normandy; Robert I fathered two children by Herlève but did not marry her.

English throne at Edward's death. William of Poitiers claims that the throne was promised as 'a lawful gift' with the assent of the magnates.[4]

Normandy's development in the period before Hastings was very different to that of England, but there were some similarities. Normandy had also been overrun by Viking invaders, and was developing into a powerful political unit. But Normandy was not a kingdom and acknowledged, however incompletely, the authority of the king of France. The most remarkable factor in Normandy's position by 1066 was its readiness to expand. Not only England, but also Spain, several parts of the Mediterranean, and especially southern Italy were to receive often unwelcome Norman visitors. Perhaps some latter-day Viking will-to-voyage endured in the only part of France where a Viking settlement had taken root; other French principalities, though equally interested in expansion, did not go so far afield in their ambitions.

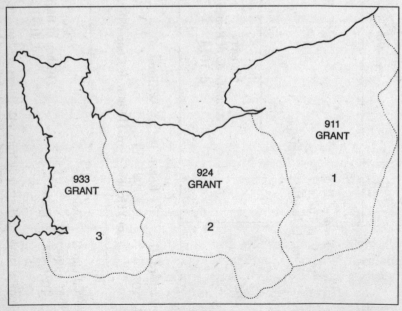

The development of Normandy under its early rulers, Rolf and William Longsword. (Map: Mike Komarnyckyj)

Normandy before 1066

Part of the explanation of Normandy's unique history lies in the kind of political unit that Normandy was. Several groups of Vikings settled on the western shores of continental Europe, and a few were able to establish some political authority, but Normandy was the only one to survive under a Viking dynasty. William the Conqueror was the direct descendant of a remarkable line of dukes descended from the first Viking ruler of Normandy, Rollo or Rolf – though the early leaders were not dukes or even perhaps counts.[5]

We need, in order to understand Normandy in 1066, to look back to the foundation of Normandy under the Viking leader Rolf. At the beginning of the tenth century, there were several similar leaders of war bands who had settled as best they could along the continental coast, mostly in regions where rivers entered the sea. There had been a series of raids against the Norman coast before any settlement occurred, for example in 841, 851, 855.

As in England, the first impact was frightening. One account tells of the consequences for the people attacked: 'I was freed from the hand of the very cruel nation of the Normans. They took me, bound me as a wretched slave, [and] sold me to a foreign land.' Having been dealt numerous blows, faced perils of the sea and storms, suffered extreme cold, nudity, atrocious hunger and a long voyage, the writer finally returned home.[6]

Rolf's group had settled along the Seine. There is no doubt these were opportunistic groups, happy to take any wealth that might offer but also eager for land, and in competition with each other for it.

The 'foundation' of Normandy came out of a policy used by the increasingly desperate rulers of Western Francia. The Viking raids were only one of several serious problems disturbing Europe at the time. The troubles had led to the splitting of the old Frankish Carolingian Empire into several component parts in 888, one of which was West Francia, and from this nucleus emerged the kingdom of France. The kings of West Francia found it difficult to survive, and their kingdom was itself in danger of splitting into yet smaller independent units, such as counties.

The struggle weakened the old Carolingian dynasty, and before the end of the tenth century it was to be replaced by the family of one of its dukes, the Capetians. However, in 911 there

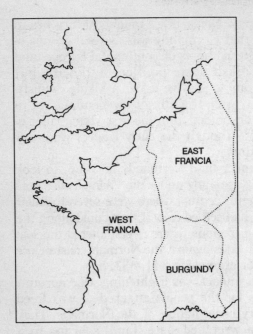

The division of the Carolingian Empire, 888: the beginnings of France and Germany. (Map: Mike Komarnyckyj)

was still a Carolingian ruling West Francia, Charles III, known rather unfortunately as Charles the Simple (898–922). Translated more accurately, his name probably meant Charles the Honest. A chronicler explained: 'during his life he was called *simplex* because of his good nature'.[7]

Charles III made the decision to try and save West Francia by allying with the Viking Rolf, the leader of one band of Vikings who had settled on the Seine. This was a bold move, and potentially dangerous for the West Franks, but it had great consequences. Charles probably had two major motives in making the agreement of 911. The first was to use Rolf as an obstacle against further Viking incursions into that part of Francia, now fighting for him rather than against him, and thus also dividing the Viking menace. He was seeking the alliance of one Viking leader not only against further Scandinavian incursions, but also against other Viking groups already settled in the region. The second purpose of Charles was to use Rolf as a buffer against the expansion of the Bretons, who had not come under the authority of the West Frankish kings, and who had been extending their power eastwards.

It is now generally accepted by historians that Charles III's grant was a sensible if risky move which, it must be said, succeeded. It is also acknowledged that it was a narrower grant than the Normans would claim a century or so later. They made the claim to justify the expansion of comital power beyond the confines of the original grant. But Rolf in 911 was the leader of one band among many and was only recognised as an ally not as a count. Whatever territories were 'granted' would have to be won and held by the recipient of the grant.

Charles III certainly encouraged Rolf to take lands from the Bretons but, in the context of 911, this almost certainly meant land which was to become part of Normandy rather than Brittany proper.

It is very doubtful that Charles III envisaged any expansion of Norman power over the whole of Brittany. No more did he wish to see a Viking Normandy. Not that he had much right, and certainly no power in real terms over Brittany or even Normandy, to make such a broad grant. However, he would have been perfectly happy to see the Normans fight against the Bretons, who at the time held land which later became western Normandy. It is unlikely that the king was more generous than he needed to be.

Rolf had recently been defeated in battle by the Franks at Chartres. So the grant came at a time of Frankish strength rather than weakness. What Charles the Simple granted in 911 was almost certainly the right of Rolf to rule in the king's name over the city of Rouen and a relatively restricted area around it by the Seine; at most it was Upper or eastern Normandy, probably the area where Rolf already held sway.

Rolf had emerged as the leader of a group settled in the area for some decades, who had recently taken over Rouen. He is thought to be of Norse rather than Danish origin, an idea supported by tradition held within the ducal family itself. It is believed that he was exiled from Scandinavia by Harold Fairhair, king of Norway (900–33), and had probably lived the life of a Viking, voyaging to Scotland, Northumbria and Ireland.[8]

Although from the evidence of a charter of 918 we can be

sure than an agreement was made between King Charles and Rolf, we are uncertain about its details. As D.C. Douglas has suggested, 'far less is known about pre-Conquest Normandy than about pre-Conquest England'. Something has been done about that by Douglas himself, and by David Bates and others since, but there is still a gap in the quantity of sources available.[9]

The problem over 911 is that the only details come from Dudo of St-Quentin, who was writing to bolster Norman ducal claims, and was doing so about a century after the event. Dudo was not himself a Norman, but had come to the court of Duke Richard I at the end of the tenth century. His *Customs and Acts of the First Dukes of Normandy* was written for the dukes, and finished before Dudo's death in 1043. Like many such works it is less reliable for the early material, but among chroniclers Dudo was particularly prone to invention. Given that we must not believe his every word, it is still worth recording what he made of the meeting which he described as occurring at St-Clair-sur-Epte in 911.[10]

At the appointed time they came to the place that had been agreed, which is called St-Clair. The army of Rollo kept to one side of the River Epte, that of the king and Robert [the Strong, duke of France] to the other. Then Rollo sent the archbishop [of Rouen] to the king of the Franks, on a mission to say to him: 'Rollo cannot conclude a peace with you, since the land you wish to grant him is not cultivated by the plough, and is altogether without herds and flocks and the presence of men. No one lives on it except by thieving and pillage. Give him rather a region from which comes nourishment, filled with riches. He will not negotiate with you unless you swear by a Christian oath, you and your archbishops, bishops, counts, abbots and all your realm, that he and his successors shall hold the land from the River Epte to the sea as a farm and an alod for ever'

Then Robert duke of the Franks and the counts, bishops and abbots who were there said to the king: 'You will not win over such a strong leader unless you do what he wants. If you do not give him what he claims from you in return for his service, give it in return for Christianity, that at last such a numerous people should be won for Christ, then you will avoid diabolical error; and, finally, [give it] in order that the edifice of your realm and of the Church should not be destroyed by the attack of his army. You should employ his defence and protection in the name of Christ. You should act as a king and a firm defender of the Church'.

The king wanted to give him Flanders on which to support himself, but he did not wish to accept that because it was marshy. Also the king offered to give him Brittany, which was on the border of the promised territory. Then Robert and Archbishop Franco told all this to Rollo, and brought him to King Charles, after an exchange of hostages, under the protection of the Christian faith. The Franks, seeing Rollo, the aggressor against all Francia, said to each other: 'This chief has great power, great courage, much wisdom and prudence, and even more energy, to have waged war in this way against the counts of the realm'.

So, placated by the words of the Franks, he placed his hands between the hands of the king, which his father, grandfather and great-grandfather had never done. So the king gave his daughter, Gisela by name, as wife to the leader, and certain lands as alods and in farm, from the River Epte as far as the sea, and all of Brittany, on which he should be able to live. The bishops, seeing that Rollo was unwilling to kiss the foot of the king, said: 'He who receives such a gift ought to kiss the foot of the king'. He replied: 'I shall never bend my knee to anyone, nor shall I kiss any foot'. But, compelled by the prayers of the Franks, he ordered a certain soldier to kiss the king's foot. The latter, at once seizing the king's foot, lifted it to his mouth and, having planted the kiss while he was standing, made the king fall down. So, much laughter arose, and a great disturbance among the men.[11]

The basic import of the agreement was that the king recognised Rolf as a chieftain (not a duke or even a count) over a territory centred upon Rouen, with the chief purpose of protecting the Frankish kingdom; 'for the safety of the realm' according to the 918 charter. In this charter Rolf and his companions are described as 'the northmen of the Seine'.[12] Flodoard, who is more to be trusted than Dudo on this, says that Charles granted Rouen and some coastal districts dependent upon that city.[13] There seems little doubt that Rolf's lands did not go beyond the River Orne to the west, perhaps not even so far; what he was given was, in essence, eastern Normandy. He also made concessions to the king. Dudo's farcical account of one of Rolf's men grasping the king's leg and pulling him over is a way of belittling what was surely some act of submission or homage, with a promise of fidelity, and does not seem credible.

Even Dudo accepts that Rolf and his men agreed to become Christian as part of the deal. Rolf and his 'companions and soldiers' were immediately baptised.[14] The slowness of Christianity to recover in Normandy suggests that the Normans were being forced into an act for which they had little enthusiasm. It was reported that, when dying, Rolf made gifts to churches, but also arranged for human sacrifices in the pagan manner. It is probable that Rolf married a Christian wife, though it may not have been Popa or Gisela, and that his children were brought up as Christians.[15]

THE EARLY 'DUKES' OF NORMANDY

The sources for the period from 911 to 1026 are not very full. We have to rely a good deal on Dudo of St-Quentin, though some other Frankish chronicles give assistance. We do not, for example, even know the date of the death of the first Viking ruler of Normandy, Rolf.

Rolf's original territory was a fertile land. Eastern Normandy contained much open country and provided valuable produce in grain and fruit. A charter of Charles III, dated to 905, shows that normal administration was operating within Rolf's territories then, so we may believe that Rolf was keeping order within his own region in eastern Normandy, which can only have improved after the 911 agreement.[16]

Rolf himself began the expansion of his lands westwards, which would culminate in forming Normandy as we know it. He probably moved his authority beyond Eu, and beyond the Orne as far as the River Vire. Rolf made the first major extension of his original grant, adding what we think of as middle Normandy, especially the Bessin. By the time of his death, Rolf had become essentially a Frankish count with his capital at Rouen.

Rolf's son, William, succeeded him in about 924. He is known as William Longsword (*c.* 924–42). Among the early rulers, the descendants of Rolf, there was no weak link. Each one in turn added something to what he acquired, and increased the strength of Normandy. In William I's case it was the second major extension of Norman authority.

To the west there was trouble between the Bretons and Scandinavian settlers along the Loire, and the Normans intervened for their own profit. By 933 William had gained western Normandy as far as the Couesnon, which it seems he had recovered from the Bretons, adding the Cotentin and the Avranchin, though comital power in these areas remained weak through the next century.[17] Normandy as we recognise it had been created, or perhaps recreated, since it responded closely to the old ecclesiastical province of Rouen and the even more ancient boundaries of the Roman province of *Lugdunensis Secunda*; it also had a rough correspondence to the Frankish region of Neustria, which it was still sometimes called. William Longsword established a family connection with Fécamp, where a palace was constructed.

William Longsword was christian and encouraged Christianity. He married a christian noblewoman, Liégarde, daughter of the count of Vermandois, though his successor was born to a Breton mistress.[18] But Christianity's revival in Normandy proved slow and uncertain. Five successive bishops appointed to Coutances were unable to reside in their see. Bishops appointed outside Rouen also found themselves unable to live in their own sees.

However, William I was known as a friend of monastic restoration, and was especially associated with the great house of Jumièges. In 942, the year of his death, William welcomed King Louis IV of France (936–54) to Rouen, which suggests that he recognised the king's authority over Normandy. Neither the emphasis on Christianity, nor the friendship with the West Frankish monarchy, seems to have been favoured by William's subjects, and may have been the cause of his assassination in

942. His death, though treated by some as martyrdom, led to a pagan revival in Normandy, and a period of disorder.

William Longsword's son succeeded as Richard I (942–96). He grew into 'a tall man, handsome and strongly built, with a long beard and grey hair'. But in 942 he was only ten years old, and as usual a minority meant disorder and difficulty.[19] Scandinavian raids were still occurring, and were a cause of disturbances within Normandy. The king of France and the duke of the Franks established themselves in Norman territory, and won a victory against the Viking leader Sihtric. They looked for the overthrow of the Viking county rather than the defence of Richard. But in 945 Louis IV was himself defeated by Harold, a Viking leader probably based in Bayeux.[20]

Gradually, over the years, Richard I emerged as a man of strength and determination. He took as his wife, though perhaps not by a Christian ceremony, a woman of Danish descent called Gunnor, from a family settled in the pays de Caux. By her he had several children, including his eventual successor. Most

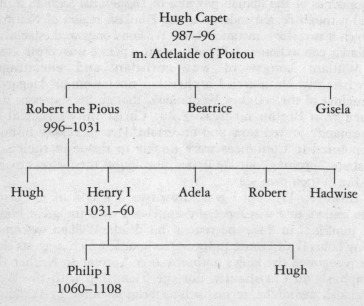

Capetian Kings of France: Hugh Capet to Philip I.

members of the Norman nobility of the Conqueror's time claimed some sort of relationship either with Richard I or with Gunnor, which brought a coherence to the ruling group that in turn added strength to their combined efforts at expansion.[21] Given the circumstances of the minority, it is hardly surprising that Richard I continued to keep links with Scandinavia, but he also made an agreement with the new king, Lothar, at Gisors in 965. For a long period after this the ruler of Normandy kept on good terms with the king of the West Franks, of importance to them both.

But Richard I did not continue his support for the old Carolingian family. He had already been closely associated with the duke of the Franks, and took as his 'official' wife, Emma, daughter of Hugh the Great, duke of the Franks (d. 956). The Normans were among the firmest supporters of this family. In 968 Richard I recognised Hugh the Great's son, Hugh Capet, as his overlord, and when Hugh became the first Capetian king of France (987–96) the Normans were among his earliest adherents. Richard also sought to restore Christianity, and from this time on paganism in Normandy waned. One of his most enduring acts was to aid the revival of the monastery at Mont-St-Michel. Richard I's reign also saw the beginnings of an important monastic revival in Normandy.

Richard II (996–1026) succeeded his father in a year marked by a peasant revolt in Normandy. The peasants called assemblies, and made 'laws of their own', but the movement was brutally suppressed by the nobility.[22] When the count of Ivry was approached by rebels to put their case, he cut off their hands and feet. But the new reign was a period of significant economic progress for Normandy. Despite being 'highly skilled in warfare', Richard II kept out of the conflicts which raged around him in north-west Europe, though he did push Norman interests beyond his own boundaries. He had 'decidedly pacific tendencies', and brought a period of significant stability to the duchy.[23]

Richard II married the sister of the count of Rennes, the 'fair of form' Judith.[24] He also had contacts with the Scandinavian world: Vikings could still be welcomed at Rouen in 1014, and a Norse poet was received at court in 1025. To Franks outside Normandy the rulers still seemed Vikings, and Richer of Reims continually referred to Richard as 'duke of the pirates'. The name given to the territory itself, 'Normandy', came from the same attitude to its inhabitants, meaning the land of the northmen or Vikings.

But Scandinavian influence was decreasing in Normandy. Place-name studies suggest that the original Scandinavian settlement did not extend evenly throughout Normandy. The names cluster along the coast and the rivers. It is clear in any case that the settlers began to integrate with the existing population through intermarriage. Some Scandinavian attitudes and customs continued but, as is so often the case, the surviving population from the old world recovered its strength, if only in influencing language and a way of life. By the tenth century French was taking over as the main language in Normandy, if it had ever been overtaken. According to David Douglas, by the eleventh century Normandy was 'French in its speech, in its culture, and in its political ideas'.[25]

The administrative system which developed in Normandy was largely Frankish, and similar to that in surrounding counties. We have a nice picture of Richard II at Rouen, in 'the city tower, engaged in public affairs'. We are told that those in attendance feared to break in upon him unless summoned by his chamberlains or doorkeepers: 'but if you wish to see him, you can watch him at the usual time, just after dinner, at the upper window of the tower, where he is in the habit of looking down over the city walls, the fields and the river'.[26]

Richard II continued the family's reputation for defending the Church, and was responsible for inviting to Normandy the reformer William of Volpiano. By this time the episcopal organisation of Normandy had developed, and the bishops were able to function normally within their sees. Under Richard II a new social structure of Normandy emerged. It is clear now that this was not the emergence of new families, but of old families in a new guise: as castellans, with stress on primogeniture and lineage. The families were not new, but their way of looking at themselves and their ancestry was.

There is, for example, no mention of the Montgomerys (one member of whom considered himself 'a Norman of the Northmen') before a charter dated to 1027 at the earliest, after Richard's death. Montgomery itself was not fortified until after 1030. The use of toponyms to define an individual and his family did not become common until about 1040.[27] It was about this time that the residence at Le Plessis-Grimoult was turned into a castle. During the period of political instability old families began to see themselves as lineages, to build castles, to latch on to offices at the ducal court, to become vicomtes in ducal administration of the duchy, indeed to threaten ducal power itself.[28]

Richard II married twice, to the Breton Judith, whose sons, Richard and Robert, succeeded him, and to the Norman Papia, by whom he had two further sons, William of Arques and Mauger, the later Archbishop of Rouen. Richard II used members of his family to rule over divisions of his territory on his behalf: at Mortain, Ivry, Eu, Évreux and Exmes. It was the acknowledgement of the rights of this second family which caused many of the problems of the subsequent period.

With local magnates called counts came the transfer of the ruler's title from count to duke, marking his superiority. Those appointed to rule over the new Norman counties, mostly in sensitive areas on or near the frontier, were members of the ducal family. Ducal government also developed, and we begin to hear of vicomtes, who were not deputies for the counts, but were all direct representatives of the count of Rouen himself, that is of the duke. During the period 1020 to 1035 some twenty vicomtes have been identified, and they represent a growing structure for comital government throughout Normandy.

NORMANDY IN TROUBLE

After the death of Richard II in 1026, Normandy underwent a long period of difficulty. The next duke, Richard III, survived only a year, until 1027. There was rumour that he had been poisoned, possibly by his successor.[29] Robert I (1027–35) was the only member of the family of Rolf who proved something of a failure, despite being known as Robert the Magnificent or sometimes the Liberal, and reputed to be 'mild and kind to his supporters', with an 'honest face and handsome appearance', and of a 'fine physique'.[30] Others, it must be said, called him Robert the Devil.

External relations deteriorated, and Normandy faced a period of severe internal disorder. Yet the duchy retained vestiges of its earlier position. When King Henry I of France (1031–60) found himself in desperate trouble in the year of his accession, it was to Normandy that he fled for refuge. Surviving gratitude for this help accounts for his aid to the young William the Conqueror during the latter's minority, the years of his greatest vulnerability.

Robert's decision to go on pilgrimage to the Holy Land is something of a puzzle. Perhaps he was overcome with piety, though his life to that date shows little sign of it. Perhaps he was overcome by remorse, for which he no doubt had good cause. However, for his duchy it was a perilous moment to depart on such a distant adventure, from which, as might have been feared, he was never to return, dying unexpectedly at Nicaea during his return journey.

One of Robert I's sins was a liaison with Herlève, variously said to be the daughter of a tanner or perhaps an undertaker of Falaise called Fulbert.[31] In any case the duke, as dukes will, had his way with her, made her pregnant without any thoughts of marriage, and thus fathered William the Bastard, perhaps Robert's chief contribution to his duchy.

When you look down nowadays from the walls of the great stone castle at Falaise (not in that state when Duke Robert lived), you are told that you are standing (presumably approximately) where Robert was when he espied the fair Herlève beside the pond below, outside the castle wall. Another story is that he had 'accidentally beheld her beauty as she was dancing'. The twelfth-century writer described William's birth, on rushes laid out on the floor, and said that Herlève had a dream about her new son: she saw her intestines spread out over Normandy and England which forecast William's 'future glory'![32]

William the Conqueror (William II, duke of Normandy, 1035–87) thus came to rule the duchy in unpromising circumstances. His father had died when William was aged about nine, possibly even younger. The duchy had passed through decades of instability, which had included a peasants' revolt and divisions among the aristocracy, while 'many

Normans built earthworks in many places, and erected fortified strongholds for their own purposes'.[33]

Added to that, William was not the legitimate son of the old duke. Bastardy was not the stain it was about to become in terms of moral attitude or right to inherit, but it was, nevertheless, a drawback, as one can see from the very fact that he was called 'the Bastard', and from the way the citizens of Alençon and others later would taunt him with his bastardy. William's reaction to this insult at Alençon shows how much it smarted: he ordered the hands and feet of thirty-two mockers to be cut off. A chronicler considered that 'as a bastard he was despised by the native nobility'.[34] The taint of bastardy added to the dissatisfaction of the nobles at having a minor succeed to the duchy.

William's own relatives were among those who stirred up trouble during his minority, suggesting the unwise nature of Richard II's acknowledgement of families by two wives. The period was marked by a series of internal rebellions and external threats. At times, William's security, and even his life, was at risk. At Valognes, he was once roused from sleep to be warned that conspirators were about to kill him; William got away half-dressed on a horse. He was protected by a few loyal retainers and given some support from the Church and by the king of France, but he often escaped by the skin of his teeth. Among those around him who were killed were his guardian Gilbert de Brionne, his tutor Turold, and his steward Osbern.[35]

The worst period of anxiety ended when Henry I of France came to his aid against the Norman rebels, enabling the young William to win his first major engagement at the battle of Val-ès-Dunes in 1047. The duke's enemies gathered in the west of the duchy and advanced to the Orne, where their way was blocked by the duke's supporters. The rebels broke, and many drowned in the river. If Wace is to be trusted, horses were seen running loose on the plain, while mounted men rode haphazardly in their efforts to escape. William of Poitiers confirms that riders drove their mounts into the Orne trying to get away, till the river was full of soldiers and horses.[36]

The Conqueror's main enemy and rival at this time had been Guy de Brionne, but the victory at Val-ès-Dunes crushed his ambitions. However, William showed little gratitude to the French king. Once freed from his greatest fears, he began to flex the muscles of his Norman war machine, and to attack neighbouring powers in a way that his predecessors had avoided. This caused growing resentment and hostility from those neighbours, and from the king.

We do not know the precise reasons, but it was in this context that the king of France joined the enemies of Normandy from 1052, and turned to attacking the duke he had previously defended. Possibly it was because of Norman participation in a rebellion against the king in the Ile-de-France. Whatever the reason, the king's hostility added considerably to Normandy's dangers in the mid-eleventh century.[37]

William was equal to the new threat, and in the 1050s transformed Normandy into a greater military power. A serious problem was posed by the building of private castles during the worst of the disturbances. Now William had to spend much of his time besieging, destroying, or taking over these strongholds. Any rebel of standing could shelter behind the walls of his own castle. In the early part of the decade his own uncles, Count William of Arques and Mauger, Archbishop of Rouen, remained the greatest internal threats, and they could now look to assistance from France and the growing rival of Normandy, the county of Anjou.

Count William of Arques' opposition turned into rebellion against his nephew by 1053. He had never readily accepted the succession of his brother's illegitimate child. In 1053 Henry I of France tried to relieve Arques, but was beaten in a conflict at St-Aubin-sur-Scie by some of the Conqueror's men, using a feigned flight. The surrender of Arques and the submission of Count William symbolise the triumph of the Conqueror over the rebels. His uncle was treated leniently and allowed to go into exile.[38]

In 1054 the enemies of William combined in rebellion and invasion, but he thwarted their attack by a great victory at Mortemer. Here, according to William of Poitiers, the invading army was decimated. At midnight, William ordered a herald from the top of a tree to cry the details of the victory to the defeated king, who then fled.[39] One of the duke's enemies in the field was the neighbouring Count Guy of Ponthieu. Guy was captured during the battle and submitted to the Conqueror, transferring allegiance to him. A few years later this move would have important consequences.

At this time, William was building a close group of familiars and friends from the Norman nobility, who would form a strong support to his activities throughout his life, men such as William fitz Osbern and Roger Montgomery, William de Warenne and Roger de Beaumont, together with his own half-brothers Robert, count of Mortain, and Odo, Bishop of Bayeux (sons of William's mother, Herlève, by the husband Duke Robert had found for her). William II was beginning to take a grip on his duchy, and the great families and the lesser lords swung in behind his lead. He was also building a sound administration, revived after the period of troubles.

But William's difficulties were far from over, and in 1057 he faced a new invasion from France and Anjou. The Angevin counts had expanded their territories in a manner even more remarkable than the successes to date of the Norman dukes. The Angevins had started from smaller beginnings, had no obvious frontiers to work towards, and were surrounded by hostile powers. At this time, Anjou was ruled by one of its greatest counts, Geoffrey Martel (1040–60). Normandy and Anjou were almost inevitably rivals since between them, and of interest to both, was the county of Maine, while both hoped to intervene also in Brittany.

William responded with energy to the new invasion and again defeated his enemies, this time at Varaville in 1057. Here William caught the invaders attempting to cross a ford on the River Dives, and attacked the rear section, when the change of the tide caused the river to rise. About half the enemy army had crossed and could not return. According to Wace, the Normans used archers and knights with lances to annihilate the men at their mercy.[40] Because of the tide, William was unable to pursue those on the far side, but Henry I was forced to flee from the duchy.

Even this victory did not ensure William's triumph. Both the king of France and the count of Anjou had escaped and continued to oppose him with some success. It is sometimes overlooked that although William made claims upon Brittany and Maine, while Geoffrey Martel lived the latter was more successful.

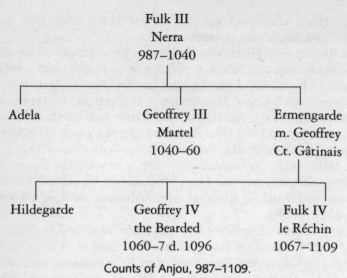

Fulk III
Nerra
987–1040

Adela	Geoffrey III Martel 1040–60	Ermengarde m. Geoffrey Ct. Gâtinais

Hildegarde	Geoffrey IV the Bearded 1060–7 d. 1096	Fulk IV le Réchin 1067–1109

Counts of Anjou, 987–1109.

For William the year which brought great change and transformed his position and his hopes was 1060. His two greatest enemies died: Henry I of France, leaving an eight-year-old son, Philip I (1060–1108); and Geoffrey III Martel of Anjou, whose death resulted in a conflict between his nephews, Geoffrey IV the Bearded (1060–7, d. 1096) and Fulk IV le Réchin (1067–1109), to control the principality.

It was at this point that William could seriously undertake a programme of expansion beyond Normandy. However, even in 1060 his first concern was not with England, where any success must have still seemed a fairly distant likelihood. His first action was against Maine, situated on Normandy's southern border. William captured the stronghold of his opponent, Geoffrey de Mayenne, by 'throwing fire inside its walls', and for a time from 1063 Maine fell under the power of Normandy.[41]

Without Geoffrey Martel, Anjou went through a period of internal troubles from which William took advantage. In the following year he moved into the second area where Norman ambitions had been thwarted by Anjou, Brittany. This was the campaign in which Harold Godwinson took part.

The reason why Harold went to Normandy is not clear. Edward

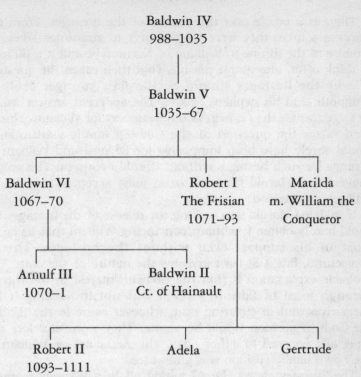

Baldwin IV
988–1035

Baldwin V
1035–67

Baldwin VI
1067–70

Robert I
The Frisian
1071–93

Matilda
m. William the
Conqueror

Arnulf III
1070–1

Baldwin II
Ct. of Hainault

Robert II
1093–1111

Adela

Gertrude

Counts of Flanders, 988–1111.

the Confessor seems to have sent him, and at least one of his aims was to try and help two relatives who were hostages in Normandy. The Durham chronicler, perhaps rightly, claims that the trip was made at Harold's initiative and against the king's advice: he 'begged the king's permission to go to Normandy and liberate his brother and nephew, who were detained there as hostages, and to bring them back with him in freedom'.[42] William of Poitiers has William the Conqueror later in England claiming: 'the king [Edward] gave me Godwin's son and grandson as hostages. What is more, he sent Harold himself to Normandy, so that he might swear in person in my presence what his father and the others whom I have mentioned had sworn . . . he confirmed in writing that the kingship of England should without question be mine.'[43]

There is a puzzle over this matter of the hostages. From the Norman sources they were handed over to guarantee Edward's promise of the throne to William of Normandy, and it is difficult to think of an alternative reason. That then raises the question of why the hostages should be Harold's younger brother, Wulfnoth, and his nephew, Hakon. The apparent answer would be to guarantee the Godwin family's support for William. This in turn raises the question of the Godwin family's attitude. It would surely have been impossible for Edward and William to arrange for such hostages without Harold's consent. This would suggest that Harold favoured or at least accepted the idea of William's succession.

If in 1064 Harold was seeking the release of the hostages, he could hardly obtain it without convincing William that he could trust in his support even without the hostages. This is conjectural, but it at least explains the nature of the oath. The probable explanation is that the Godwin interest in the throne through most of Edward's reign was not in seeking it for themselves, but in ensuring that, whoever came to the throne, the Godwin position would be secure. They were therefore not especially opposed to either Edgar the Aetheling or William, if their own family position was guaranteed.

The Tapestry shows Harold setting off in a leisurely manner, perhaps hunting on the way. He rested at his own manor of Bosham, where he feasted before boarding ship in Chichester Harbour. It was probably a storm which blew him to the shores of Ponthieu where he was arrested by Count Guy and taken to his castle at Beaurain. What Guy hoped to gain is uncertain, perhaps to use Harold as a bargaining counter with William.

The Conqueror was informed of the event, and ordered Harold's release. Count Guy was no great friend of the Norman duke, but he had been forced into recognising his overlordship after being among the defeated at Varaville. At any rate, Guy decided not to oppose William and escorted the captive to the duke, to whom he was handed. The act of obtaining his release gave William an advantage over Harold, whose ability to act freely in Normandy is uncertain.

William received Harold in the palace at Rouen. The Tapestry refers to some now forgotten scandal there between a woman with an English name, Aelfgyva, and a cleric, and then shows William setting off with Harold on the Breton campaign.[44] They passed by the great coastal monastery of Mont-St-Michel. Crossing the River Couesnon some of the Norman soldiers got into trouble in the quicksand, and were saved by the heroic action of Harold.

Their first objective was the castle at Dol, which the Tapestry shows as a wooden keep on a mound, a motte. It also shows Conan II, count of Brittany, escaping down a rope, though chronicle sources tell us that he had gone before the Normans arrived. They took Rennes and moved on to Dinan, which resisted. These two castles are also portrayed as wooden towers on mottes. Dinan was fired with torches, and the Bretons handed over the keys in surrender.

The Breton campaign had been successful, though its effects were soon to be reversed. William recognised the English earl's contribution, and 'gave arms to Harold'.[45] The Tapestry version is surely the portrayal of a knighting ceremony. It probably means that Harold recognised William as his lord, and must be taken along with the oath in defining how the Normans viewed Harold's subsequent actions.

So the victorious Norman army, having temporarily imposed its authority on eastern Brittany, rode back to Bayeux, where William's half-brother, Odo, was bishop. It was here, according to the Tapestry, that Harold took the famous oath to William.[46] Chronicle reports say it took place earlier and elsewhere, and Bonneville-sur-Touques, which is named for the event by William of Poitiers, is the most likely location. The Tapestry, in naming Bayeux, may have been trying to puff up the role of Bishop Odo, for whom the English artist was probably working.

There can be little doubt that an oath was made. What its exact content was we shall never know. Nor can we be quite certain if Harold was forced or tricked into swearing. The Norman interpretation was that Harold had made a promise to support William, perhaps as his man. William of Jumièges says that Edward sent Harold to 'swear fealty to the duke concerning his crown and, according to the Christian custom, pledge it with oaths'. William of Poitiers confirms this, saying that Harold promised to do all in his power to ensure William's succession to the English throne. He goes on to say that Harold promised to hand Dover to William with various other strongholds in England. We cannot take the Norman view without retaining some doubts about its accuracy on the detail, but it is impossible to discount the oath altogether, and William's actions throughout point to his belief that in 1066 Harold betrayed his trust.[47]

The theme of the Tapestry is that Harold had made a sacred oath, he is shown swearing on a reliquary; by taking the English crown he therefore broke his promise. The implication is that Harold had promised to aid William in getting the English crown, though the oath may not have been so specific; but it surely at the least promised Harold's fidelity to William. In any event Harold was able to return to England. One of the hostages, his nephew Hakon, was released, but Harold had to leave his brother Wulfnoth in Norman hands: this smacks of a compromise.

The Tapestry's portrayal of Earl Harold reporting back to the Confessor suggests that his trip was seen as a failure and a humiliation. Had he been sent merely to inform William of a promise, this would not be the case. Perhaps it means the partial failure to get a good deal on the hostages. Perhaps Edward no longer favoured William's succession; his attempts to bring over Edward from Hungary suggest this. It is also possible that Edward returned to the idea of William for the succession, as the Normans have it.

The other possibility is that Edward was toying with the thought of Harold succeeding. If so he may have been disappointed at the dilemma Harold had created for himself in Normandy. The comment of the author of the *Vita Aedwardi* that Harold was 'rather too generous with oaths (alas)' further suggests that Harold had promised more than was thought good, which would not be the case if Edward had sent him expressly to promise support to William for the English crown. Edward's general reluctance to make public promises belies the idea that Edward arranged for Harold to take a solemn vow in public about the English succession. In short the Tapestry suggests that what had happened in Normandy was not at the wish of the king, and hints that support for William as king may not have been welcome in England.[48]

It seems that William had, on an earlier occasion, visited Edward the Confessor in England, and been given some promise of the succession. William was related to Edward, whose mother we recall was Emma of Normandy. Given that Edward had no children, William's claim by relationship was as good as anyone else's. Harold's was, at best, through his sister, Edith, who was married to the king. William's interest in England was opportunistic. Had the chance offered at another time, he may well have had to ignore it. But in 1066 he could contemplate a military venture.

When Harold took the throne, William began to make plans to invade England. It is impossible to know exactly what happened in all the behind-the-scenes negotiating about the succession; almost certainly Edward gave out conflicting signals. Although we rely on Norman sources which have a bias, it is most likely that their version is close to the truth: that Edward promised William the succession, and that Harold took some oath to support William.

The Norman interest in expanding beyond the duchy was becoming a reality by the 1060s. Roger de Tosny and Robert Crispin led forces against the Muslims in Spain, helping in the recapture of Tarragona and Gerona. Probably the most interesting of the projects, apart from England, was the Norman venture into southern Italy. A Norman principality was established at Aversa by 1030. In time they would conquer the southern mainland of Italy and by 1061 were ready to begin the invasion of the island of Sicily, where they established a new Norman kingdom in the twelfth century.

An Italian chronicler recognised the adaptability of these conquerors: 'the Normans are a cunning and vengeful people . . . they can endure with incredible patience the inclemency of every climate'. It has recently been argued that at least some of the adventurers were not of Norman origin, including some of the more important such as Roger de Tosny in Spain.[49] It may be that part of the impetus was too tight a ducal control at home rather than Viking spirit. But there is still no doubt that men from Normandy played a vital role in expansion from north-western Europe and especially in opposition to the power of Islam. Norman efforts in the early crusades and in the eastern Mediterranean underline this ability to utilise their military abilities in varying circumstances. The point is the desire to leave Normandy for distant lands. But until 1066 such ventures had not been led by the duke with a ducal army.

The invasion of England was made possible by a combination of factors. William had been freed from many of his continental anxieties by the 1060s, but there were other considerations. He needed support. First he must be secure in Normandy. In 1055 a monk at Marmoutier could write that William was 'ruler of his whole land, something which is scarcely found anywhere else'.[50] By the 1060s practically every major family had accepted his authority, even ones on the fringes of the duchy found it advisable to have representatives at his court.

Officials in Normandy such as steward, butler, constable and chamberlain were not new, but the duke's authority over them was stronger. The Peace of God, introduced into Normandy in 1047, was repeated in 1064, guaranteeing peace from violence in the duchy from Wednesday evening till Monday morning: only the ducal forces were allowed to use arms during that period. With William II power reverted to the duke, and his government became dominant in the duchy. He dispensed justice at his court, and could even afford to indulge in informal acts, as when he made a grant while sitting on a carpet outside a house at Bernouville.[51]

He also needed to be sure that powerful neighbours would not take advantage of his absence overseas. His most important move was to marry Matilda, daughter of Baldwin V, count of Flanders (1035–67). She was thought 'a very beautiful and noble girl of royal stock', and is believed to have been just over 4 feet tall.[52] The marriage was forbidden by Pope Leo IX (1048–54), probably because of too close a blood relationship. But William went ahead with the ceremony in either 1050 or 1051 at Eu. This made Flanders an ally rather than a threat, and indeed a number of Flemings came with William on his invasion.

The Conqueror also desired the support of the Church in his venture. This was threatened by that selfsame marriage, since William had ignored the Church ban in order to marry. He was condemned for not awaiting papal approval, but he and his wife managed to placate the Pope, in part by building two great religious houses at Caen: St-Étienne for men, and La Trinité for women. In 1059 the Church gave formal approval of the marriage. By 1066 the Church was prepared to sanction the English venture, and a papal banner was given to the duke and proudly displayed for propaganda purposes when the troops embarked.[53]

William had prepared the ground well. By 1066 he was safe at home with firm authority over the ducal administration. After the death of the king of France and the count of Anjou he was free from major concern about neighbouring powers. He had made a marriage alliance with the most important of these, Flanders. He had also overcome difficulty with the papacy regarding his marriage and won not only acceptance but support for his venture in England. If ever the time was ripe to cross the sea and seek his fortune across the Channel, that time was in 1066.

FOUR

ARMS AND ARMIES

Much has been written about the advantages which one side had over the other in the battle of Hastings; in fact, in terms of the arms used there was very little difference. The state of war and its technology spread beyond any single state, county, duchy or kingdom. The English and the Normans had more in common than they had differences in 1066. On the Bayeux Tapestry, one can not easily tell English from Norman by either the arms they carry or the armour they wear. Indeed, to show a difference the artist often resorted to the use of distinguishing hairstyles: short for the Normans, long for the English. Both sides wore similar helmets and armour, both used similar swords and spears.

Historians have been clear for a long time now that the English army was well armed and well organised. Any lingering ideas that readers might retain of native troops armed only with clubs or similarly crude weapons, called together haphazardly and acting as a rabble rather than a trained army, should be dismissed at once. It seems probable that every army called into being in England by the kings consisted largely of trained men, if not quite professionals in our modern sense.

The main composition of the fyrd or army consisted of the household warriors and landed retainers of the king and of the great men who owed him allegiance. They might be seen as 'royal war bands' rather than national armies in a modern sense. The royal force, or indeed a local force acting for the king, could call upon shire levies too. Local shire levies seem to have been prepared to act in an emergency, for example, against invasion. Men from Somerset and Devon turned out against Harold

Godwinson when he returned to England against the Confessor in 1052. But even shire levies consisted largely of the middling to higher social ranks, armed men mostly with some experience of war. This is not to say that no men of lower rank participated. Ceorls, not the lowest of the low, did join the fyrd, as we see at Maldon, and the poem called the *Carmen* speaks of peasants at Hastings.[1] But it is not likely that large numbers of untrained troops were used. The whole process of assembling an army was geared towards ensuring the reverse: bringing together selected men, chosen because they would be useful in war.

Housecarls were military retainers, probably introduced by the Danish Cnut, and they were to be found in the household of an earl or ealdorman as well as that of the king. Such men appear to have been paid wages, and may in a sense be seen as mercenaries or stipendiaries, as probably were the Danes employed in the royal fleet in 1015.[2] But housecarls were sometimes granted lands and a place to live. They were not so much mercenaries or some sort of standing army as they were household men.

Military households are a common feature of the medieval world, both before and after Cnut. The meaning of 'housecarls' after all is household servants, and this is essentially what they were. There were 15 acres of Wallingford where housecarls dwelled, presumably employed as a garrison there, and Domesday Book records various other examples.[3] We shall look at the English system in due course, and find that it provided well-trained men quite capable of fighting any force of the day.

Increasingly too it is becoming apparent that although there were some social distinctions between English and Norman society, and although armies were raised by slightly different methods, that the differences were not as great as once thought. This is not the place for a lengthy discussion on feudalism and what we mean by it. It was not a medieval word for a start. For our purposes, what can be said is that although the actual process of raising forces was not quite the same, the underlying rationale was not so very different. Both powers, for example, raised some troops on the basis of the land held by individual warriors, and the service owed in respect of that land.

There were some differences in the composition of the

armies. Two stand out and will need to be considered in detail. Firstly, at Hastings, the Normans had archers in some numbers whereas the English appear to have had few. Secondly, the Normans made considerable use of cavalry whereas the English, although they had horses and were experienced riders, seem not normally to have fought as cavalry. In the end these two factors might be said to have made the difference between two well-matched forces which stood against each other in the field for practically the whole length of a long autumn day. It is important to examine the reasons for these points of contrast.

ARMS AND ARMOUR

Let us begin by examining what in general the two sides had in common, the normal arms and armour of a fighting man in the middle of the eleventh century. Archaeology has provided very few useful objects from this period, virtually none from England and Normandy. Until this is remedied, we rely heavily on the images in the Bayeux Tapestry.

There has been some discussion over the date and provenance of this remarkable work. Suffice it for the present to say that there is general consensus, about which we see no need to quarrel, with a date very shortly after the battle, in the late eleventh century probably between 1077 and 1083, and also with its being made in England and possibly at Canterbury. The artist is anonymous, and he was not present at some of the events portrayed, but by and large the more research goes into the Tapestry, the more respect historians have for the accuracy and care of his work.

There are some details over which one is uncertain of the artist's intent, and there may be some errors since he was probably not a man with military experience, so we must beware of accepting everything without question, especially when the Tapestry seems at odds with surviving contemporary chronicles; but for the most part we can accept the Tapestry as the best evidence for the arms and armour of the time.

Let us examine what the typical soldier on the Tapestry is wearing, and what arms he is carrying. Firstly, let us consider those troops portrayed as fighting on foot. Occasionally on the Tapestry one gets hints of clothing worn under the armour. This obviously existed, but from its nature is impossible to describe with any certainty for this period. Almost certainly both head and upper body would have been covered with enough clothing to give some padding effect to metal armour.

The two main pieces of armour were a helmet and a byrnie, or hauberk. The eleventh-century helmet was made of either leather or metal, and was conical in shape: Normans, English and Scandinavians all wore much the same kind. Leather helmets were not much more than caps but offered protection against the weather as well as against weapons. Better armed soldiers, and especially wealthier ones, would have had a metal headpiece. This could be made of one piece of metal, as is proved by a surviving example in the Museum of Armour at Vienna. Most of the helmets on the Tapestry appear to be of the type made of separate plates of metal, riveted together on to a framework of metal strips. In one helmet from the early Saxon period, the plates of the helmet were made from horn.[4] The most important feature of the helmet of our period was the nasal. This was normally made from a metal strip in the centre at the front, projecting down beyond the level of the helmet so that it covered the nose, thereby offering some protection for the eyes and face.

Some Tapestry helmets appear to have projected at the back in order to cover the neck. One must assume this to be an occasional rather than a regular feature. A helmet found in York from the Viking period has a curtain of mail fixed to cover the neck.[5] The head could also be covered, under the helmet, with chain mail. This might be in the form of a hood attached to the main mail coat, or as a separate piece. The word 'hauberk' itself derives from Frankish 'halsberg', meaning neck protection, so the hood may have been an original feature.

The hauberk became a symbol of status, only a man of some rank would own and use one. When his horse was killed at the battle of Dreux in 1014, Hugh of Maine buried his hauberk, put on a shepherd's cloak and carried shepherd's gear on his shoulder as disguise in order to escape.[6] Indeed, the unit of land which provided military service was known as the 'fief de hauberk'. The byrnie, or hauberk, or mail coat, was shaped rather like a tunic or tee-shirt, and had to be donned by slipping it over head and body.

Both infantry and cavalry wore a similar mail coat, as seen on the Tapestry. William of Poitiers confirms that the second line of the Norman army, consisting of better armed infantry, wore hauberks.[7] Modern efforts to reproduce this form of armour are illuminating in terms of giving some idea of the difficulties and advantages to be gained from the garb. It feels quite heavy to lift, and it was thought a feat of strength that the Conqueror on one occasion returned to camp smiling, having carried his own and the rather large William fitz Osbern's hauberk on his shoulders for some distance. And yet, once put on, the mail coat balances on the shoulders and is less restrictive to movement than one might suppose.[8]

The hauberk is constructed from circles of metal looped through each other. There are various possible variations on this method of production, some coats given double or even triple layers of protection; some being soldered, some riveted. It is also possible to assist the comfort and usefulness of mail by varying the size of the metal rings: smaller rings at the edges make it fit more snugly to the body. Mail provided some protection from certain blows, more from slashing than thrusting efforts; but it could always be pierced, for example, by a direct shot from an arrow, bolt, spear or lance, and it did not cover the whole body, so that there were always vulnerable spots – the face, the hands, the lower part of the legs.

There are some points to examine with regard to the armour of cavalrymen. Their hauberks were much the same as those of the infantry, but two possible differences need to be considered: the appearance of a rectangular piece on the chest, which in the Tapestry and elsewhere seems to be applied to cavalry rather than infantry armour; and the question of how the tunic shape would need to be adapted in order to make riding possible and comfortable.

There is some interest in a feature of some mail coats in the Tapestry, and elsewhere, which have a rectangular shape over the breast. They do not appear on all examples on the Tapestry, and feature most prominently in a section before the battle. They are not worn always by the great men. It could be that the artist only included when he felt like it, what was actually a normal feature.

One explanation of this rectangle, which seems to be edged with leather, is that it was an extra plate attached in order to give added protection to the chest. Illustrations other than the Tapestry look as if this could be the case, where the piece is coloured differently and looks like a single piece of plate armour. However, on the Tapestry there appears to be mail within the rectangle, though it could still be a separately made piece.

The best explanation seems to be that this was the way the hauberk was made easier to put on, having an enlarged opening which could be closed up once it was on, like buttoning up a shirt at the neck once in place. At any rate, a story that, on arrival in England, the Conqueror put on his hauberk the wrong way round does suggest that the tunic was not uniformly constructed front and back. The suggestion is made that the rectangle, clearly visible in the illustration above, was a flap of mail, part of which needed to be secured by tying in place. The only question then is why it appears to be rectangular, an L-shaped flap might seem more likely. One suggestion does not necessarily exclude the other: it is possible that an extra piece of armour was tied on over the neck opening.

Another suggestion is that it might have been a contraption of leather straps to allow the shield to be tied in place. One Tapestry illustration shows a Norman grasping part of a rectangular arrangement of straps, which looks exactly like the rectangle over the chest, but is clearly independent of the mail.[9]

The other question is whether hauberks were made differently for mounted men. Ian Peirce believes that they may have been trousered, and certainly that is how some appear on the Tapestry. This would have been extremely uncomfortable for mounted men and very inconvenient. It is more likely that they were always, for both infantry and cavalry, tunic-shaped. The tapering of rings towards the edges would have made the metal cling round the limbs and give a trousered appearance.

The shield portrayed on the Bayeux Tapestry is mostly the long, tapering, kite-shaped type. The same type of shield seems to have belonged to both infantry and cavalry. It is shown held over the arm, and slung round the neck when not in use. It was not to have a long history after this period. For infantry the tendency was towards a slightly shorter and more manoeuvrable shield with a straight-edged top. For cavalry the kite shield must have been unwieldy and awkward, and it is not surprising that it was replaced by various types of smaller shield, some similar to infantry shields, some round. In fact, some of the soldiers on the Tapestry, notably English infantry, one of whom seems to be Gyrth Godwinson, are using a smaller shield, which is circular and more convex in shape.

The straps shown on the Tapestry seem of simple design, about a quarter of the way down the shield, from side to side, so that when held in action the top of the shield could comfortably protect the face. Some of the shields are shown with bosses placed at the centre of the broader part, and some have a few rivets – four, six, nine, even eleven – probably to hold together the planks of wood making up the shield, perhaps to help fasten on a leather covering, and perhaps also to hold the straps. The boss, like the rivets, was of iron and some shields had a metal rim, some an iron bar inside for the hand-grip. Various woods could provide the basic material for a shield, but alder and willow were the most popular in England.[10]

The Tapestry shields are decorated but, unless the artist was ignorant of such designs, were not heraldic in nature. It seems significant that the body of Harold Godwinson could not be recognised after the battle; had he been wearing distinguishing heraldic arms this would not have been the case.[11] The Tapestry artist is probably to be trusted.

Individual and family arms, passed by descent and with modifications, were just about to begin their appearance at this time, probably first in France. The earliest manuscript with apparent heraldic shields on is the Stephen Harding Bible, a Cistercian work of the early twelfth century, and even that is an imaginary depiction of biblical scenes. Some Tapestry designs no doubt did show who were their possessors, as did some of the standards, but they seem to be purely individual affairs.

Some of the standards displayed on the Tapestry have a broader significance, for example, the dragon (the wyvern of Wessex) held for Harold Godwinson. We know that Viking leaders commonly used a raven standard, which had religious significance as the mark of Odin. These had an ancient and sometimes religious as well as national importance. They represent the whole force behind the banner in some sense.

The arms of the English infantryman were the common weapons of such soldiers over centuries: sword, spear and less commonly, axe. The sword was already the weapon *par excellence* of the noble warrior. Its manufacture had developed over the centuries, and would continue to improve in design. But by the eleventh century, swords were well advanced and even in some areas manufactured in bulk.

The early medieval sword at its best was perhaps the Viking sword, a weapon developed for cutting rather than thrusting, with the emphasis on the sharp edges. At least in legend, it was said that such a sword was so sharp that on one occasion a man was sliced: 'so cleanly in two as he sat in his armour, that the cut only became apparent when, as he rose to shake himself, he fell dead in two halves'. Most of the main weapons of this period depended upon the skill of the smith who had first worked the iron. Forging methods had improved particularly from about AD 900, and the blade could now be made longer and lighter.

Frankish swords were also improving, and the makers – either individuals or 'factories' – seem to be Frankish. Sword makers' names were sometimes engraved on the blade: the name 'Ulfberht' appeared in the tenth century, 'Ingelri' from about 1050 for the type X sword with a broad, flat blade with a rather rounded point, and type XI, also eleventh century, with the name 'Gicelin', which was rather longer and narrower in style.

There were several processes for producing the blade, which was normally double edged. The handle or hilt resulted from a careful assembly of parts: a guard to protect against blows sliding up the blade, with a pommel which served the dual purpose of fixing the handle on to the blade, and balancing the heaviness of the blade so that the hand could be comfortably at or near the pivotal point in terms of weight.

The spear had two main components: a wooden shaft and a metal head. It could be used for thrusting, but was certainly at times employed for throwing, as can be seen on the Tapestry. It was generally the weapon of the ordinary soldier, but nobles could also have one. At Maldon, Dunnere, a ceorl, 'shook his throwing spear'; but the commander, Byrhtnoth, himself 'brandished his slender spear' when he spoke to the men. It is interesting, and suggestive of the importance of the weapon in general, that there are eight Old English words for a spear.[12] The shaft was commonly made of ash, indeed 'ash' was one of the eight words meaning spear, but various woods might be used.

The cavalry lance on the Tapestry looks very much like the infantry spear, and perhaps at this time there was no great difference. One might expect the lance to be longer, but there is no sign yet of the elaborate hand guards and heavier design which would mark the later cavalry lance. It is true that spears themselves might be long. The Aberlemno stone depicts such a spear.[13] In 1016 at Sherston we hear of 'spear and lance', which suggests a longer infantry weapon.[14] And Wace did say that when the horseman dismounted to fight on foot he broke his lance in half, obviously suggesting that the cavalry weapon was longer, but then Wace was writing in the twelfth century. The shaft of the cavalry lance, like that of the spear, appears to be quite straight, with no special holding point.

The lance was not yet used for a concerted charge, that is, held couched underarm by all the men charging together with lances levelled so that its force came upon impact. On the Tapestry one does see the lance sometimes couched, but more often it is held overhead, and can be both thrust and thrown. It has been argued that it might have been used in this manner in response to the problem of riding against an enemy on higher ground. But it seems more likely that as yet cavalry did not operate as one large unit in a charge together, and that the way of using the lance was a matter of individual preference. There was more improvisation and less organisation about charges than would be the case a century later.

A number of the English soldiers are shown using a battle axe. This seems to be already a somewhat antique weapon. It had been a favourite of Scandinavian armies, and it does still appear from time to time in later conflicts. Its use in England may also have depended chiefly on Scandinavian influence, the two-handed weapon does not seem to have been used before the later Anglo-Saxon period.[15] An axe could still be handed to King Stephen at the battle of Lincoln in 1141. In the twelfth century, by which time its use was rare, it was seen as the typical Scandinavian weapon by one chronicler, writing of the defender of the river crossing at Stamford Bridge using 'his country's weapon'.[16]

The axe was a fearsome and devastating weapon, but not easily wielded and less flexible than a sword. An axeman required a good deal of space around him in order to be effective, and this could leave the line vulnerable to charging cavalry. It must also have been a particularly tiring weapon to wield through a long day of battle. Nevertheless, it was favoured by some of the English.

One cannot be certain about the Tapestry's accuracy on size. The art form of the age did not attempt exact reproduction in size. In people, size probably denoted rank rather than height. If it is to be trusted in this respect, then the Tapestry seems to show two types of axe: a smaller hand axe, which might have been thrown, and the long-shafted battle axe, which could only be used in the hand. There is a particularly vivid example of the latter held at the very front of the English line at the moment when it came face to face with the Norman cavalry. Another view shows Leofwin Godwinson wielding an axe, and it may have been primarily an aristocratic weapon.

At the other end of the social scale, the bow in war was usually the weapon of the lowly, though this had not always been the case in Scandinavia. Most of the archers shown on the Tapestry are small and not well armoured, both signs of humble rank. Only wooden bows made from a single piece of wood appear on the Tapestry. Given the size problem with the art, and the dwarf size of the archers portrayed, it is quite probable that the bow was in fact about longbow length. This would be necessary to give it sufficient impact. So the bow used by the Normans was similar to a longbow, a single stave tapered at the extremities, held by a string.[17]

The armour of the cavalryman, which for Hastings means the Norman cavalryman, differed little if at all from that of the well-armoured infantryman: they also wore helmet and hauberk and carried a kite shield. The only instance where there might be a difference was in the styling of the hauberk. In later periods it was common to split the hauberk at front and back towards the lower edge, so that it could spread out like a skirt. This would mean that the rider could sit astride his mount without having uncomfortably to sit upon a tunic of mail. This is probably the method used in 1066.

The cavalryman's weapons were similar to those of the infantryman: the same type of sword and a lance which was not unlike a spear. As we have seen, the more specialised cavalry lance was not yet developed. However, the rider would not use the battle axe, a purely infantry weapon, nor in this instance did he use a bow. The aristocracy saw bows as weapons for hunting, but in war it was the weapon of those of lower social rank. However, during the pursuit after the battle, one Norman is shown mounted and drawing a bow.

Perhaps the main weapon of the cavalryman was his horse. Its weight, speed and impact could have great effect. Before long, the Frankish cavalry would be proving its worth against different style armies in the East during the crusades, when those seeing it in action for the first time were greatly impressed. Anna Comnena thought that 'the first charge of Frankish cavalry was irresistible'; the Frank could 'drill his way through the walls of Babylon'.[18]

The cavalry horse was a special animal, more valuable than any other horse. It had to be specially bred and specially trained. It was large without being too clumsy. In battle, as the Tapestry makes abundantly clear, warhorses were stallions. The fact that the Normans went to all the trouble involved in bringing their own horses by sea suggests how important the special animals were. This process is demonstrated on the Tapestry, and described in the *Carmen*.[19]

Warhorses had bridles, reins and large saddles, raised at front and rear to give a solid seat. In the Tapestry the saddles appear to be held by a strap round the horse's chest, and sometimes a strap under the animal's belly may also be seen. As yet the horses themselves do not appear to have been protected by armour. By this time stirrups were well established, which made fighting from the saddle more feasible and the couched lance effective.

Glover thought that the Norman horseman was 'for the most part a mounted javelineer', but the pictures of the Tapestry showing a lance held in couched position suggests this is too restrictive on methods. By the time of the First Crusade, lances were used in the couched position. Anna Comnena describes the southern Norman Robert Guiscard tucking a lance 'under his arm' as he prepares for action.[20] The rider wore spurs, not a new invention, but important for control in the tense situation of battle.

ARMIES

Both the English and the Norman systems of raising troops were effective. In the normal course of warfare, large armies were rarely required. Often the need was to defend on a wide geographical scale, and therefore the bulk of the troops raised were distributed to key points on frontier or coast according to the threat of the moment. The nature of England's geography, and the history of Viking raids and invasions, meant that naval defence was a necessity, so fleets and seamen had also to be assembled. It has been argued that the lithsmen of late Anglo-Saxon England composed a permanent force, and they made up a fleet. But this is uncertain, their usual function seems to be that of hired men for specific purposes and temporary rather than permanent, usually being paid off at the end of their period of use.[21]

Throughout northern Europe it was expected that all mature men would be prepared to fight in defence of their country or state or whatever power held their allegiance. But for larger forces, which needed to be kept in the field a length of time, there was always a problem in taking men away from their usual employment. Armies habitually relied not on forces raised in temporary emergencies, but on more or less professional soldiers.

There were two main sources of such men. Firstly, all kings, dukes, counts, earls and great men of this kind had their own households, perhaps the most significant element of which was the military household. This consisted of trained and often experienced soldiers. They lived with their lord, they accompanied him in war and peace, they defended and protected him. Their loyalty was demanded, often with an oath to guarantee it, his protection and maintenance of them was expected. In battle such men would fight as an integrated group, and group loyalty and comradeship was also a feature of such troops.

The second type of professional soldier were mercenaries or stipendiaries. They served for pay, and were hired for the purpose. There was often little distinction between mercenaries and allies; men who agreed to fight for you and expected rewards and who were paid in some sense. Both the Anglo-Saxon and Norman systems allowed room for hiring experienced soldiers.

The line between mercenary and loyal household man could be thin; one might easily become the other. Because troops were paid certainly did not mean that you could expect them to be unreliable and disloyal. They often prided themselves on giving good service, and on many occasions outshone other men in their dogged fighting for their lord. Sometimes such men also came in groups and were hired under a leader, but the age of captains of large mercenary troops was in the future.

Such professional troops were the backbone of armies, but in order to fulfil all the demands of war, other men were required: for garrison work and field armies when the threat was greater, when, for example, invasion was anticipated or undertaken. Northern Europe as a whole had developed systems which obliged the more solid citizens and farmers to undertake military duties. The systems varied, rather as creatures vary with evolutionary development, but the purpose was the same, and the methods at least in such a close area as northern Europe were quite similar.

The differences between the English and the Norman systems are often stressed, but in truth the similarities were more numerous and perhaps more important. Thus in one way or another the primary link was between landholding and military obligation. Maldon in Essex had to aid the royal host by sending a horse for the army. Under King Aethelstan, a law read 'every man shall provide two well-mounted men for every plough', and that king also took 'no small mounted force' with him against the Scots.[22] Even to the possession of horses, this is not unlike the demands made on Normans of a similar rank.

This matter has been distorted by the long historical debate over feudalism. Historians have strained to define it, not surprisingly because in a sense it only exists in their imaginations. This in effect means that any historian can define what he or she sees as feudalism. Our only need is to try and see what actually existed. And of course something did exist: there was a system in each area.

If we avoid talking about feudalism, we may reasonably examine how these systems operated without too much heartache. However, it needs to be made clear that, if not a system, there were certainly areas of land which had been given out in both England and Normandy on the understanding that military service was attached to them. In England, king's thegns probably held in this way. An early law stated that 'if a noble who holds land neglects military service, he shall pay 120s and forfeit his land'.[23]

In England as in Normandy, men's first allegiance was to their immediate lord, whether he was the king, the duke or another. Before the word fee or fief was used, Church lands in particular had often been granted as benefices, with military obligations attached. English bookland had originally been ecclesiastical. Such land had been given to the Church without any services attached, but much of it was later recovered in order to support military obligations. And English loanland compared closely in function to a benefice, neither being necessarily military in origin. In Domesday Book 'feudum' or fief was sometimes the word used for loanland.[24]

The English had developed a method of raising forces which depended upon land assessment. This had been deliberately initiated for the purpose of raising armies during the years of threat from Scandinavia. In essence, land was assessed by a unit known as the hide. This was referred to by Bede as a unit for a family, and no doubt had a real basis in the minds of its inventors, but like all units of assessment (compare, say, the rating system in England of recent times, or the council tax going through the same process now) it became a unit in its own right not exactly related to any other unit of land or money.

The hidage assessment needed to be reviewed and altered from time to time and so moved further and further away from its origins. Some areas received privileged ratings, others developed after the system had begun and so on. But it proved such a useful method that it was retained for centuries, and was still an important unit in Domesday Book even after the Norman Conquest. Roughly speaking, so many men were demanded for military service according to how many hides an estate had been assessed at. If this was gradually altered to allow men to pay so many shillings instead of performing personal service, it still led to the raising of forces.

The common soldier of the royal army was not, in England any more than in Normandy, the lowest social being in the state. A recent work defines the royal fyrd or army as 'a royal levy composed of privileged landowners and their own retainers, reinforced by the king's military household and stipendiary troops'.[25] All this confirms a long-held suspicion among historians that neither army at Hastings was probably very large. There is no way of being certain, but figures such as the 1,200,000 given by the *Carmen* for Harold's force can certainly be ignored.[26]

Probably the main group of people called up were the thegns, men of some high social rank in terms of the populace as a whole. The term thegn underwent a change of meaning because the thegn underwent a change of status at the Conquest. The thegn of the England of Edward the Confessor was the ordinary man of rank throughout the realm. However, there were gradations in the rank of thegn itself.

It is becoming clearer that a king's thegns were a special group. These owed their military obligation to the king directly. Therefore, they are strikingly like the lords who owed military service to the Norman duke for their lands. We need not debate in detail the relation between hides and military service, and there are several problems and uncertainties about it. There may not have been a nation-wide arrangement, but certainly in some areas there was a definite link between the land one held, valued in hides, and the amount of military service given: typically one well-equipped soldier from every five hides. Possession of five hides was also seen as a qualification for the rank of thegn.

It used to be said that English thegns owed their military service because of their rank, while Norman lords owed their service for their lands; but the distinction has become increasingly difficult to maintain. Both groups held lands and both groups owed service. It is doubtful that they made the distinction over purpose that historians have when called to the colours. They came because it was their duty to do so. A Norman or an Englishman would need a good excuse to evade a call from duke or king to join an army of invasion or a defence force against invasion.

The main difference between the composition of the English and Norman armies was neither the system of raising nor the type of man who responded, but the circumstances which made particular demands on either side. Harold was calling on his normal national and local system to face invasion; in 1066 to face a double invasion, which made for rather exceptional demands. We shall see this in practice when we examine the events of that year. But it meant that Harold raised a field army from his own resources and from as many shires as he could use, as well as a fleet. His northern earls also raised forces in the emergency from *their* resources and from the local shires.

William's position was quite different. He had to persuade men to join him on a dangerous expedition which was beyond the normal demands of military service. He therefore had to search more widely for men to come, and needed to cope with the problem of keeping a force beyond the usual time limits. Only the offer of extraordinary rewards could succeed. It used to be thought that William had a fully organised feudal system by which to raise his forces. Now this is less clear. It is certainly true that, as in England, there were Normans who owed military obligations. But a good deal of the duchy was held in alods, without obligations. The duke, like the English king, also relied on household troops and mercenaries. In a campaign against the Angevins we hear of him paying fifty knights.[27]

One problem of troops raised through obligation related to land was the attachment of an understanding of the time limit for it, whether it be forty days, or two months, or whatever. If an army were to be kept in the field for a considerable length of time, there must be additional rewards offered, and therefore even troops which came to fulfil an obligation might stay to be paid, and could in a sense also be considered as mercenaries.

There was also the important and related problem of provisioning an army for a prolonged period: food and the necessities could be collected for distribution, but in the end there would be a resort to foraging. Harold found the problem of keeping a force in the field difficult in 1066. By September 'the provisions of the people were gone, and nobody could keep them there any longer'.[28] Harold in fact disbanded his fleet before the vital battles occurred, having to recall it in the emergency. For William the problem of fighting overseas made more acute the problems of both long service and provisions.

With the glittering if uncertain rewards offered by the possible conquest of England, and thanks to the high military reputation he had won by 1066, William was able to attract into his ranks a variety of men who might term themselves allies or who had some link to him but who could not be described as obligated: men, for example, from Flanders, the county of his wife, Brittany, Maine and other parts of France.

William also put efforts into not only collecting ships but also building anew. The Tapestry portrays both the making of ships and the loading of provisions, including wine, for transport over the Channel.[29] Success in war depended as much on the ability to keep a force in the field and to feed it, as it did upon tactical brilliance. In 1066 both Harold and William showed themselves to have abilities above the average in these respects.

Both sides had fleets and sailors available. The Norman fleet was hastily raised, collected and built. The Viking founders of Normandy had maritime expertise, and Normandy has a long coastline with many inhabitants who made their living from the sea. But Normandy had not engaged in naval war and had no naval traditions, apart from its Viking past. William's fleet was a temporary expedient. It served its purpose, since William's primary need was for transport.

The English had the more difficult task of using a fleet for defence, but they had a well-ordered naval organisation going back over many years to King Alfred. In 1008 Aethelred II had ordered the building of new ships, one from every 310 hides.[30] On other occasions it seems land assessed at 300 hides was expected to provide a ship. The English ships, like those of the Normans, were probably derived chiefly from Viking models. There is a lengthy description of one ship given to Edward the Confessor by Earl Godwin:

> A loaded ship, its slender lines raked up
> In double prow, lay anchored on the Thames,
> With many rowing benches side by side,

> The towering mast amidships lying down,
> Equipped with six score fearsome warriors.
> A golden lion crowns the stern. A winged
> And golden dragon at the prow affrights
> The sea, and belches fire with triple tongue.
> Patrician purple pranks the hanging sail, . . .
> The yard-arm strong and heavy holds the sails.[31]

And John of Worcester recorded 'a skilfully made galley with a gilded prow' given to Harthacnut.[32]

Men were obliged to serve at sea in much the same way as in the army on land. A number of ports had special obligations in this respect. The Isle of Wight seems often at this time to have been used as a base for the south coast. But in September 1066 Harold had to disband his fleet because it had been kept active too long, and William luckily, or perhaps through good planning, was able to cross without opposition. Harold did recall the fleet, and it posed some threats again to William's security in England.

THE KEY DIFFERENCES

We have already suggested that there were two vital differences between the armies which met at Hastings: the Norman possession of groups of archers, and the Norman use of cavalry. Each of these factors helped to decide the outcome of the battle, and deserve careful consideration.

Why the English did not have many archers at Hastings is not easy to explain, but it does seem to be true. None of the sources give any indication that English archers played any important role in the battle. None of the reliable literary sources mention English archers. On the Bayeux Tapestry there is one solitary archer among the English ranks, but not portrayed as in any way significant in the fighting, and his bow looks rather unimpressive in size. Yet the word bow itself is an English word, appropriately meaning 'flexible' or 'that which bends'.[33]

Before 1066 there is not a great deal of evidence about English battles, let alone about the composition of English armies, but there is sufficient to believe that the English did possess archers, as indeed probably to a greater degree did the Scandinavians, so that unlike the matter of cavalry it was not a question of any fundamental difference in the way battles were normally fought. Indeed, whereas the difference over cavalry troops is explicable, the lack of archers in Harold's army remains puzzling.

The eighth-century Franks' Casket (from Northumbria) shows a man using a bow in defence of his home. At the beginning of the tenth century, an archer killed a noble by shooting him with an arrow through the window as he relieved himself in the privy. At Maldon in 991, 'bows were busy', though it is not said on which side. Elsewhere in the poem there is mention of a Northumbrian hostage, Aescferth the son of Eglaf, who 'did not shrink back at the war-play,/rather he sent forth arrows swiftly –/sometimes he hit a shield, sometimes pierced a warrior,/time and again he dealt out wounds'.[34] Riddle number twenty-three in the *Exeter Book* is about a bow, spelled backwards, which must be guessed: 'Wob's my name, if you work it out;/I'm a fair creature fashioned for battle', which clearly suggests that these weapons were not only for hunting. A letter of Aldhelm confirms this, with 'the warlike bowman in the midst of battle', though he is quoting from a classical source.[35]

Snorri Sturlusson, the thirteenth-century Icelandic author of the *Heimskringla* sagas, has the English using bows in the battle of Stamford Bridge. There is no reason that this should not be right, but Snorri's version of the battle is late, garbled and unreliable, and without confirmation it is dangerous to accept his version as correct. In his account, the Vikings had bows and arrows, while the English attacked with 'spears and arrows', with the Norse king being killed by an arrow in the throat.[36] There is perhaps some confirmation in an addition made to the C version of the *Anglo-Saxon Chronicle*, not about the battle, it is true, but about crossing the river, when 'an Englishman shot an arrow' at the defender of the bridge, though without dislodging him.[37]

Two main answers to the puzzle of why the English used archers on previous occasions but not at Hastings seem possible. The first is that, excluding Snorri, these other occasions were much earlier and possibly what had once been a customary method of fighting had become more or less obsolete. There is no more proof for this than for a second contention, but the second seems more likely.

Archers came from certain regions, normally where there were woods or forest. This sort of region made for the use of archery on a larger scale than elsewhere, providing easy sources of material for equipment and plentiful targets for hunting. It is noticeable in later history how often one hears of archers coming from, say, the Forest of Dean or Sherwood Forest. Methods of fighting also tended to be regional, and archery may well have been more popular in Northumbria than Wessex: one notes how many of the early instances of evidence come from the region of the old northern kingdom. Later on, Gerald of Wales wrote that Gwent was noted for its archers whereas other parts of Wales were better known for producing spearmen.

We know very little about the composition of the English armies at either Gate Fulford or Stamford Bridge. Possibly archers fought in one or other or both of these, in which case those same would not have been available at Hastings. As relatively lowly infantry they would be recruited in the local levies. At Hastings, Harold gathered men from as wide an area as he could in the brief space between Stamford Bridge and his fight with William, but the local levies for Hastings inevitably came largely from the south and probably not for the most part from regions especially noted for archery.

In other words it may just be an accident of events that deprived the English of archers at Hastings: the unusual circumstance of having three important battles within the space of a few months and the location of the third and last of them being in the south. We know that the Weald did later produce archers, and perhaps some from there were at Hastings. It may be also that Harold was more concerned about his élite troops, the swordsmen and axemen. Only these men who came from the wealthier social class would possess horses and be able to ride from Stamford Bridge to Hastings. The infantry would be what the local levies provided, and the evidence of the battle suggests that they were chiefly spearmen.

The Normans certainly possessed and used archers at Hastings. Norman archers were also reputed to be lowly. There is a story in William of Jumièges where Bernard the Philosopher puts on poor man's clothes and then takes up the appropriate weapon, a bow, in order to gain the attention of Duke Richard II by pretending to shoot him. He was arrested, but later pardoned.

The Normans had archers in sufficient numbers to use them in tactical groups. At Hastings, Norman archers were put at the front of the army in the opening phase, played a significant role in the battle, and accounted for the life of Harold Godwinson. Nor was this the first occasion that we hear of Norman archers; they were used, for example, at Varaville in 1057.

Judging by their sophisticated tactical employment at Hastings, archers were a fully integrated part of Norman forces, probably having been employed over a considerable period of time. Both the Franks and the Vikings had archery traditions, so the Normans could have inherited either or both. The bow shown on the Tapestry is always the wooden bow. The likelihood is that this was of length sufficient to be compared to a longbow, and was certainly of the same construction. Actual bowstaves which have been found confirm the point that longbow staves were common over a long period: some forty were found from the late Roman period, one from the seventh century, others from the Viking period. A reconsideration of the artwork of the Tapestry suggests that many of the bows there were probably the height of a man.

Literary sources make it clear that the Normans also possessed crossbows. There is no reason not to believe this possible. The crossbow has a long history, from ancient China to the Romans and the Franks. We have no detailed description and no depiction on the Tapestry, but probably in the eleventh century these would be of relatively primitive construction, perhaps using a forked piece of wood as the basis. It was, nevertheless, thought a powerful weapon. The author of the *Carmen* says that shields were of no use against crossbow bolts.[38]

The crossbow was mechanical in operation, with a trigger. It shot a shorter, heavier missile than the wooden bow did, called usually a quarrel or a bolt. One advantage of crossbows was that men could be more easily trained to use them. We can only guess why crossbows are not illustrated on the Tapestry. The most likely explanation is that they were rare in England; we hear nothing of them before the Conquest, though it has been suggested that one is pictured on a seventh-century Pictish carving.[39] Since the Tapestry was designed by an English artist, we may guess that he was unfamiliar with this weapon.

As to the Norman possession of cavalry, this is more explicable. The English again had, to a degree, the capacity to use horses in war, and occasionally before 1066 they had done so. Likewise the Scandinavian conquerors; when Cnut crossed the Thames in 1016 it was 'with many men on horses'.[40] When Harold was sent by the Confessor against the Welsh in 1063, he went with 'a small troop of horsemen'; later he met his brother Tostig who commanded a small 'equestrian army'. It is even true that an Englishman of rank was expected to ride: 'a noble should be on a horse's back'. An early scene on the Bayeux Tapestry shows Harold riding to Bosham with his retainers, called 'milites', and they are mounted. There are Englishmen in Domesday Book referred to as 'milites', though it is not clear what their military function was. It is not for war, and the horses are probably not warhorses, but the similarity to Norman mounted warriors is unmistakable.

Similarities were marked by the English themselves, and their word for the French 'chevalier' is the one which has established itself in the language: 'cniht' meaning retainer as the origin, of course, for 'knight'.[41] But the English ethos of war, like that of the Vikings, was an infantry one. Swordsmen and spearmen, in the Scandinavian case even archers, were the admired warriors. The known English burials of warriors demonstrate that the weapons of an infantryman were those considered precious enough to take into the other world, reflecting their values in life. The English warriors expected to stand side by side, comrades together around their leader, to hack, or thrust, and trade blows. The *Carmen* poet wrote 'the English scorn the solace of horses and trusting in their strength they stand fast on foot'; and he also stated that at Hastings the English had horses which they left to the rear when forming for battle.

The shield-wall, or war-wall, was a poetic description of this put into practice: a solid line of men standing shoulder to shoulder to face the enemy. At Sherston in 1016, the best men were placed in the front line, which was probably normal practice. At Hastings, the English were described as all on foot and in close ranks.[42] The ideal was to advance towards victory or to die.

Cavalry, with its capacity to ride off to safety, was not an admired kind of troop. A telling phrase in the *Anglo-Saxon Chronicle* relates to the flight of the English under Earl Ralph at Hereford in 1055, 'because they were on horseback'. In the poem of the battle of Maldon, Byrhtnoth told his men each to let go of his horse, 'to drive it far off and to march forwards'. This attitude lasted well into the age of cavalry, when it could often be a mark of courage to abandon the horse and its promise of escape, and to stand alongside your men.[43]

There is plenty of evidence that the English had horses and used them for war, sometimes that they even did fight from horseback. There are early, again northern, stone carvings of cavalry in battle.[44] There are countless examples of horses being used for transport, and no doubt at all that the English aristocracy could ride and did ride. Harold's quick journey from Stamford Bridge to Hastings was not made on foot. The attempts of some ill-informed individuals to do the trip on foot to test its feasibility seem rather pointless. There was no serious problem in covering the distance on horse as Harold and his household and professional or noble troops clearly did. There are also plenty of examples of horses used in raids and for pursuits after a battle. The horses possessed by English warriors were clearly held in the vicinity and used as required.

But actual cavalry fighting in battle is another matter. It required three things at least which the English lacked: a desire to fight in this way; trained warhorses for use in battle; trained men used to fighting from the saddle. The Normans possessed all three, perhaps derived from Frankish connections. A ninth-century proverb in Francia claimed that training for cavalry should begin before puberty, since after that it became difficult to acquire the knack. Young men, such as Robert de Grandmesnil, trained to fight on horseback in William's household. Such young men were no doubt the 'boys' encouraged by Bishop Odo at Hastings on the Tapestry.[45]

Certainly the English had horses and bred them. We hear on occasions of the Vikings taking English horses for their own use during their campaigns. But the Vikings used them as the English did, not for battle. The Normans needed their own specially bred horses, such as they took with them to Sicily, such as they transported across the Channel in 1066. The young Norman warrior learned to fight from horseback as a noble pursuit. The idea of a mounted élite was already forming in Norman and northern French minds in a way that was yet to happen in England. The heroes of English poetry were warriors who fought on foot. The warfare of Normandy, like most of north-western continental Europe, relied heavily on development from the Frankish Carolingian Empire. Fortified strongholds or castles, and warriors trained to fight on horseback had developed over a century or so. The Bretons, for example, 'gave themselves to arms and the equestrian art'.[46]

There is still a question mark over the degree of continuity from Carolingian Neustria to Viking-ruled Normandy. There is little sign of those things we consider 'feudal' before 1100: castles, knights, mounted warfare. It may be significant that the great families of the Conquest era, such as the Beaumonts, Warennes and Montgomeries, do not appear much before 1100 either. This does not mean the families did not exist, but perhaps it signifies a change in attitudes to the importance of family and especially the concept of inheritance and lineage.

Both features, castles and mounted cavalry, were emerging as newly dominant in warfare in the mid-eleventh century. Western medieval cavalry methods developed very gradually, with the first evidence from the Merovingian age, and with less dominance in the Carolingian period than once thought. But when the Conqueror aided by the king of France fought at Val-ès-Dunes in 1047, there were probably cavalry attacks from both sides.[47] The less reliable and later writer Wace, a Channel Islander, gave a graphic account: 'horses were to be seen running loose over the plain, and the field of battle was covered with knights riding haphazard for their lives . . . the Orne swallowed soldiers and horses in great numbers'.[48]

There is one reference to English cavalry fighting in 1066, but it is made by Snorri Sturlusson. He has an English cavalry charge at Stamford Bridge, not confirmed in other evidence of that battle, and oddly similar in his account to the Norman charges at Hastings. It is likely that Snorri, writing an heroic saga at a much later date, used the only detailed evidence of a battle from the period (for Hastings) to fill out the account of the battle which mattered more to his work, in which occurred the death of his hero, Harold Hardrada, king of Norway. No evidence can be ignored, but Snorri's is far less convincing than that from the period itself.

Perhaps the most telling piece of evidence in this debate is the one clear example of English fighting on horses close to this period. In 1055 Ralph, earl of Hereford, fought a skirmish against the Welsh. Ralph's background was continental, he was the Confessor's nephew by his sister's marriage to the count of Mantes. Edward knew him during his own Norman exile, and brought him to England after he gained the throne. Ralph was then rewarded with his earldom. He was trained in the continental methods of war, albeit he was not a greatly renowned warrior, and indeed in England earned the epithet of 'timid'. According to John of Worcester, against the Welsh, Ralph ordered his English troops 'to fight on horseback, against their custom'.[49] They were not successful. From this we may reasonably deduce that there were some continentals in England who were keen to develop cavalry fighting, but who found that at this time it was difficult. It would take time and the will to undertake drastic change. We may conclude that the English by 1066 had chosen to prefer their trusted infantry methods against the considerable changes that would be required to produce not simply cavalry forces but to make their élite troops into mounted warriors.

The development in Normandy may have been later than once supposed, but it had happened. At Hastings, his men were astonished to see William fighting on foot at all.[50] The Norman nobility began to see mounted warfare as a part of being the warrior élite. When the Conqueror himself was knighted, sword, shield and helmet were part of the ceremony, as were lance and the reins of his horse. So also were promises to protect the Church and the weak, to act justly. We see the beginnings of chivalric ideals.[51]

The Normans now used well-armed mounted cavalry as a regular feature of their warfare. In 1041, during the course of their rise to power in southern Italy, a Norman force beat the Byzantine Varangian Guard at Monte Maggiore by a mounted charge. At Civitate in 1053, Richard of Aversa led a successful charge against the opposing papal force, and had the ability to regroup and return to the fray, thus winning the battle. In Normandy, we hear of William commanding forces of three hundred knights; and it was the speed of the charge at Varaville, cutting off the enemy when only half were across the River Dives, which gave William victory in 1057.[52]

They had also, by 1066, developed some tactical achievements. It used to be questioned whether medieval cavalry was capable of the feigned flight, and some historians wrote off this feature at Hastings as coming from the imagination of writers. It is now widely accepted that feigned flights were possible, and had indeed been employed by various Frankish armies and others over a period of time, for example, by the Alans, Huns, Byzantines and Magyars. The Bretons employed the feigned flight against Fulk IV, count of Anjou. The Normans used the feigned flight on several occasions before Hastings, for example, under Walter Giffard at St-Aubin in 1053: 'the Normans succeeded in drawing away a considerable part of the army and, as if in flight, they led the French into a trap. For suddenly the Normans who seemed to be fleeing, turned round and began violently to cut down the French.' Walter Giffard, incidentally, probably fought for William at Hastings.[53] The Normans also made a feigned flight to draw the enemy away from the walls of Messina in Sicily in 1060.

Later Norman armies were organised in small tactical groups, sometimes called conroys, and there is little reason to dispute the likelihood that these had a long history. Wace suggested that the conroys were based on men from the same geographical area. The conroy is unlikely to have numbered much more than about twenty men.

There was a third major difference between English and Norman warfare, but its significance is less vital so far as Hastings is concerned. The Normans built and used fortifications which we call castles, the English on the whole did not. There were fortifications in England, but their nature was different. From Alfred onwards there had developed a network of over thirty fortified strongholds, virtually towns – the burhs. Some of these were fortified with stone walls, as Towcester, while some towns already possessing walls had them repaired.[54] But these were on a national basis, and were large enough to contain urban populations and offer shelter to those living in the neighbourhood. Nevertheless, it may be significant that our word for 'castle' derives from the word the English used for their own fortifications.[55]

There was at least one private fortification, found at Goltho in Lincolnshire, which suggests that the English were moving along the same sort of path as the Normans. It has been called 'a pre-Conquest castle', and its function like that of a castle was as a 'defended residence', though Goltho's defences were not as massive as those of a typical castle, and at present it is a unique site. When it did become a castle in about 1080, it was a particularly small one, but was still more strongly defended than its English predecessor.[56]

The continentals brought to England under Edward the Confessor had, it is true, built a handful of such buildings, including Pentecost's Castle and Robert's Castle, so the English were not entirely unfamiliar with this kind of fortification. It is interesting to find Harold Godwinson making earthwork defences with a ditch around Hereford in 1055. Given time and without the Conquest, castles would almost certainly have developed in England, but the rate would have been slower.[57]

Equally truly there do not seem to have been so many castles in Normandy, nor were they built so early, as was once believed. Normandy was certainly not the base or centre of castle-building, and seems to have adopted the practice which grew up probably first in the Loire region. In England there were no more than half a dozen castles at the most before the Norman Conquest.

In Normandy, castles were at this time mostly what we might call citadels, fortifications built within towns. But there were some separate structures and a few at least were earthwork and timber (i.e. motte and bailey). There is mention of large ditches cut to defend both Arques and Domfront. When the Conqueror besieged Brionne for three years from 1047, he constructed earthwork fortifications on the banks of the River Risle; similarly at the siege of his uncle's new castle at Arques, William built a mound for the protection of his own men, and again no less than four mounds at Domfront. At both Domfront and Alençon, previous dukes had permitted the erection or rebuilding of castles.[58] There were pre-1066 towers at Ivry and Brionne, as well as 'The Tower' at Rouen. J. Yver believed that the length of some sieges meant that the castles concerned were probably constructed of stone.

Breton castles are shown in the Bayeux Tapestry's account of the Conqueror's campaign there probably in 1064: at Dol, Dinan and Rennes. The Tapestry also shows the castle of Bishop Odo, the Conqueror's half-brother, at Bayeux; and at Beaurain where Harold was held prisoner; and probably William's own fortification at Rouen. There is reference to the Conqueror building a new castle at St-James-de-Beuvron. The use of castles may seem less relevant to Hastings than the possession of archers and cavalry, but it is not entirely without significance, when one considers how William used Pevensey and constructed a castle at Hastings in the period immediately preceding the great battle, and indeed how the Conquest was carried through in the years after Hastings.[59]

FIVE

THE YEAR 1066

By 1065 Edward was ageing: 'with locks of snowy white he blooms', but he was still seemingly in good health.[1] The question of the succession was as open as ever. Probably more as a political counter than from any great favour for one or the other, Edward had at various times given hope of the succession to William, duke of Normandy, and Harold Godwinson, earl of Wessex. One can make this interpretation since both were able apparently with confidence to believe they were Edward's choice, and yet the old king had never made any formal or public declaration of his intentions.

If he favoured anyone it was probably for a time his relative Edward the Exile, son of Edmund Ironside and grandson of Aethelred II, whom he had sought out in Hungary and invited to England. That Edward the Exile was brought to England after the Confessor's promise to William seems fairly convincing proof that if the king ever had favoured the succession going to William, he had changed his mind by the late 1050s. It is true that William was his first cousin once removed, which marauded as a claim after the Conquest, but in truth gave faint right. Even fainter was Harold's claim, as the king's brother-in-law, no right by heredity at all. Neither William nor Harold, nor for that matter Harold Hardrada in Norway, had any close claim to the English throne by descent, so that Edward the Exile seemed the most likely choice to continue the line of old Wessex kings. His only real rival, in terms of relationship, was Ralph, earl of Hereford, who was Edward the Confessor's nephew. Ralph's parents were Edward's sister Godifu and the count of Mantes. He too had been shown favour by the

The Year 1066

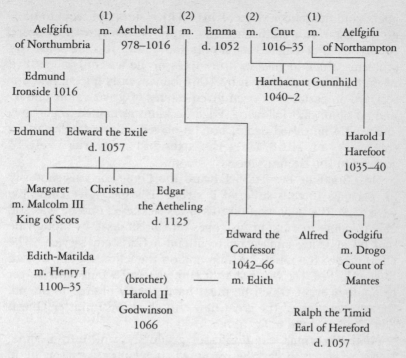

The relatives of Edward the Confessor.

Confessor, who had brought him to England after his accession, and made him an earl. But Earl Ralph died in 1057.

Edward the Exile had three children including a son, Edgar the Aetheling, who had come to England with him. But, as we have seen, Edward the Exile died on arriving in England, also in 1057, and with him probably died any clear intentions of the Confessor for the future of his throne. With the deaths of his two closest relatives, Edward probably accepted Harold Godwinson as the powerful claimant nearest to the throne, but it is unlikely that he felt any great enthusiasm that his crown should go to a commoner who was the son of his old rival, Earl Godwin. There were some who, now that the father was dead, did favour Edgar the Aetheling for the throne, perhaps initially this even included members of the Godwin family and Harold himself.[2]

But Edward the Confessor, no doubt contemplating difficult times ahead and the tender years of his relative, does not seem to have given Edgar the Aetheling his support. Many others were concerned that Edgar was simply too young to cope with the problems which loomed for the successor; he was only about five when his father died. Even by 1066 he was only fifteen, had not received an earldom or been given estates of great value, and so had no significant following. Edgar's claims remained important, and would be raised again, but he played only a small part in the events of 1066. Only the strongest man was likely to succeed in the circumstances.

On Christmas Eve 1065 Edward the Confessor was seriously ill, perhaps having suffered a stroke. His piety overcame his weakness, 'the holy man disguised his sickness', and he was still able to come to table in his robes on Christmas Day, though he had no appetite, and go on to attend a Christian service.[3] The effort proved too much for him, and on the following day he had to stay in bed. He was not well enough on 28 December to get to another event which he must have greatly desired to attend, the consecration of the great new church at Westminster. Queen Edith had to stand in for him.

After Christmas, the Confessor gradually sank into a coma. However, after two days he recovered consciousness sufficiently to retail a rather garbled vision which he had experienced. He told of a dream about two monks he had once known in Normandy, both long dead. They gave him a message from God, criticising the heads of the Church in England, and promising that the kingdom within a year would go to the hands of an enemy: 'devils shall come through all this land with fire and sword and the havoc of war'. This certainly smacks of a tale told with hindsight. There followed a strange forecast relating to a green tree cut in half.[4] This was probably no more intelligible to his hearers than it is to us. His wife went on compassionately warming the old man's feet in her lap.

This may have given rise to the suggestion that Edward's mind was disordered. Those at the bedside whispered together about the king's words. They included Harold Godwinson, Robert fitz Wimarc and Archbishop Stigand. The latter, no doubt irritated by the visionary reference to failings among those at the head of the English Church, suggested that 'the king was broken with disease and knew not what he said'.

But the deathbed wishes seem utterly sane and sensible. As those close to him wept at his condition, he made his last requests. He praised Queen Edith, who was there beside him, for the zealous solicitude of her service: 'she has served me devotedly, and has always stood close by my side like a beloved daughter'. He asked Harold to give protection to Edith: 'do not take away any honour that I have granted her', suggesting that he was aware of the bad feeling which had grown up between brother and sister over their brother's fall.[5]

The king also asked Harold to protect foreigners in England. This implies that he feared the hostility of Harold and others to his continental friends and courtiers. It is also clear that on his deathbed he saw Harold as his likely successor, who might be able to carry out his last wishes. It is impossible to know Harold's mind, but one interpretation that would fit most of the details we are given by the sources is that Harold in 1064 still had not seen himself as becoming king. He and his family had apparently been happy to favour Edward the Exile until his death. It seems likely that Harold went to Normandy freely, and there is no evidence that he was forced into making oaths to William. He was not the duke's prisoner, as is often said. He went with the duke on campaign and was knighted by him. In other words, it seems possible that it was only after 1064 that Harold began to consider taking the throne.

The *Anglo-Saxon Chronicle* states that Edward had 'entrusted the realm', had 'granted' the kingdom to Harold, while the *Vita* records that he commended 'all the kingdom to his protection'. Even the French chronicler William of Poitiers spoke of Harold 'raised to the throne by Edward's grant on his deathbed'. Wace, with his usual vivid embroidering, has Harold demanding 'Consent now that I shall be king', to which Edward replies, 'Thou shalt have it, but I know full well that it will cost thee thy life'. The deathbed scene is vividly portrayed on the Bayeux Tapestry, with the unshaven archbishop in attendance on the dying king. Wace has the Confessor going on to mutter: let the English decide to make Harold or William king as they please. But there seems little doubt that at the end Edward was prepared to name Harold as his successor.[6]

In the early days of the new year, 1066, probably on 5

January, Edward the Confessor died. According to the *Vita*, his beard gleamed like a lily, and there was a rosy blush on the face of the corpse, and pale hands held as if in sleep. On the following day, the king was buried at Westminster, built for him in what was then a beautiful spot near the river and open fields, its 'most lofty vaulting surrounded by dressed stone, evenly jointed', the roof of wood covered with lead.

John of Worcester wrote that the king was 'most bitterly mourned, not without tears, by all who were present'.[7] When the Confessor's tomb was opened in 1102, Osbert of Clare described what they found when the stone slab was lifted: the body wrapped in a pall, sceptre by its side, crown on head, ring on finger, sandals on feet. They cut through the pall to reveal a bearded face. Osbert also mentioned a perfumed fragrance. By this time, men were beginning to think of Edward as a saint and the preservation of his body as miraculous. When the tomb was opened a second time, later in the twelfth century, the crown and sceptre were missing, presumably kept by those who had uncovered the tomb in 1102.[8]

The Tapestry portrays the funeral: the body wrapped and tied in its pall, in a decorated bier marked with a cross at either end. The bier was borne by eight men, four at the front and four at the rear. Beside it are portrayed two small figures, probably their size indicating their humble social rank, who are ringing bells. The bier was followed by a procession of clergy, one carrying a crook, and two carrying what are probably psalters. They move towards the new church of Westminster with its rounded arches and domed tower, the most apposite site for the body of the pious king.[9]

In England there seemed a general acceptance that Harold Godwinson should be king. Many must have had reservations, but few were prepared to oppose him, and the majority probably thought him the least of the various evils, which included rule by another Scandinavian (Hardrada), by the foreign and unknown William, or by a boy, Edgar, who would find it difficult if not impossible to fight off the rivals. For men in Wessex, Harold was their obvious lord; for earls in the north, he was at least the devil they knew and perhaps respected. Events in any case moved so fast that it is difficult to see any other immediate choice.

On the day of Edward's burial, Harold Godwinson was proclaimed king, and crowned in the new church at Westminster. The Normans would later claim he had acted with indecent haste, but they could hardly deny that England had accepted him. Those magnates who were in London, no doubt anticipating the old king's death, favoured Harold. He had achieved some recognition of a special position in the kingdom, being referred to as 'dux Anglorum' (duke/general of the English) and 'subregulus' (sub-king). The *Anglo-Saxon Chronicle* says that Harold took the crown 'as the king had granted it to him, and as he had been chosen'. Even the Bayeux Tapestry, made after the Conquest for a Norman owner, shows the English offering the crown to Harold.[10]

However, the Tapestry also shows Stigand beside the throne in the next scene, with Harold on the throne.[11] Stigand was already under fire from the papacy, and after the Conquest would be displaced as archbishop. To show him, apparently involved in the coronation, hints at its illegitimacy. William of Poitiers directly states that Stigand carried out the ceremony. But it is not certain that this is so. English sources say that Harold was crowned by Eadred, archbishop of York, who had always been on good terms with the Godwin family. Stigand had received the pallium from the antipope 'Benedict X' (1058–9), who had been deposed in 1059. The previous archbishop, as we saw, was ejected, and Stigand's position always remained precarious. But he was still in place as archbishop, and remained there until 1070, and the ceremony was seemingly accepted by the Church, whoever presided. There seems little reason to believe that Harold's coronation was not legitimate. Comments to the contrary stem from Norman propaganda. Harold Godwinson was king but, as the *Anglo-Saxon Chronicle* tersely comments, he was to have 'little quiet'.[12]

One week into the new year of 1066 and England had a new king in Harold II (January–October 1066). According to the *Vita Aedwardi*, he was a man who looked the part he now took on, and had a suitable temperament: strong, handsome, graceful, tall, used to living hard as a warrior, with a mild temper and a willingness to understand others, able to act with restraint.[13] His most obvious rival was William of Normandy. Others still lurking in the wings were the young Edgar the Aetheling, Sweyn

II Estrithsson, king of Denmark (1047–74), and Harold III, king of Norway (1047–66; this was Harold Sigurdsson, better known to us as Harold Hardrada). The success of Cnut in England had linked England to the Scandinavian polity. Cnut had ruled both Denmark and Norway, and his successors as kings in those countries could make some sort of claim to succeed him in England. In turn, each of those kings would attempt to do so.

But the joker in the pack, who initiated the first drama of the new reign, was Harold Godwinson's own brother Tostig, former earl of Northumbria. Upset by Harold's failure to assist him in the north, he turned elsewhere for support, anywhere else. He voyaged around northern Europe from Flanders to Norway, contacting the count of Flanders, as well as William the Conqueror and Harold Hardrada. It was Tostig himself of the invaders in 1066 who made the first appearance.

King Harold II had little chance to make anything of his reign. Indeed, we know almost nothing of his acts as king. John of Worcester records promises made at the coronation and says, in a general way, that he did destroy iniquitous laws and establish just ones, and show some favours to the Church. He ordered ealdormen and sheriffs to arrest thieves and wrongdoers, and he made efforts to improve land and sea defences. We know that he placed infantry forces, presumably as garrisons, at key points along the coast.[14]

The chronicles move immediately to the dramatic events of the year, and there are sadly few administrative documents to inform us. There was little enough time for anything to be done, and what was done was probably thought best forgotten or destroyed once the Conquest had occurred. Harold at least had time to establish himself as king. The successes of his reign were themselves considerable in such a short space. Had the Conqueror lost at Hastings, Harold would have appeared to be a great military figure. There are plenty of signs that he was a man of determination, vigour and ability. But what might have happened remains conjecture. What did happen in his nine months as king is virtually unknown, apart from the conflicts of the year.

One of the few acts we know of was his marriage to Edith, the sister of the northern earls Edwin and Morcar and widow of Gruffydd, Harold's former enemy in Wales, who had been killed in 1063. The new marriage was an interesting move, and augured well for his good sense on the throne. He had already decided against attacking Morcar, who had displaced his brother in Northumbria, thus alienating Tostig. By the marriage, Harold united the major powers within the kingdom, and its effect was to keep the support of the northern earls in the various invasions of the year.

Harold in the early part of 1066 went to York, presumably to cement his relationship with the family of Leofric. We know that Harold had a long-term mistress in Edith Swanneck, who probably bore him five children, and who was never discarded. But, as so often in this period, the new king was prepared to make a political marriage too. Despite the brevity of his marriage, he apparently had two children by his wife, twins called Ulf and Harold, born presumably after the death of their father.

There is also a strong tradition that during his brief reign, Harold was seriously ill. This stems from material related to his foundation at Waltham Abbey, where he is said to have prayed before his recovery. One source, from that abbey, suggests that he suffered a stroke while the Confessor was alive, and recovered after receiving a holy cross. These are not particularly reliable sources, but there may be some truth in the illness.[15]

Harold was at Westminster at Easter in April, and soon afterwards Halley's comet appeared in the sky, inspiring the various prognostications of disaster we have already noted. The *Anglo-Saxon Chronicle* records that it was first seen in England on 24 April, and 'shone all the week'. Soon afterwards came the first hostile arrival on the shores of the country. In May Harold's brother Tostig brought a fleet of some sixty ships to the Isle of Wight, 'as large a fleet as he could muster', together with money and provisions which he had been given.[16]

Tostig received aid from the Orkneys, which is significant since the islands were under the authority of Hardrada, and that king would soon arrive there himself. It suggests strongly that Snorri was right, and Tostig had made earlier arrangements with Hardrada over the attack on England. This is partly confirmed by John of Worcester's account, which says Tostig joined Hardrada 'as he had previously promised'.[17] Other aid was probably from the count of Flanders, who perhaps expected

Tostig to aid William of Normandy's efforts rather than those of Harold Hardrada. Tostig's own intentions were most probably to recover his lost earldom of Northumbria. He moved on eventually to Thanet, where he was joined by his former lieutenant in Northumbria, Copsi, who brought with him seventeen ships from the Orkneys. They made several damaging raids on their way, and sailed northwards into the Humber.[18]

When Tostig had reached Sandwich, news of his arrival reached his brother in London. Harold then mobilised his own land and sea forces, the former 'larger than any king had assembled before in the country'.[19] This was partly because Harold was unsure of the nature of the reported force. The *Chronicle* says that 'he had been told that William the Bastard meant to come here and conquer this country', but this invasion was not led by William, and the early mobilisation had unfortunate consequences for Harold later in the year.

The king's new brothers-in-law, the northern earls Edwin and Morcar, now repaid his attentions to them. They heard of Tostig's raid in Lindsey, and came to deal with him. They drove him off, and some of his men deserted. Eventually, Tostig sailed to the safety of Scotland with only twelve small ships, where Malcolm Canmore gave him refuge. Malcolm's predecessor, Macbeth, had offered threats to northern England, and these increased under Malcolm. After the death of Earl Siward, Northumbrian power had declined, so that the Scots offered a very real threat. Northumbria itself was not a clear political unity and in effect was often two separate entities, with centres at Bamburgh and York.[20] Malcolm's interest in Tostig shows that his own interests in northern England were not dead; from 1054 he attacked Northumbria on five occasions. But the reduction in size of Tostig's force demonstrates the degree of success of the attack by the northern earls against him.

Tostig's arrival proved a minor probe as the events of the year unwound. He was but the herald of more threatening invaders. The second force to reach the shore came from Norway and was led by Harold Hardrada. Hardrada had led a spectacular and heroic life, which made him a hero in later literature, especially in the sagas of Snorri Sturlusson. Some of this work, written in the thirteenth century in Iceland, is clearly dubious factually, but nevertheless, it gives some interesting material on Hardrada's career, seen by the editors of Snorri as 'one of the most remarkable and memorable of the medieval kings of Norway'.

Some of Snorri's writing was based closely on older lost works and where these can be identified Snorri can be useful – sometimes he tells us the source. Some of Hardrada's life was taken from the earlier *Saint Olaf's Saga* (about Hardrada's brother), but other sections are less reliable and possibly invented. The following account of Hardrada's career, from childhood until his arrival in England, is taken largely from Snorri's *Heimskringla*, and should be treated with the care that material from such a source deserves. But, even if partly legendary, it is the only full account we have of Hardrada's life, and it presents a picture of the king which rings true in its general effect, if not always in its detail.[21]

As a child, according to Snorri, Hardrada showed his individual character. When the king pulled faces at his two older brothers they both were so afraid that they wept, but Harold simply stared back. When the king then pulled his hair, he retaliated by pulling the king's moustache. Another story was that Harold with his two brothers was asked on one occasion what in the world they most wanted. The others answered corn and cattle, but Hardrada's answer was warriors.

Hardrada's brother, St Olaf, was killed in the battle of Stiklestad near Trondheim in Norway in 1030, fought during an eclipse of the sun. Hardrada stood beside him bravely in the battle and was wounded. Afterwards he found refuge in a farmhouse while his wounds healed, and then was forced to flee Norway for Sweden and then Russia, eventually going to Byzantium with five hundred men. He sought employment in the imperial service, and was hired by the Eastern Emperor Michael IV, the Paphlagonian (1034–41). During this period he helped suppress pirates in the Greek islands, took part in the Byzantine conquest of Sicily between 1038 and 1041, aided the suppression of revolt in Bulgaria by Peter Delyan, and went on an expedition to the Holy Land. Under Michael V (1041–2) and then the Empress Zoë, Hardrada was commander of the Varangian Guard. By this time, Harold wished to return to Norway. When he was repeatedly refused permission, his attitude led to imprisonment, and on his release he simply left. Snorri explains this as part of a love tangle with the Empress and her niece, both of whom wanted to marry Harold, and his release as occurring with the aid of his saintly brother's appearance from beyond the grave. It is difficult to know how much of all this can be accepted as fact, but there is little doubt that Hardrada did serve in the imperial guard.

Then Harold returned to Novgorod, where Snorri says he married Elizabeth, the daughter of King Jaroslav.[22] Back in Scandinavia, Harold soon began to play a part in local politics. Magnus I the Good, the son of Hardrada's brother St Olaf, had become king of Norway (1035–47) and of Denmark (1042–7). Magnus and Hardrada were soon at loggerheads, but eventually agreed to share the crown of Norway. In return, Harold gave his nephew a share in the wealth he had brought back with him. Hardrada assisted Magnus in the restoration of authority in Denmark, and on Magnus' death, Norway went to Hardrada and Denmark to Sweyn II Estrithsson (1047–74). The latter was the son of Earl Ulf, formerly regent of Denmark for Cnut, and Cnut's daughter, Estrith.[23]

King Harold Hardrada married a second time, to Thora, daughter of Thorberg Arnason, by whom he had two sons. Hardrada was reputed to be a domineering ruler; 'scarcely anyone dared to argue with him', his great height and strength no doubt enforcing his arguments. He treated opposition ruthlessly. A spokesman for opposing farmers, Einar, was simply hacked to pieces in the king's presence, while farmers who opposed him or refused to pay taxes had their homes burned down: 'flames cured the peasants/Of disloyalty to Harold'. He alienated some of his own supporters, including his nephews Asmund and Guthorm, as well as Earl Hakon who deserted to Sweyn.

It was not long before Hardrada also quarrelled with Sweyn Estrithsson. The Norwegian king assembled an army and a fleet and headed south, his great ship with seventy oars moving 'like an eagle with wings flapping'. He fought against Sweyn in the sea battle of Nissa in 1062, in what is now Sweden, where 'blood gushed into the ocean'. Harold is said to have used a bow during the battle. In the end, the Danish fleet broke, and Hardrada boarded his rival's ship, though Sweyn himself managed to escape.

The Year 1066

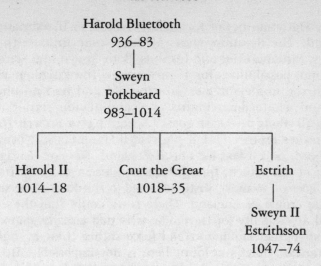

Harold Bluetooth
936–83

Sweyn Forkbeard
983–1014

Harold II
1014–18

Cnut the Great
1018–35

Estrith

Sweyn II
Estrithsson
1047–74

Kings of Denmark.

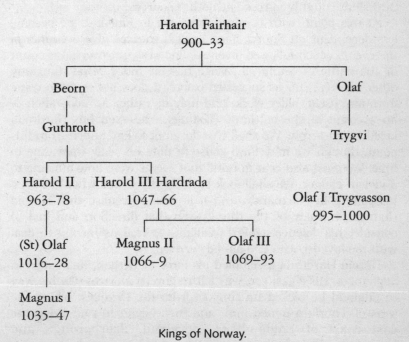

Harold Fairhair
900–33

Beorn

Guthroth

Harold II
963–78

Harold III Hardrada
1047–66

Olaf

Trygvi

Olaf I Trygvasson
995–1000

(St) Olaf
1016–28

Magnus II
1066–9

Olaf III
1069–93

Magnus I
1035–47

Kings of Norway.

Now Hardrada began to interest himself in the situation in England. The Scandinavians all had some links with that country, through Cnut and his sons. Both Sweyn and Hardrada saw some possibilities for themselves in the kingdom where Edward the Confessor was growing old and had no obvious heir, and where descendants of Scandinavian settlers were strong all along the east coast. According to Snorri, Harold Godwinson's brother Earl Tostig visited Hardrada in Norway at Oslo Fjord, and asked for aid in England. He says Tostig was aiming at the crown, though this does seem unlikely. Indeed, Snorri goes on to make Tostig offer aid to Hardrada if he should seek the crown of England. There is no doubt that the crown seemed a possibility for Hardrada, who had already gained one kingdom by determination and force rather than by right or inheritance. Snorri's account here is not impossible. He then says that Harold Hardrada determined to invade England, and Tostig went on to Flanders. Snorri's figure for a fleet of over 200 ships roughly agrees with other sources.

At this point, with Hardrada arriving in England, we become less dependent on Snorri since English sources give accounts of the events which followed. Even so, Snorri's controversial account of the battle of Stamford Bridge has far more detail than any other version. But, as suggested before, it does not seem to come from any useful older work, and may be rather an adaptation of an account of the battle of Hastings – he even has Hardrada killed by an arrow. We shall therefore not follow Snorri from this point, though we may have cause to note his view from time to time. We must also bear in mind that events were now building to a violent climax. We shall look back shortly to see what has been happening in Normandy, and it is vital to realise that Harold Godwinson knew of the threat from that direction and had to consider his defence against William, as well as having to deal with the invader who had already arrived.

Harold Hardrada assembled his force at Bergen, and sailed in September. His eldest son was left to govern Norway. On his way to England he picked up support from the Orkneys, where the sons of Thorfinn joined him, and then began to raid along the east coast of England: at Cleveland, Scarborough and Holderness. The northern earls, Edwin and Morcar, had seen off

Tostig, but the latter rejoined Hardrada at some point before Stamford Bridge, probably before Gate Fulford.[24]

Hardrada landed at Riccall and advanced towards York. The army of the northern earls emerged from the city to face him as he approached the River Ouse. The first of the three major battles in England during the year was then fought on 20 September at Gate Fulford, just south of York – now a suburb of the city. The battle lasted 'for a long time', but the English were defeated, and many died escaping across the river or being pursued into the swampy ground nearby, making 'a causeway of corpses'. The two earls survived and made their peace with the Norwegian king.[25]

Harold Godwinson, it will be recalled, had summoned his forces early in the year. By September, when the most common period for invasion was over, he could hold his men together no longer, and the land and sea fyrds were dismissed. The ships were to dock in London. This did not, of course, leave him without any troops at all, but it did weaken the coastal defences, and it was clearly an exhausting year for both the troops who remained in arms and those who would shortly be recalled. John of Worcester's description of this move suggests strongly that Harold retained the mounted part of his army.[26] When Harold Godwinson heard of the landing of Hardrada in Yorkshire, he desperately sought to assemble a large force once more. But he could not do miracles, and the first line of defence had to be the local force of the northern earls, which had been defeated at Gate Fulford.

Hardrada rested on his laurels. He made an agreement with the citizens of York, and used his fleet at Riccall as a base. According to Gaimar, the invaders carried off cattle, but part of the agreement was for provision of food. The Norwegian king also demanded 150 hostages, leaving an equal number of his own men in the city.[27] So while Harold was making a rapid and draining march north, Hardrada was replenishing his strength. Hardrada, awaiting the fulfilment of the agreement, brought his army to the fields near the River Derwent, close by the crossing at Stamford Bridge. But Hardrada had only occupied the site for a day when Harold of England made his unexpected appearance.

It would be of great interest to know what unmounted men Harold Godwinson had at his disposal. It is unlikely that men marched on foot from the south, while many of the northern men had been involved at Gate Fulford, and Harold's haste did not allow time to wait and magnify his force. The *Anglo-Saxon Chronicle* says that he went north 'as quickly as he could assemble his force'. The parallels between this situation and that of Hastings are not often noted, but they are clearly worth consideration. Probably it was survivors from Gate Fulford, and some from areas near to Yorkshire, that provided the infantry for Harold at Stamford Bridge. At any rate, Godwinson raised a good army, 'with many thousands of well-armed fighting men'. Harold's march north has been seen by the historian of the battle as 'one of the greatest feats of military manoeuvre in medieval history', which is laying it on a bit thick, though it was certainly a creditable performance.[28]

The rapid march paid dividends. The invaders were taken by surprise. Godwinson reached Tadcaster on 24 September, less than 10 miles from York. There he rested overnight and then set

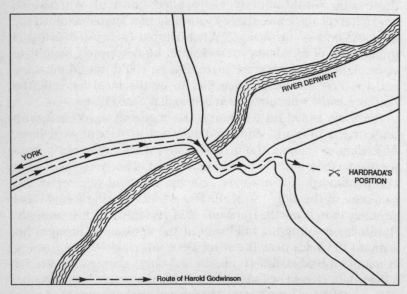

The battle of Stamford Bridge, 25 September 1066.
(Map: Mike Komarnyckyj)

off early next morning, Monday 25 September, to deal with Hardrada. He marched straight on through York, which shows that the citizens were not prepared to make any military effort to back their agreement with Hardrada. Godwinson headed eastwards from York, towards the Derwent and the enemy.

There is a bridge over the Derwent at Stamford Bridge now, and there was one then; the river is wide and deep and difficult to cross so the bridge was vital. It has been suggested that it was placed differently, but it is probably close to its ancient position.[29] Hardrada's army was in the open countryside on the far side of the river. It is flat, open ground, as it was then, damp and rather swampy. One reason to discount Snorri's account of English cavalry is that the ground would have been most unsuitable for such warfare.[30]

The enemy army was in disarray. The alarm came too late. Some of the troops were still miles away with the fleet in Riccall. Hardrada's only hope was to hold the bridge, and a few men made a valiant effort to do this. Early accounts, not only later legendary ones, mention the defence of the bridge by a big Norwegian, who held off the men trying to cross.[31] He was overcome, or perhaps undercome, when the English sent a boat along the Derwent and a man from below thrust a weapon, probably a spear, through the planking of the bridge, killing the hero in a particularly painful manner. This story presents a problem: if the English had archers here, as generally accepted, why did they not shoot the man? If they did indeed have archers, the story would seem to be a fabrication. We are left with a doubt over both the presence of English archers and the tale of the defender of the bridge.

The English crossed the bridge. The Norwegians were still frantically attempting to get into some order, Hardrada prominent in his blue tunic. They tried to hold the area known as Battle Flats, slightly higher than the surrounding ground. Snorri says that the Norwegian king's hauberk was called Emma, and that he fought two-handed with a sword.

The English charged straight in and broke the Norwegians apart, though fighting continued until 'late in the day'.[32] Snorri has men from the fleet arriving while the battle was in progress, and one of them, Eystein Orri, took up Hardrada's fallen banner

Landwaster, thus prolonging the battle. The conflict was 'very fierce fought on both sides', becoming 'a most bitter battle', but it turned into a massacre.[33]

There was a massive slaughter. A few escaped, among them Hardrada's marshal, Styrkar. Snorri gives an account of how he got away in just a shirt and helmet. He came upon a cart whose driver had a leather coat and offered to buy it, but the man said he knew Styrkar was a Norwegian and refused. Styrkar cut off his head, took the coat and the horse, and rode to the coast. The English pursued the defeated troops to the coast, where some of the ships were set on fire.[34]

Three hundred invading ships had arrived, five hundred according to one account, and twenty-four at most sufficed to take away the survivors.[35] Hardrada's son Olaf was one of those allowed to go. Among the dead left on the field were the old warrior Harold Hardrada, and Tostig, the embittered brother of the English king. The local legend that Hardrada survived to live the life of a peasant in a hut may safely be discounted. According to Orderic Vitalis, there was still in his day 'a great mountain of dead men's bones' marking the field.[36]

Harold Godwinson's career and reign was short and tragic, but he had his moment of glory. The Norwegian invasion was probably greater in terms of numbers than the Norman one which followed. Harold must have gained enormous confidence from his decisive victory. Had Hastings gone the other way, he would have been seen as one of our greatest warrior kings, which indeed he was. In the long run, Stamford Bridge had important consequences: it narrowed the field of competitors for control of England to two, and it did much to shift England away from the Scandinavian threat which had dogged it for a long period.

And so we move in our narrative to the last and most fateful invasion of England in 1066. William of Normandy had made careful preparations. We have seen how he made the marriage alliance with Flanders, repaired the damage that had been done to his relations with the papacy, and pushed Norman power beyond his frontiers so that he now had little fear of attack. According to William of Poitiers, he had also obtained a promise of fidelity from Sweyn Estrithsson, king of Denmark.[37] Some

'These people marvel at the star'; Halley's comet on the Bayeux Tapestry.
(The Bayeux Tapestry – 11th Century. By special permission of the City of Bayeux)

Statue of Alfred the Great, Winchester.

The small kneeling figure adoring Christ is St Dunstan, Archbishop of Canterbury, the great tenth-century church reformer. The writing above the small figure may be in Dunstan's own hand. (Dunstan's Classbook, Bodleian MS Auct. F. 4. 32, f. 1r)

Corfe Castle, on the site where Edward the Martyr was killed in 978. He had reigned for only three years and was succeeded by his brother Aethelred.

Winchester, the West Gate.

Shaftesbury, with the Abbey ruins in the foreground.

Bosham, where Harold possessed a hall and from where he set out across the Channel on the journey that resulted in him meeting William, duke of Normandy.

Dover, the scene of the clash which brought to a head the differences between King Edward and Earl Godwin.

Jumièges Abbey, Normandy, which produced Robert, Archbishop of Canterbury, and to which he retired. (Dr N. Higham)

York, where two hundred of Tostig's men were attacked and killed by Northumbrian rebels in 1065.

A page from *The Customs and Acts of the First Dukes of Normandy* by Dudo of St-Quentin. (Bibliothèque Municipale, Rouen, MS Y II, f. 1)

Vire, which came under Rolf's authority by about 924.

This scene of the Tapestry shows the Conqueror in his 'palace' which was probably at Rouen. (Michael Holford)

The Conqueror's army passes Mont-St-Michel on his campaign into Brittany. (Michael Holford)

Falaise, the birthplace of William the Conqueror. The stone towers of the castle were built after his death.

Detail of William seated in his palace (probably at Rouen). (Michael Holford)

Harold at Bosham Church before crossing the Channel. (The Bayeux Tapestry – 11th Century. By special permission of the City of Bayeux)

On arrival in France, Harold is arrested by Guy, Count of Ponthieu. (The Bayeux Tapestry – 11th Century. By special permission of the City of Bayeux)

Top: The enigmatic scene suggesting a scandal in Normandy between a clerk and a lady called Aelfgyva, whose identity is uncertain. The sexual nature of the scandal is indicated by the blatant posture of the male figure and perhaps by the shape of the candle in the bottom margin. (Michael Holford). Bottom: Harold rescues two soldiers during the march into Brittany. (The Bayeux Tapestry – 11th Century By special permission of the City of Bayeux)

Harold is knighted after taking part in the Breton campaign. (The Bayeux Tapestry – 11th Century. By special permission of the City of Bayeux)

Bishop Odo's castle at Bayeux; note the elaborate decoration.

Harold reporting back to King Edward after his eventful excursion to Normandy. (Michael Holford)

Caen, the main ducal stronghold in western Normandy.

The Bayeux Tapestry represents Englishmen, as at Bosham on the left, with longer hair, while the Normans, on the right in William's palace, have their hair cut shorter, especially at the back.
(The Bayeux Tapestry – 11th Century. By special permission of the City of Bayeux)

Wallingford, looking towards the castle.

The Normans prepare to invade England, loading arms, armour and provisions on their ships; note especially the hauberks carried on poles. (Michael Holford)

Norman cavalrymen with the rectangular shapes on their chests.
(Michael Holford)

Straps in a rectangle, attached to the inside of a shield. (Michael Holford)

The cavalryman carries a kite-shaped shield, while the infantrymen have smaller circular shields. (The Bayeux Tapestry – 11th Century. By special permission of the City of Bayeux)

Shields on the Stephen Harding Bible have heraldic-style decoration. (Bibliothèque Nationale, Paris, MS 14)

Cavalrymen with swords, and one has a bow. (The Bayeux Tapestry – 11th Century. By special permission of the City of Bayeux)

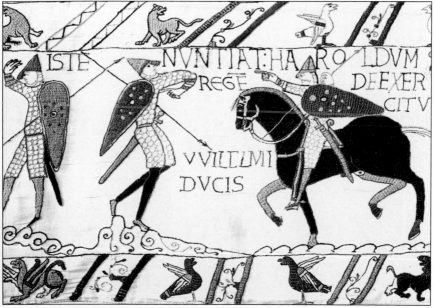

Two infantrymen with spears and a cavalryman with lance at rest.
(The Bayeux Tapestry – 11th Century. By special permission of the City of Bayeux)

Of the two cavalrymen here, one uses the lance couched, the other overarm.
(The Bayeux Tapestry – 11th Century. By special permission of the City of Bayeux)

The English shield-wall holds the first Norman cavalry charge.
(The Bayeux Tapestry – 11th Century. By special permission of the City of Bayeux)

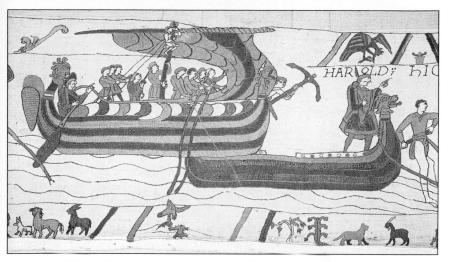

Ships of the period owed much to the design of Viking ships.
(Michael Holford)

The solitary English archer on the Bayeux Tapestry. (The Bayeux Tapestry – 11th Century. By special permission of the City of Bayeux)

On the Tapestry, those Englishmen riding with Harold to Bosham are called 'milites'. However the text is translated – as soldiers or knights – this is none the less an illustration of English soldiers on horseback. (The Bayeux Tapestry – 11th Century. By special permission of the City of Bayeux)

The Anglo-Saxon shield-wall.
(The Bayeux Tapestry – 11th Century. By special permission of the City of Bayeux)

The modern town of Hastings, viewed from the height of the castle.

Westminster Abbey, built by Edward the Confessor, was consecrated on 28 December 1065.

Edward's body being taken to Westminster Abbey for burial. (Michael Holford)

Harold Godwinson being presented with the crown of England. (The Bayeux Tapestry – 11th Century. By special permission of the City of Bayeux)

Waltham Abbey, Essex, founded by Harold Godwinson.

The mill pond on the Derwent, near the crossing point of the river.

The Normans loading provisions and arms for the invasion of England.
(Michael Holford)

Dives-sur-Mer, the assembly point for the Norman invasion fleet. William's
journey did not begin well, and he proceeded cautiously. (Dr N. Higham)

William's ship, the Mora, and the invasion fleet crossing the Channel.
(The Bayeux Tapestry – 11th Century. By special permission of the City of Bayeux)

In this work by Orderic Vitalis, William of Jumièges is shown presenting his chronicle to William the Conqueror.
(Bibliothèque Municipale, Rouen, MS Y 14, f. 116)

One of the several places in the Tapestry where two pieces of the linen are joined. The join occurs just to the right of the leading figure on foot. (Michael Holford)

The last scene in the Tapestry, as it survives today. (The Bayeux Tapestry – 11th Century. By special permission of the City of Bayeux)

The so-called 'kebabs', cooked by the Normans while on the Sussex coast.
(Michael Holford)

The crossed D of Gyrth is an example of Old English lettering on the Tapestry, and evidence of an English contribution to its making. (The Bayeux Tapestry – 11th Century. By special permission of the City of Bayeux)

The earliest manuscript of the Carmen, in early twelfth-century handwriting. (Bibliothèque Royale de Belgique, MS 10615–10729, f. 229v, col. ii, vv. 549–66)

The first page of Book III of the Ecclesiastical History by Orderic Vitalis, in his own handwriting. (Bibliothèque Nationale, Paris, MS lat 5506, vol. ii, f. 1)

Part of the wall of Pevensey Castle, Sussex, close to where the Norman invaders landed.

Normans foraging in Sussex after the landing.
(Michael Holford)

Bishop Odo and the Normans eating during the wait on the coast. The scene is rather daringly based on a depiction of the last supper, with Odo taking the place of Christ.

Battle Abbey: the memorial built to mark the spot where Harold was said to have been killed.

The Norman cavalry makes its first charge: note the couched lance of the figure on the right. (Michael Holford)

The death of Harold. After being struck by an arrow, Harold is depicted as being hacked down by a cavalryman with a sword (left). (Michael Holford)

The triumphant Normans pursue the English from the field.
(Michael Holford)

The motte of Berkhamsted Castle, the probable site where many of the English
submitted to the Conqueror

Normans were keen on a conquest of England, but the Conqueror had also to persuade unenthusiastic nobles, and partly for this purpose held councils to seek advice – at Lillebonne, Bonneville and Caen. Wace says the barons were summoned, and the debate lasted 'a great while' over what animals and what aid they could afford. Some claimed they had no obligation to serve over the sea. William resolved the problem by talking to the barons individually.[38]

The Conqueror had prepared the way by propaganda. It seems as if William at least was convinced that Edward had offered him the succession to the English throne. He had enforced upon Harold an oath which, whatever its exact contents, to Norman eyes meant that Harold should have supported William's rights in England. When Harold himself accepted the crown, William began his preparations to make it his by force. All the Norman sources give Harold's perjury as the justification for William's invasion.[39]

William needed men. Some came to him from obligations enforced in Normandy. Some were loyal military men in his household. Others came as allies or hired men, sometimes the distinguishing line was thin, from Flanders, Boulogne, Brittany, Maine and other parts of France. William of Poitiers says that men were attracted by the justice of the cause, and by the generosity of the Conqueror, by which he presumably means either in pay to hired men or in promises of what might be gained on the expedition. Orderic Vitalis saw them 'panting for the spoils of England'.[40]

The constant attempts to calculate a figure for William's force seems unprofitable. Unless we believe Wace's 696 we do not know the number of ships involved, and we do not know how many of which type; there are no reliable figures from contemporary evidence for any section of the force.[41] Of course, one can get a rough idea from the length of time to disembark, from the ground covered in the battle and so on, but beyond such a rough guess – 5,000 to 10,000 as a grand total is a usual figure – there seems no point in making apparently precise but in effect meaningless estimates.[42]

William also needed ships. Normandy like England has a long coast, and fishing was an important industry. Some ships were certainly available. But the Norman duchy, despite its Viking past, had not given much attention to naval warfare, and in 1066 perhaps the major need was a large fleet of transport ships. There had been minor expeditions to England in support of the claims of the sons of Aethelred II, and the Normans had used a fleet for the invasion of Sicily.[43] But the expedition of 1066 broke new ground, requiring the transport of a full ducal army of invasion, including warhorses. Wace says that all the ports of Normandy were in a stir.[44] William needed to augment his fleet. His allies, including Flemings and Bretons, probably gave some aid, but he also needed to build ships, which we see being accomplished on the Tapestry. Men are shown felling trees with axes, trimming them, and using drills, hand axes and adzes to build the ships.[45]

In the case of William's activities, we are well informed. William of Poitiers was the duke's chaplain. It is true that he only came to England after 1066, and did not take part in the expedition of that year. His description of it, and of the battle, is therefore at second hand. But he was well placed to get the facts from the best informed men. These were, of course, for the cleric, all on the Norman side, and his account is inevitably biased. We need to beware of this, but we do not need the same provisos over knowledge which had to be made in the case of Snorri writing about Hardrada.[46]

William of Poitiers tells us a little of his hero's youth: of his being knighted, holding reins, sword, shield, helmet and lance, wearing 'princely garb'. At that time, he made vows to protect the Church and give good government. But mostly the early days are an account of the dangers and rebellions which we have already followed. The writer's bias is shown, for example, by an account of William's taking of Alençon, but without mention of either the insults about his bastardy or the vicious revenge that the Conqueror took. The chronicler clearly says that the Confessor promised William the crown of England 'by a lawful gift' and as his heir, and that the English magnates assented. He says that the hostages, Harold's younger brother Wulfnoth and his nephew Hakon, were given to guarantee this promise. Poitiers adds that Harold's visit was on the Confessor's orders, and to confirm the offer of the crown. He details Harold's promises as being to do all in his power towards gaining the throne. Wace, with hindsight, goes so far as to say that Edward forbade him to go in case he was drawn into a snare.[47]

When Edward the Confessor died, William of Poitiers says that Harold took the throne without waiting for a proper election, thus 'breaking his oath'. The duke then decided to take his revenge and at once ordered the building of ships, the collection of equipment, arms and men, according to Poitiers assembling an army of fifty thousand soldiers. The Conqueror kept his eyes and ears open for developments in England; spies were used by both sides. William of Poitiers tells of an English spy captured by the Normans and sent back with a message to Harold which contained a warning. William's advisers also informed him of Harold's strength in England, and tried to dissuade him from his project, but he began to make arrangements for how Normandy should be governed in his absence. William proclaimed, 'we have enough ships. Soon we shall have triumph, honour and glory.'

Then followed a period of waiting which must have tried the nerves of William and all his men. It is possible that he deliberately delayed to some extent, knowing of Hardrada's invasion. It would suit William well to let his two rivals hammer out their differences, leaving him with one rather than two enemies to defeat. He may also have thought that the later he left it the more likely that Harold would have problems keeping his army and fleet at the ready. The eventual timing of his trip worked perfectly. But it cannot have been all calculation.

The Norman sources make it clear that he had to wait for a favourable wind for the vital crossing, and chafed at the delay. The weather was against him for several weeks. William of Poitiers says they waited a month in the mouth of the Dives, at Dives-sur-Mer, which was not far from Caen and lay between Varaville to the west and Bonneville to the east. He kept his troops under strict discipline, provisioning them well and forbidding forage. 'Weak or unarmed, any man might move about the district at his will, singing on his horse, without trembling at the sight of soldiers.'[48]

According to the *Carmen*: 'for a long time foul weather and ceaseless rain prevented [William] from leading the fleet across the Channel, while [he] awaited the favour of the winds; and the troubled sea forced [him] to put back, and gusts of the east wind curled the ocean waves'.[49] It is almost certain that William would have come to England earlier had the weather allowed it, so he had fortune as well as planning on his side.

His fleet assembled at the mouth of the Dives, and in neighbouring ports. On 12 September he was able to move, but only as far as St-Valery-sur-Somme, at the mouth of that river, and that with difficulty. Probably from the weather, William suffered a set-back on the short journey from the Dives to St-Valery, and men were drowned. William of Poitiers says they were buried in secret, obviously so as not to dishearten the army. Perhaps to rebuild morale, and to ask for a favourable wind, William organised a religious ceremony, parading the relics of St-Valery before the men. It was at St-Valery that William of Poitiers says they received the standard (vexillum) from Pope Alexander II (1061–73), which put them under the protection of St Peter.[50]

The *Carmen* says that at St-Valery they faced another 'long and difficult delay' . . . looking 'to see by what wind the weathercock of the church was turned'; it was 'cold and wet, and the sky hidden by clouds and rain'.[51] A recent article has discussed the problems for William's fleet facing the possible dangers of a lee shore, the difficulties of the tricky Channel tides, and the weather conditions most likely caused by Atlantic lows.[52] There is no doubt that William was wise to be cautious in deciding when to sail. He may also have been well informed as to developments within England, with his own frigates operating at sea during the period of waiting.[53]

At last on 27 September the wind relented, and the crossing began. Masts were raised, horses brought on board, sails hoisted, arms stowed. Soldiers flocked on to the ships like doves into a dovecote.[54] A herald announced the positions for the ships in the fleet on the voyage. By evening, the force was embarked and they set sail, to the sound of drums, trumpets and pipes, anchoring just out to sea. William's ship was the *Mora*, given him by his wife Matilda, which further enhances the likelihood of a considerable input to the fleet from Flanders. Wace says it had a figurehead of a boy with a bow and arrow, which pointed towards England as they sailed.[55]

When they began the invasion crossing, William's own ship led the way with a lantern fixed to its mast for others to follow, while a trumpet was used for signals. It must have been a somewhat motley fleet, gathered from all possible sources as it was, and with leaders who had little experience of such endeavours. Much of the fleet consisted of transports, and many were loaded down with men, provisions and horses. William's ship found itself moving too far ahead, and contact was lost with the fleet.

Whether by fortune or by planning, the English fleet as well as the men of the land fyrd had been disbanded when William sailed, and such troops as could be raised had been taken off north, so there was no opposition to the crossing or the landing. At first light, the look-out from the masthead could not see the fleet. The Conqueror's ship weighed anchor and waited until the others appeared. William, to show he was not dismayed, ate a breakfast accompanied by spiced wine, 'as if he were at home'. Then the look-out spotted the first four ships, and soon the fleet hove into view 'like a forest of sails'. Before long they were reunited, and sailed into Pevensey Bay where they disembarked on 28 September, completing the process during the afternoon. It was said that very few men were lost on the crossing; one who did perish was the unfortunate soothsayer, who had failed to forecast his own demise.[56]

SIX

THE SOURCES FOR THE BATTLE

It is time to pause before we look at the actual conflict. We have already made use of most of the sources which give accounts of the battle.[1] Use of Wace, for example, has often been preceded by some modifying remark to warn of his relative unreliability. Some sources are clearly invaluable, and our whole look at the period depends on them. But now we come to the crux of our present business, the battle itself. Any interpretation depends not only on the contemporary and near-contemporary sources, but also on interpretation of them. History is not a precise science. We never have perfect materials on which to work. The degrees between good, reliable material and difficult, unreliable material are many and slight along the way. Some works themselves are rather like the curate's egg, good in parts. What each historian chooses to use or to disregard makes his own view individual. One historian will disagree with another, but there is no absolute right and wrong. However much care we take, we can get it wrong. Indeed, we do not truly know if we get it right or wrong; we can only do our best. It is necessary to make a careful evaluation of sources but, in the end, interpretation of them is subjective rather than objective, since none of us knows the absolute truth of what happened in the past.

The battle of Hastings is well covered as medieval battles go, and we know much more about it than most conflicts. It was quickly recognised as a major event, and was treated as such – headline news for any chronicler writing on the period. The major lack in the Hastings sources is of an eyewitness account. This is a serious gap, and we have no way of filling it. No one who was on the field of Hastings has left us an account of what happened. All our narratives are therefore at second hand. Even then, in nearly all cases, we can only guess at where the chronicler obtained his information, and how much reliance can be placed upon it. Our primary concern though must be to try and gauge which chroniclers were best placed to receive accounts from participants and give good information.

We also must try to determine the viewpoint of the writer, since we know how much this affects his account. We try to detect bias and partisanship, and it is often apparent; medieval writers made little attempt to be neutral as modern journalists sometimes pretend to be. And they were all human; each one lived a life which gave a particular view to the events at Hastings. One would be a monk, hearing accounts from knightly guests; one would be a chaplain in a noble or royal household, listening to the table chit-chat of battles past; another would grow up in a house where the elders told tales of valour in days gone by. In a way, the openness of these opinions is an advantage, because the bias is often clear, and allows us to counter it. At Hastings, the most obvious bias would be whether the writer was pro-Norman or pro-Saxon. As it happens, nearly all the sources for the battle are Norman in viewpoint, and this creates a problem in trying to make a fair balance.

The other major consideration (we do not have time to go beyond this in our discussion) is the date at which the writer was putting quill to vellum. Obviously the nearer to the event the more valuable the account tends to be. Unfortunately again, precision on dating is not always possible. We usually begin from undated manuscripts, sometimes only copies without originals, sometimes only printed copies with the originals lost. Dating manuscripts is a whole science on its own, and dating works where we do not possess the autograph work by the writer is even more difficult. That said, we can usually come to some conclusion, an approximate date which gives at least a suggestion as to the likely value of a source.

Let us then survey briefly our major sources, and try to give some indication of their main values and weaknesses. There is still a certain amount of dating debate over the two main Norman chronicle accounts, but they are both eleventh century.

In most people's estimation, the major source for Hastings and the Conquest is William of Poitiers' *Gesta Gulielmi Ducis Normannorum et Regis Anglorum* (Deeds of William, Duke of the Normans and King of the English).[2] The original manuscript belonging to Sir John Cotton was copied and printed by Duchesne in 1619 and never seen again. The original may have been burnt in a fire in 1731. For dating we must rely on evidence within the contents of the account. There is a good modern edition of this by Raymonde Foreville, with a French translation, and sections are printed with English translations in all modern collections of sources relating to the Conquest and the battle. The main reason for recognising its value is twofold: it is the most detailed account of events that we have, and it is by someone who was in a position to be well informed. William of Poitiers may be treated as virtually the mouthpiece of the Conqueror. It was also written down early, Foreville believes by 1074, most others would agree by 1077. We know a little about the writer: he came from a noble family in or near Préaux, related to the Beaumonts, and had apparently early in life been trained in military discipline. But his sister became an abbess, and he became a priest at about the age of thirty. He had been born in Normandy in about 1028 and for some time studied in Poitiers, hence his toponym. He had legal knowledge and was for a time Archdeacon of Lisieux. He entered the household of the Conqueror as a chaplain, and this of course is why his work has such value. He did not cross to England in 1066, but he did come at some slightly later date. He treated the Conqueror as a hero who could virtually do no wrong, which is where we treat him with some circumspection. What we have goes up to 1067, but his account up to 1075 is probably used and preserved by Orderic Vitalis.

The second important Norman source is the *Gesta Normannorum Ducum* (Deeds of the Dukes of the Normans) by William of Jumièges.[3] In contrast to William of Poitiers, this work does not concentrate on the Conqueror. It is a history of all the dukes. The early section is almost a direct copy from the work of Dudo of St-Quentin, which makes one wonder about William of Jumièges' historical acumen. But it does come up to his own period, and he was writing in the early 1070s. He was a monk at Jumièges, a great Norman monastery with old links to England in its associations. His work was added to by other writers in the versions we have, in particular by Orderic Vitalis and Robert of Torigny. This has been known for some time, and there are two modern editions. The best and the most recent is by Elisabeth van Houts, and has an English translation with the Latin, and clear indications of whether the work we are reading is by William of Jumièges or one of the interpolators.

The chief English source for the Conquest is the *Anglo-Saxon Chronicle*, which is actually several different versions of a work begun in the time of Alfred the Great.[4] It is a year by year account of events. Additions to the annals were kept in several monasteries, and so different versions of the *Chronicle* developed. This became more complex over time, as one house borrowed a version from another house and then began to make its own additions. There are five main versions, known as A, B, C, D and E. The one which gives the fullest account of the Conquest is version D, the manuscript for which is written in a late eleventh-century hand. Both D and E may come from a version which had been made in York, sometimes called the northern recension. They are pretty well the same until 1031. D then continues with its interest predominantly in the north, probably still being kept at York. It continues till 1079. From 1031 E was probably being written up at Peterborough; it continued later than other versions of the *Chronicle*, until 1154. These versions, D and E, are therefore mainly from the point of view of northern and eastern England, where Scandinavian influence was strongest, not in the heartland of Godwin power. The writers are Benedictine monks but, so far as we know, without the major contacts that benefited William of Poitiers. Nevertheless, the D version in particular is valuable material as the main English view of what happened, and told in Old English. The easiest version of the *Chronicle* to use is that edited by Dorothy Whitelock and others, which places the versions side by side in columns so that comparison is easy; but for the original Old English one needs to go to other editions.

John of Worcester may be taken in conjunction with the *Chronicle*, since its earlier part is almost a Latin version of it.[5] The Anglo-Saxon material used to be called the work of Florence of Worcester, but its recent editor argues that we should call the work John of Worcester's. Here we have another

Benedictine house, Worcester, keeping an annal. The value of the Worcester account is that although close to version D on the Conquest, it is at least another English view of events.

The other major source for the Conquest is that invaluable and unique embroidery and document in one, the Bayeux Tapestry.[6] We all know that it is really an embroidery and not a tapestry as such, but it would be pedantic to call it by anything other than its familiar name. Those who view it in its present setting are often surprised that it is only 20 inches high, but also marvel at its 230 foot length, which cannot be appreciated in full in the usual book reproductions in separate plates. Indeed, the way the artist has designed the scenes to move fluently along from one event to the next is masterly. The backing is of bleached linen, and the embroidery is in five main colours of wool, with three less used colours. An artist sketched the scenes, and the embroiderers filled in the outlines with laid and couched work, stem stitch and outline stitch. It is made of eight sections pieced cunningly together so that one has to search hard to find the joins. The original end is lost, probably because of the manner in which it used to be kept rolled up. It is thought that perhaps 9 feet are lost, and that the missing section may have contained scenes of William's entry into London and his coronation. The latter would be a fitting conclusion, since we have the Confessor on his throne at the start and Harold's coronation in the centre. Apart from the main narrative beginning with Harold's trip to Normandy and ending with the English flight after Hastings, there are top and bottom margins, which sometimes add to the main story, sometimes retail myths and fables, and also provide delightful illustrations of such things as harrowing, scaring birds, hunting and boat-building. It is now widely accepted that the work was made for Odo, Bishop of Bayeux. It is possible that some of the minor figures on the Tapestry – Wadard, Vital and Turold – were tenants of Odo, who soon became earl of Kent.

The Tapestry may have been specially made for display in Bayeux Cathedral at its dedication in 1077. Some critics have thought certain scenes on the Tapestry too bawdy to be intended for such an ecclesiastical setting, but this seems to come from modern rather than medieval sensibilities. Certainly, an inventory of 1476 shows that the Tapestry was at the cathedral then, and was put on view annually. Some efforts have been made to devalue the Tapestry. A recent suggestion was that the 'kebabs' were too modern and that the work dates from the nineteenth century. But although it is clear there were some repairs done to the original, we can still feel safe that it is an early and valuable contribution to our knowledge. Its particular value is that it gives pictorial versions, and therefore information not otherwise available. Indeed, it is not merely visual evidence but a great work of art.

The Tapestry also has a written legend, a brief account of the events portrayed. From its tone this is almost certainly the work of a Norman, or at least a pro-Norman, though it does have one or two interesting touches of English sympathy, such as the rescue carried out by Harold on the Brittany expedition. It completely ignores the invasion by Hardrada. The Tapestry magnifies the role of Odo of Bayeux, who barely appears in the chronicle accounts.

It was probably made in England and worked by English embroiderers, perhaps at Canterbury: some of the scenes seem to have been adapted from manuscript art in Canterbury works. English working seems evident in such places as the use of a crossed d in names and in the English version of the Hastings place-name.

A printed copy was published in 1730 by Montfaucon, the drawings done by A. Benoît. The original was nearly lost during the French Revolution, when it had to be rescued from being used to cover a wagon. It was taken to Paris, and returned for exhibition at the Hôtel de Ville in Bayeux in 1812. It is known that repairs were done in 1842, which can be recognised from the use of different colours in the wool, and restoration marks on the linen. Modern examination has included such details as stitch marks which suggest how the original looked.

Then there are a number of sources to which we choose to give a secondary place, either because there is some question mark over their reliability and/or because they are late in time compared to the sources already mentioned. The most interesting of this group is the *Carmen de Hastingae Proelio* (The Song of the Battle of Hastings).[7] This is a long poem about the battle. It is very detailed and many historians have considered it a prime source, and some still do. To a degree the jury is still out on the *Carmen*, though all would agree it has *some* value. The manuscript was rediscovered in 1826 by G.H. Pertz. There was no title on the manuscript, indeed its subject matter is really 'The Norman Conquest' rather than simply the battle. It was written by an educated person, with plenty of biblical and classical references. It has been thought that this was a work mentioned in the twelfth century by Orderic Vitalis, a poem about the Battle of Hastings by Guy, Bishop of Amiens. This being so, it would be an early source, earlier than William of Poitiers. But the surviving manuscripts, one main and one tributary, which come from Trier, have been dated to about AD 1100 from the handwriting. If written by Guy, then it was by a respected and important noble, who came to England with the Conqueror's wife a couple of years after Hastings. The poem retains a mysterious dedication with initial and not names: 'L . . . W . . . salutat' – which could be either L greets W, or W greets L. Those who name Guy as the author fill in 'Lanfrancum Wido salutat' (Guy greets Lanfranc (Archbishop of Canterbury, 1070-89)).

But R.H.C. Davis made a serious attack on the attribution of the work to Bishop Guy. In an article, in *English Historical Review*, he suggested that too much of the poem is of a style and content that would fit with a later date. The present author found that argument convincing and still does; others have been less sure. Davis argued that the poem is not as hostile to Harold as Orderic had suggested Guy was. He thought that the *Carmen* borrowed from William of Poitiers, though others believe it is the other way round. The most convincing argument is that the *Carmen* introduces legendary and incredible material which could only be later. This includes the story of Taillefer, the giant who opens the conflict. He appears in none of the accredited early sources, and the tale has the touch of legend about it. Then there is the killing of Harold, by four men, identified as Duke William, Eustace of Boulogne, Hugh, the heir to Ponthieu, and Walter Giffard. The first, presumably William, cleaved through Harold's breast, the second smote off his head, the third pierced his belly with a lance and the fourth cut off his thigh and carried away the leg. If this were true it is not credible that the main Norman sources would have ignored the fact that

William actually participated in the killing of Harold. We can agree with Davis that this, and other examples he quotes, is 'literary embellishment'. One possibility, though probably beyond proof, is that the *Carmen* is a work of about 1100 which is either based on the poem by Guy of Amiens or is an embellishment of it. This would leave it with importance, but the need for care must be stressed. It seems that as our knowledge stands at present it would be unwise to give the *Carmen* the credence that we give to William of Poitiers, the *Anglo-Saxon Chronicle*, or the Bayeux Tapestry.

Another difficult work to assess, though its author and date are known, is the *Roman de Rou* by Wace.[8] This is undoubtedly a late work, as Wace was not born until about 1100. He was born in the Channel Islands, though the handwriting for his native island could be interpreted as either Jersey or Guernsey, we are not sure which. He at least tells us the source of his information: people he spoke to who had witnessed the events. He said, 'I talk to rich men who have rents and money, it is for them that the book is made.' He described himself as a 'vaslet' or varlet, which it is thought might mean that, like William of Poitiers, he had some knightly training in his youth. A recent article shows that he had a good knowledge of warfare, which gives his work value for our purposes. He was educated at Caen in Normandy, and in the French realm, later returning to Caen. He was patronised by Henry II, who gave him a prebend at Bayeux cathedral. He held this post for nineteen years, so it is nearly certain that he was familiar with the Tapestry. He was a prolific writer, and his works included verse romances, one called the *Roman de Brut* and another the *Roman de Rou*. Rou is a version of the name Rollo or Rolf, the Viking leader who became the first ruler of the new Normandy, so the work was a kind of verse history of the dukes. He probably wrote it in the second half of the twelfth century, and died in 1184. The problem with the *Roman de Rou*, apart from its latish date, is that it is a romance. Wace was a literary writer, he was looking for effect, he liked a good story and was not always fussy about accuracy or borrowing from one situation to enliven another. He is the sort of medieval author who is most difficult for historians to use: too useful and too lively to ignore, but too risky to trust.

The use of Wace in this book is to allow passages about which there is no serious concern, but to have great caution with any lines which have the feel of legend or invention about them. As said before, history is not an exact science.

Finally, we need to consider a group of twelfth-century historians who covered the history of the battle. By this time, the Norman Conquest was well established, and its significant consequences were apparent. This coloured views of events, and William's position is usually seen as the correct one: the winner is always right in history, as some would say. We do not have time or space to look at all the later sources which deal with Hastings, so this is simply a selection of those which seem the most useful or important. It should be said that, because of their dating, they must generally be given second place behind the earlier sources when trying to assess their relative significance. But often they will confirm what appears in the earlier sources; usually, of course, they are based on one or more of them, and sometimes on sources which are lost – and this will give an added value.

William of Malmesbury was a major twelfth-century English historian. His *De Gestis Regum Anglorum* (Deeds of the Kings of the English) includes material on the period of the Conquest.[9] William was a Benedictine monk, but he was unusual in that he explains to us something of his methods, telling us that he travelled about in search of documents. He was also able to read Old English as well as French and Latin. He wrote a vast number of works, and was a stylish and lively historian. He was probably born in the last decade of the eleventh century, and is thought to be of mixed Norman and English parentage. He says he collected historical information at his own expense, which suggests that his family was fairly wealthy. He became librarian at Malmesbury, and perhaps precentor. William is selected because he was an outstanding writer rather than because he gives especially important information.

Orderic Vitalis, like William of Malmesbury, was a product of the Conquest, son of a Norman priest and an English mother. He was born at Atcham near Shrewsbury in 1075. His father may have been in the household of Robert of Montgomery. Orderic received some local education and was then sent as a boy of ten to train to be a monk in the Norman house of St-Evroult. There he stayed for the rest of his life, until 1141 or 1142. An early work consisted of his additions to the chronicle of William of Jumièges. He then spent some thirty years working on his great opus, the *Ecclesiastical History*, which was a long and rambling work, whose intention and structure changed with the years. As a result, it is full of the sort of titbits which make history fun, tales of people he knew or heard about, the occasional scandal.[10] Orderic comes across in his writing as a likeable man who enjoyed life, and his work has a human touch which some medieval chronicles lack. We have Orderic's work in his own beautifully neat script. His English background gives his work interest from its attitude. He is the only one to give us the name for the battle location as Senlac, and he has some criticisms of the Conqueror's actions.

A third English historian of note is Henry of Huntingdon.[11] He was Archdeacon in Huntingdon, a secular cleric rather than a monk, a father of children as well as the son of a priest, a man of the world. He was well travelled and visited Bec in Normandy, and Rome. He had a historian's, almost a journalist's nose for information, and wrote 'there is nothing in this world more exciting than accurately to investigate and trace out the course of worldly affairs'. He tells us that he used 'compilations of the chronicles preserved in ancient libraries'. His *Historia Anglorum* is a great wide-ranging history of the English. His outlook has a strong East Anglian slant. He was born in about 1080, began writing in about 1133 and, after adding new work to his original effort, brought it down to 1154. It was a popular work of its day with many known copies. One of his virtues was that he could read Old English, and used the documents to which he had access. Henry's work is now available in one of the first-rate Oxford editions, with Latin alongside an English translation.

Finally, because it has a special significance, we must consider the value of the *Chronicle of Battle Abbey*.[12] This too is now in an excellent modern Oxford edition. The chronicle is undoubtedly late in date, after 1155, but it was written in the abbey built on the site of the battle - so it tells us – its very name depending upon the event. It was written by a monk with a great interest in the law. The trouble is that his modern editor has caught him out. He used documents forged in the abbey to make a case, and there is little doubt that some of his claims are false. The difficulty is to know if others are true. He was certainly trying to boost the importance of his abbey. The chronicle consists of two separate texts, of which the first is an account of the Norman Conquest, and both mention the abbey's foundation. The main value of the chronicle is its local knowledge. It gives detail not known elsewhere: the name of Hedgland on Telham Hill, and the story of the Malfosse. The modern editor of the chronicle has shown the problems over this location, and we shall look at them in the following chapter. The even more basic problem is that if this chronicler is unreliable, can we trust his story of the abbey's foundation on the spot where Harold was killed? This also we shall return to. The uncertainty over the *Carmen* is added to by the fact that there are incidents which only appear, other than in the *Carmen*, in Wace and the Battle chronicle. We seem to be looking at three sources which are all beginning to enlarge on original facts with dubious tales.

There are numerous other sources, but we must call a halt. We conclude that William of Poitiers is our primary source of information, that he is followed by several valuable early works in William of Jumièges, the *Anglo-Saxon Chronicle*, and the Bayeux Tapestry. All the other sources, to some extent, depend upon these early versions. The only other account which *may* be early and original is the *Carmen*, but our decision is to relegate this to the second division of sources. Here it joins forces with later and less trustworthy accounts, depending either upon hearsay, third-hand material or invention. The difficulty is that these include some of the most detailed works and some of the most lively, Wace and the *Carmen*; and some by the best historical writers, William of Malmesbury, Henry of Huntingdon and Orderic Vitalis. We must pick our way between their accounts. In the end, our objective is the truth. We cannot be certain we find it, but we must be certain that our attempt is honest. Such is the historian's task, every historian's task, from professorial academic to humble student.

SEVEN

THE BATTLE

When William jumped on to the beach at Pevensey, he stumbled forwards. Some were ready to see this as a bad omen. William of Malmesbury's version of the incident was that: 'as he disembarked he slipped down, but turned the accident to his advantage; a soldier who stood near calling out to him, "You hold England, my lord, its future king."'[1] Wace, whatever his faults, knew something of the sea, and described or perhaps rather imagined the landing, seeing the Norman invaders

> Sally forth and unload the ships,
> Cast the anchors and haul the ropes,
> Bear out shields and saddles,
> Lead out the warhorses and palfreys.
> The archers disembarked,
> The first to set foot on land.[2]

The landing had been easier than any invader could have expected. Harold is generally seen as a good commander, and one knows of the problems he faced keeping his force in the field, and having to deal with Hardrada. Even so, the complete lack of any opposition to William speaks of some neglect. It suggests that Harold was not as well informed as William, and believed that William would not come so late in the year.

But William must have felt very satisfied with the success of the crossing. The first major obstacle had been overcome. The period that now followed was for him a game of nerves. The two leaders pursued very clear policies in the short campaign.

Harold soon decided to act as quickly as possible, and made all his efforts in that direction. William chose not to push inland against a major town, perhaps London, as most invaders would. He decided instead to wait, which was a bold and risky choice. He did his best to bring Harold to him by making as big a nuisance of himself as he could on the coast. But how long could this game have continued had Harold not accepted the bait?

The Conqueror did his best to protect his position, another good reason for staying near his base. He had chosen his landing place well. Pevensey and Hastings offered harbour for his fleet. He must also have gained information on the fortresses of the region. His demand for Harold's promise to gain, fortify and hand over to him the stronghold at Dover as part of the oath, demonstrates William's thinking. He must already then have been considering the possibility of bringing a force to England, and thought in terms of the most powerful naturally defended site on the southern coast, one still important because it marks the shortest passage across the Channel.

We have no way of knowing why William did not land at Dover; possibly it did not offer such good beaching facilities as Pevensey, possibly Harold might expect him there after the 1064 demands. One positive reason for landing in Sussex was that the shire was Godwin territory. Godwin's first appearance in history was in Sussex, and the family still held considerable lands in the county. It was from Bosham that Harold set out in 1064; he also had manors in the Hastings region of East Sussex.[3] William's intention of bringing Harold to him was enhanced by the fact that it was Harold's own family possessions that were suffering most from the Norman invaders.

At any rate, Pevensey offered a good defensive position and a ready-made fortress. The coastline was somewhat different in the eleventh century, offering better conditions for embarkation. But one thing that was much the same was Pevensey 'Castle'. Pevensey had been noted by the Romans as a good site, easily defended from the land direction because access was narrow and difficult. They had built one of their Saxon Shore forts on the site. Unlike earlier Roman forts, it was irregular, roughly oval, filling the good land over the marshy ground around. Those well-constructed walls still stood in 1066, and still stand now, albeit having been repaired from time to time. William built a smaller defence within the walls, though the whole space offered a good temporary protection for the invading army. The later Norman stone castle was constructed within one sector of the walls: a castle within the Roman walls, using those walls as a bailey. It is generally thought that William's temporary castle had been on this same site.

Before long, however, William moved along the coast and made use of an even more powerful naturally defended site on the cliffs at Hastings. Some historians have queried this, suggesting there was no road to follow, but the chroniclers make it clear that this was his first move and that it was by land. Here he built another castle. The Tapestry beautifully illustrates the construction of the motte: a noble supervising, men carrying tools, two of them fighting, others picking and shovelling to make the earthworks. The castle is portrayed as a motte with a wooden keep on top, just as the Breton castles shown earlier were depicted.[4]

The Tapestry also shows various scenes of William's activities during this period in a way that no chronicle could do in words.[5] We see the sails and masts being removed and the ships beached; horses being brought ashore. If William had forbidden forage during the wait in Normandy, he made no such proviso now. The troops, including mounted men, seized food from the locals. We see one holding a sheep, another looming over it with an axe, while a cow forlornly looks on. One man returns with a pig over his shoulders, another leading a packhorse.

We also see the invaders cooking on the beach: birds and meat on skewers, a pot slung from a pole fixed in place by uprights, heating over flames on a stand that looks not unlike a modern barbecue. Elsewhere, a bearded man is removing hot cooked food from a grill, using a sort of pincer implement to save his fingers. He is putting the food on a plate ready to be eaten.

Other servants are carrying food on skewers to the nobles at an improvised table made from shields. On these are placed a variety of containers, dishes and plates, while one man refreshes himself from a drinking horn. At what looks like an actual table appears William's half-brother, Odo, Bishop of Bayeux. This scene, rather cheekily, seems to be inspired by contemporary artworks of the last supper, with Odo positioned in the place taken by Christ, and with a cooked fish before him. The artist was clearly aware of the Christian significance of that creature. No doubt the intention was to enhance the role of Odo, the patron of the Tapestry, but perhaps also to reflect the Norman belief in God's blessing on the invasion. Odo is shown in the act of blessing the food and drink before them.

William did more than forage to anger Harold and bring him south. He also attacked property and people in the area, much as if it were a Viking raid. Some intending conquerors might try to placate their future subjects; this was not William's concern at that time. Primarily he needed to bring on a quick decision. Battle-seeking was not always the policy of William, though some historians have made it so. Like all good medieval commanders he engaged in battles sparingly. John Gillingham has pointed out that the Breton campaign, on which Harold had been able to observe William's methods, was a typically cautious one.[6]

But now a quick battle was the duke's best option, unless Harold would take the offered compromise and surrender the throne – which was unlikely. That being the case, William could not succeed unless Harold was removed from the throne by force. As Harold approached, as the English fleet moved in to cut off possible retreat, as supplies began to dwindle, William's position would become increasingly difficult: at the very least he must fight his way out of a trap. Both commanders at Hastings settled for a battle, but neither can have been entirely lacking in anxiety in a situation which offered much but also would have dire consequences for the loser.

The foraging itself was not necessary. Plenty of provisions had been loaded on board before sailing, and they had certainly not yet run out or even run low. The foraging would provide useful additional provisions, but its main purpose was to harass Harold's Sussex people. William of Poitiers wrote: 'when he heard that the territory around the Norman camp was being ravaged, Harold was so furious that he hastened his march. His plan was to make a sudden night attack and to crush his enemies when they were least expecting him'; though the chronicler could not have known the thoughts of the English king. But provocation was in the Conqueror's mind, and we find him burning down houses and turning people from their homes.

One of the most graphic scenes in the Tapestry is of what appears to be a mother and son outside their house as Normans set torches to it and the roof goes up in flames.[7]

The Tapestry shows a messenger from Harold coming to William.[8] If we can take this at face value it means that Harold knew about William's coming very soon after it occurred, with time to give instructions to a messenger to reach the invader's camp. Some of the sources also give information on an exchange of messages. If Harold's came first, as the Tapestry suggests, it was probably to offer some sort of deal. But the Norman sources only tell us about William's messages, telling Harold to give up the throne. If he did so, he was offered position and lands. But now that Harold was king it must have been clear that such offers were highly unlikely to be accepted. The negotiations were perforce brief, their content superficial, going through the motions: neither leader showed any signs of compromising. It was in such circumstances that medieval battles were often fought.

Harold may have heard the news of William's landing while he himself was in York. His decision to move south was taken immediately. He returned to London, but was already set on heading straight for William. He could not immediately know William's plans, and needed to consider some defensive moves. It was quite possible that William would move on to Dover, or would strike at either London or Winchester. London was a good base.

It says much for the English military system that despite two draining battles in the north, the king could still at such short notice raise a solid army. John of Worcester points out that powerful men of England had been lost in the northern battles, and that half the army was not assembled. For once the words of Wace are acceptable on the loss of men from the north, 'the Danes and Tostig having much damaged and weakened them'.[9]

The housecarls of Harold's household and the mounted fyrdmen had come to London from Stamford Bridge. Poitiers says that Harold received some aid from Denmark.[10] It is probable that the battle had not been quite so prolonged as later sources said. The nature of it, with the surprise attack resulting in victory, normally would speak of a relatively brief conflict. It had been prolonged by the arrival of reinforcements from the coast, but the English army must have escaped without enormous losses. Had Stamford Bridge been too damaging on Harold's men, he would not have been able to contemplate another battle. The signs are that the victory had been so great that few men were lost.

Nevertheless, the journey north, the battle, the journey back to London had to be exhausting. Harold waited six days, during which reinforcements arrived or were summoned to meet him. A few days' rest in London helped to recover strength and determination, but it must have been a weary force that made its way down towards Sussex.

Some historians in the past marvelled at the stamina of men on foot who did all of these things. It cannot be proven certainly, but it is generally accepted that men on foot did not attempt such feats. The housecarls and the fyrdmen who travelled those distances were on horseback. They fought on foot but rode long distances. The men who bulked out the army to greater numbers almost certainly came from local levies, in the main shire levies. This would also help to explain a differing kind of force in different regions of the country. Those recorded as dying at Hastings came mainly from the Midlands and the south. Certainly some could have assembled in London and marched to Hastings on foot, the distance makes that quite possible.

Harold had to take his decisions fast, and he was a decisive man. His military successes had depended upon it. Above all, the victory at Stamford Bridge had come from the bold move of heading fast to York, despite knowing that northern reinforcements would be restricted because of the events at Gate Fulford. His push on through York had taken Hardrada by surprise and the result had been a great victory. Such a victory would put his men in good heart and give them confidence in his leadership.

It was in London that Harold made the vital and fatal decision of when to move on. With hindsight, most would agree it was the wrong decision. According to Orderic, those close to him advised delay or that he himself should not command the army. He responded with anger, and when his mother clung to him to prevent him going 'he insolently kicked her'.[11] These details sound like invention, though there must have been some

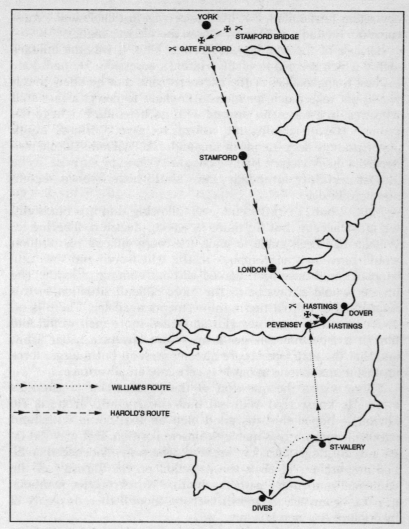

The routes to Hastings of the rivals. (Map: Mike Komarnyckyj)

opposition to the plan. But his choice was justifiable and almost came off. He had a good army whose morale was high.

Because of the way he had become king, it was the military ability which seemed to justify Harold's accession. He had done his best to make allies of the northern earls, but he knew that it would not take much for men in England to desert a monarch who was, in essence, an upstart with no hereditary right to the crown. Harold could not afford to give William much opportunity to seek friends in England. Like William, Harold also needed a quick victory. Had he caught William by surprise, as he almost certainly intended, there could have been a second Stamford Bridge.

But . . . but . . . in the end, even allowing that it is hindsight, we must accept that he made a wrong decision. The longer William had been made to wait, the more difficult his position would have become. Supplies in the end would run low, and supplies could have been denied without coming to battle. The invader would always be in the more difficult situation in this respect. Also, Harold had reinforcements available. There is no doubt that with every day Harold waited more men would join him. It is true that a larger army is not always a better army, and that the core forces were already present, but a larger force against a smaller one in battle is certainly an advantage.

There is also the question of the composition of Harold's force. He knew that William had cavalry and archers. He obviously hoped that his good men on foot could withstand cavalry if given a reasonable defensive position. But why did he go into Hastings with few archers? The only evidence that he had any archers at all is the depiction on the Tapestry of the one small and rather pathetic figure.[12] No chronicler mentions any use or impact of English archery, though there is plenty of mention of Norman bowmen.

The conclusion must be that Harold had very few archers. Yet, as we have seen, archery was a well-known activity in England, and there must have been some available, even if the northern battles had diminished the pool. We are getting into difficult territory, and we do not know where archers came from or how many might have been available to Harold. But at Hastings, against the Normans, from a good position, archers would have been invaluable. Harold ought to have obtained some, even if it meant waiting. In any case, Harold decided on a rapid march to catch the Conqueror off guard as he had done with Hardrada. He rapidly moved southwards to London with the best of his mounted troops. He spent a few days in London, the minimum necessary to organise a new army for battle, raising southern levies. Then it was on to the south coast.

Harold marched on the road from London, through the forest of the Weald. William of Jumièges wrote: 'Hastening to take the duke by surprise, he rode through the night and arrived at the battlefield at dawn.'[13] He arranged for an assembly point on the southern exit from the wooded heights. The place was marked by an old apple tree. We now need to consider the site where the battle was fought. Historians have agreed. There is no doubt. Vested interests would be upset if the accepted site was wrong. It is probably correct, but the 'probably' needs to be emphasized. When first suggested that evidence could be interpreted to indicate a different site, one might have expected enraged howls from various quarters.[14] In the event, nobody seemed to notice, not even more recent works on the battle. This is odd because the point is a serious one. The *best* evidence for the location of the battle is not at all definite about the accepted site, and we should recall that none of the eleventh-century sources was the work of an eyewitness, or probably of anyone who ever visited the site. So far as we know, the twelfth-century Battle Abbey chronicler was the only author of any of our sources who actually knew the ground. We should therefore examine the matter of location in more detail.[15]

The reason that historians assume they know where the battle was fought is that they accept without question the statement in the *Chronicle of Battle Abbey*. Allen Brown, whose account of Hastings remains the best, wrote: 'we know the site of the engagement: we know with an unusual degree of precision where it was fought'.[16] But the Abbey *Chronicle*, as we have seen, would not normally be considered a prime source of evidence: it is late, it contains demonstrable distortions and economies with the truth, and it has reasons for manufacturing or exaggerating this particular point. The reason it is taken seriously is because it is a local source: the writer would have known abbey traditions and

The Battle of Hastings

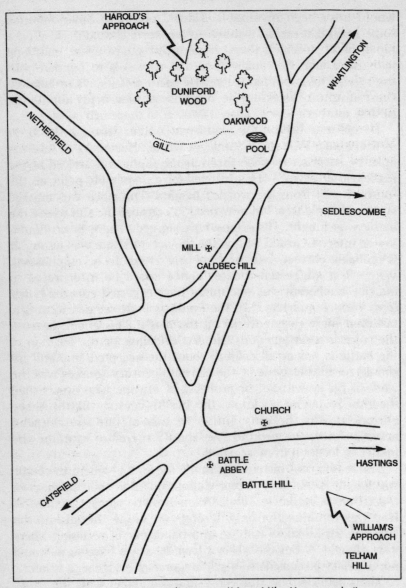

Battle and the surrounding area. (Map: Mike Komarnyckyj)

local lore. But he was writing a century after the event, his knowledge is all at second hand, and the source of his information is not passed on to us. The chronicle tells us that, in building the abbey, the Conqueror was fulfilling a vow that had been made long before on the continent, and the modern editor suggests we should treat this tale with circumspection. We ought to treat all his tales with circumspection.[17]

He wrote that four monks were brought over from Marmoutier and they 'studied the battlefield and decided that it seemed hardly suitable for so outstanding a building. They therefore chose a fit place for settling, a site located not far off, but somewhat lower down, towards the western slope of the ridge . . . This place, still called *Herste*, has a low wall as a mark of this.' But when the Conqueror was told, 'he refused angrily and ordered them to lay the foundations of the church speedily and on the very spot where his enemy had fallen and the victory had been won'. He adds that 'the English had already occupied the hill where the church now stands'. He then goes on to say that 'they prudently erected the high altar as the king had commanded, on the very place where Harold's emblem, which they called a standard, was seen to have fallen'.[18]

This has convinced many, and it may be true, but in accepting this chronicler we must realise we are taking much for granted. The tale has the same sort of pseudo-realistic ring about it as the vow story. The writer himself says that the Conqueror never visited the site. The building was certainly not ready until many years after the battle. They started in one location and finished in another. The writer was keen to enhance his abbey's reputation with the tale of the vow; one cannot but suspect that he at least firmed up the foundation story to suit the abbey's purpose. We should have reservations about swallowing the tale without question. It is some cause for concern that the altar story does not emerge until a century after the event: it is surprising that no earlier writer knew of and repeated such a vivid detail.[19]

The reason all this is being laboured is that we shall now do what we recommended should always be done, look at the early and best evidence. Only from its being local can the *Chronicle of Battle Abbey* possibly be thought 'best'. The early chronicles in fact do not clearly identify the location, and there are some comments which are a little worrying to the acceptance of the traditional site. The most important of these is the one chronicle written by an Englishman in Old English and close to the event, the D version of the *Anglo-Saxon Chronicle*. This is a brief account of the battle, but it makes a clear statement of location: 'King Harold was informed of this [William's landing and activities] and he assembled a large army and came against him at the hoary apple tree.'[20] It does not say they assembled there and then moved on a mile and fought, but that is where they fought. This also indicates that it was no chance location, but one that was well known and selected well in advance as a meeting point, perhaps with the prime intention of preventing a Norman march northwards to London.[21]

The location of the apple tree oddly enough has been investigated and settled to most people's satisfaction. It is thought to have been on the summit of Caldbec Hill, where there is now a windmill. This is a place where the boundaries of three hundreds met, and such old trees often marked important boundary points of that kind.

The odd thing is that historians have settled the position of the tree, but never considered that the D version might be correct. It is an eminently suitable position for the sort of battle the chronicles describe. Caldbec is a hill with slopes steeper than those at Battle. In fact Caldbec, 300 feet above sea level, dominates the area, and Chevallier, again without considering there might be other significance to the statement, thought that before victory was won the Normans would have needed to control Caldbec. And what of our best source for the battle, William of Poitiers? He wrote: 'They stationed themselves in a position overlooking him, on a hillside adjacent to the wood through which they had advanced', which again fits rather better with Caldbec than with Battle.

The *Carmen* gives some detail of the English taking up position. (We shall keep to our determination to treat the *Carmen* as a second rank source.) The poet says that the Normans first saw the English while they were still among the trees: they could 'see the forest glitter, full of spears'. The action begins thus:

Suddenly the forest poured forth troops of men, and from the hiding-places of the woods a host dashed forward. There was a hill near the forest and a neighbouring valley and the ground was untilled because of its roughness . . . they seized this place for the battle. On the highest point of the summit he [Harold] planted his banner.

This could fit either hill, but the remarks about woodland are of interest.[22]

Caldbec Hill was right on the edge of the heavily wooded land. Domesday Book allows us to say this with some hope of being accurate, since it indicates which parts were cultivated. The Battle chronicler says there were woods around the abbey, but from Domesday it seems likely that if troops emerged from 'forest' they would first come on to Caldbec, which after all was the appointed meeting place. We shall leave the identification of the Malfosse to a later point in our discussion, but it fits as well and perhaps better with a battle fought on Caldbec than one on Battle Hill.

It might be thought that Orderic's description, though a late one, confirms the abbey account. He wrote: 'a great multitude of the English flocked together from all sides to the place whose early name was Senlac . . . Reaching the spot they all dismounted from their horses and stood close together in a dense formation on foot.' It is important that Orderic uses an otherwise unknown place-name, and it has been universally applied to Battle Hill, but without any evidence. Orderic knew a name for the place, but which place? Senlac means literally 'sand-lake', and there is no lake close by Battle Hill, though people have conjectured that there may once have been.[23] The hill itself would certainly not be called 'sand-lake', and there is no reason to think that Senlac means Battle Hill.

However, there was a lake, or at least a pool, close by Caldbec Hill, close to Oakwood Gill on the edge of the wooded area. We also note that taken as it stands, without prior knowledge of where Senlac is, Orderic's account sounds more like that of the *Anglo-Saxon Chronicle*, as if the English dismounted and fought at the point of assembly, rather than marching on a mile or so, and that Senlac was the name of the assembly point. His account is that they came to Senlac and 'Reaching the spot they all dismounted from their horses'. The Bayeux Tapestry, just as it moves to the story of the battle, depicts three trees – none have been shown since the Norman felling of timber for building the fleet.[24] This seems to confirm that woods were in the vicinity of the fighting, though in this case seen from the point of view of the Norman advance, which also shows a hill on the approach.

There are a few minor points which might cause this pause for thought to seem worthwhile. The battle accounts have always left a few puzzles when historians have tried to relate them to the actual ground of Battle Hill. There are questions about the 'hillock' on the Tapestry.[25] One has been identified in the flatter ground before the abbey, but it hardly fits, and is very small. The 'hillock' also appears on the Tapestry before even the rumour of William's death. Later, it will be suggested that there was no hillock to look for. Then there is the matter of where the 'Malfosse' was, if that is the correct name even to connect with an incident in the battle.[26]

It is puzzling given the enormous interest in Hastings, that despite the digging of foundations for the abbey, for the old primary school, for all the houses along the main road, all the digging in gardens, the archaeological digs at various points in the abbey grounds, the road making, not a single trace of the battle has been found. There are a few tales about finds, but none which have ever been verified and which would prove that Battle Hill had been the site of a great battle. Have people simply been looking in the wrong place?[27]

Here we shall end this debate. There is no certainty that the battle of Hastings was fought at Caldbec. What needs to be said is that the evidence is not decisive. There are question-marks against placing the site on Battle Hill, and we should keep a more open mind on the matter than has been the case to date. I did not put this case with any particular pleasure. I have had a long association with Pyke House and the traditional battlefield. I shall be perfectly happy if some further proof appears which confirms the traditional location. It is simply that if one looks at the evidence objectively, questions have to be raised. I must confess to a wry grin at the thought that the traditional site just might be wrong, and at all those people who have so carefully measured Battle Hill to calculate how many men stood on it if each had 3 feet of ground, the little signs all over the place to mark who stood where, the confident guides in the abbey, or whatever. . . .

The case for Caldbec Hill as the battle site has been put at some length because it has never been done before, not because it is necessarily correct. Yet whatever reservations we have about the Battle chronicler, it does seem likely that the abbey called after the battle would have been built where the battle was fought, and that the monks, who did not know the land or the country, would have sought advice from any one of the thousands who had fought there. But stranger things have happened. We may also question whether the altar is actually on the summit of the hill and was Harold's command post. But on the ground of probability, there remains a good case for the traditional site.[28]

Harold certainly placed a banner to mark his command position on the summit of the chosen hill. Harold may have had two banners: the Wessex dragon banner sometimes called the Wyvern which is shown on the Tapestry, and perhaps also his own personal banner of the Fighting Man. William of Malmesbury says that after the battle the Fighting Man, embroidered with gold and precious stones, was sent to the Pope by the victor.[29]

The following account of the battle will be based on the early chronicle evidence, and will not assume a known site, though locations will be discussed where it becomes important to do so, for example, over the Malfosse business. Before we can move to the actual conflict there is one other disputed matter to settle. Did the English set up some kind of palisade or defence to protect themselves during the battle? We can answer fairly certainly: no they did not. The wall comes either from a mistranslation and misunderstanding of Wace, or from Wace himself if you believe he meant a palisade rather than using that simile for the shield-wall. The palisade in front of the English was popularised by Freeman as a 'development of the usual tactics of the shield-wall', and has survived in various accounts since, despite Round's thorough demolition work on it in the last century.

I have changed my mind over this since 1985. I then believed that Wace got it wrong and had the idea that a shield-wall must be some sort of real wall. This is possible, the matter depends on a translation of a difficult section of his French, and in particular on the translation of 'escuz', which could mean either shield or wall/fence. I now feel that Round may have got it right, and that Wace did not mean a solid wall at all, that he realises perfectly well what a shield-wall was, and that his passage is a poetic flight intended as a simile, and that he no more meant an actual wall than Shakespeare thought the sea was a real wall around the scepter'd isle. It is the word 'escuz' which persuades me, as it persuaded Round. I think we can credit Wace with deliberate poetic punning. What he is saying is that the shield-wall was *like* a real wall and so on, with somewhat exaggerated emphasis and detail. Of course, one can always be wrong on such debatable matters.[30] In any event, Wace, with his knowledge of twelfth-century warfare, is often interesting on tactics, and added a point we may accept without difficulty in an imagined speech by Harold: 'all is lost if they once penetrate our ranks'.[31] The English did form a solid mass together on the hill, close together, an imposing sight, a difficult obstacle.[32]

A secondary question relating to the ancient apple tree is why Harold needed an assembly point. It usually seems to be assumed that it was to allow the army with him to sort itself out. But the terms in the chronicles very much suggest a meeting point. It was surely here that Harold had arranged to meet troops raised in the southernmost counties. Given the haste of his march and the very minimum of time for troops to answer any summons, such a meeting place was a necessity. In the situation, it again is possible but seems unlikely that he then advanced further towards William and was halted again. If we are right and this was a broader assembly point, it would be a place where Harold would be forced to delay; troops which are assembling do not all arrive and place themselves neatly within minutes. We know that William was informed of Harold's movements, the likelihood is that he caught him at the assembly place. It is a small point, and given medieval accuracy not one to press, but John of Worcester specifically says that the march was 9 miles, though Battle is only about 7 miles away.[33]

Harold probably did intend to march on southwards to the

coast and catch the Normans as he had caught Hardrada, though he may have been happy enough to stand on a good defensive site and await the Normans' coming; again we cannot be certain, though the former always seems to be assumed. Harold was no novice in war, and he had organised something of a trap for the Normans. He had now re-formed the English fleet, and ships had been sent to block any return passage that the Normans might attempt. Orderic says seventy ships performed this task.[34]

In any case, William roughly knew Harold's position and had his army on the alert for a sudden move. We need not take William of Malmesbury's account of the night before the battle too seriously, he was trying to explain away the result in terms of the godliness, or lack of it, in the conduct of the two armies: 'the English as we have heard passed the night without sleep, in drinking and singing . . . the Normans passed the whole night in confessing their sins, and received the sacrament'. Wace as usual makes the most of this idea, carried away with thoughts of English drunkenness: 'All the night they ate and drank, and never lay down on their beds. They might be seen carousing, gambolling and dancing and singing; Bublie they cried, and Weissel, and Laticome and Drincheheil, Drinc-hindrewart and Drintome, Drinc-helf, and Drinc-tome . . .', while the Normans and French 'betook themselves all night to their orisons, and were in very serious mood'.[35]

William had already been told by Robert fitz Wimarc, who had been in England for some time but acted as an informant for the Normans, of Harold's victory in the north. According to William of Poitiers, he warned the Conqueror to avoid battle. The chronicler also tells us that there were Norman scouts watching the approaches and informing the Conqueror. William of Jumièges remarks on the duke's readiness for action: 'taking precautions in case of a night attack, he ordered his army to stand to arms from dusk to dawn'.[36]

The warning of approaching troops came on the night of Friday 13 October. William got his men ready and made a battle speech, reminding those around of the courage needed, that 'there was no way available for retreat', and that defeat would mean death. Poitiers says: 'without losing a moment, the duke ordered all those in camp to arm themselves, although that day a large section of his troops had gone off foraging'. William also arranged for a mass, in which he himself participated. He placed around his neck the relics on which Harold had sworn the oath he was to break.

It is about 7 miles from the coast to Battle. In his own haste the Conqueror put his hauberk on back to front, but laughed off the mistake so as not to make it appear a bad omen. No doubt, as Gillingham has suggested, it was the result of William feeling nervous about what was to come. William of Malmesbury says he exclaimed over the hauberk 'thus shall my dukedom be turned into a kingdom'.[37] Then they prepared for the march and set off in the very early hours northwards.

They moved forward behind the papal banner. 'In the first line William put infantry, armed with bows and crossbows; in the second line he placed more infantry, better armed and in hauberks; finally came squadrons of cavalry, with William in the centre with the stronger force.'[38] William took the normal route which brought him to Telham Hill, the summit of which is Blackhorse Hill.

It was here that his look-outs spotted the English and that William prepared his men in order for a battle. The *Anglo-Saxon Chronicle* says: 'William came against him by surprise before his army was drawn up in battle array.'[39] Had both armies been on the march, Harold would have been in no more disarray than William. If he were ready to deploy on Battle Hill he would have been in better state than William. The suspicion recurs that William caught Harold at the assembly point.

The *Anglo-Saxon Chronicle* also suggests some disloyalty in the English ranks, commenting that Harold was aided only 'by the men who were willing to support him'. John of Worcester confirms this point.[40] Harold had failed to catch the Normans in the way he caught the Scandinavians, but he did have time to arrange his army in a good defensive position on the crest of a hill, whichever hill. 'They immediately dismounted from their horses and all packed densely together on foot.' There can be no doubt that the English army fought as an entirely infantry army. No source says otherwise. Even if late in date the opinion of the *Carmen* is interesting: 'the

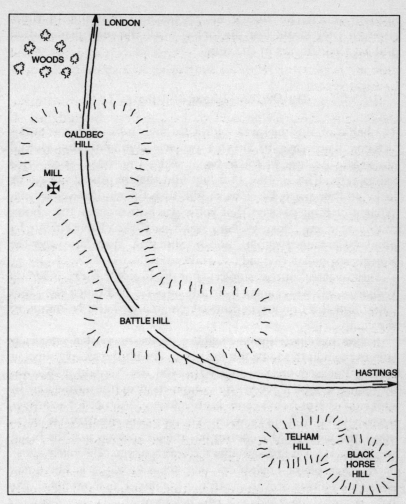

The area in which the battle was fought: Caldbec and Battle Hill.
(Map: Mike Komarnyckyj)

English scorn the solace of horses and trusting in their strength they stand fast on foot . . . all the men dismounted and left their horses in the rear'.[41]

THE OPENING PHASE OF THE BATTLE

The battle of Hastings was fought through most of Saturday 14 October. Wace says, in another unlikely comment, that Harold chose the day on purpose because he had been born on a Saturday and his mother had told him that he would always be lucky on that day. If Wace was right, then the mother was wrong. William of Jumièges says that battle was joined at the third hour, that is at 9 a.m. Duke William was able to direct movements by hand, by arranged signals, and by shouting. Wace also says the Normans shouted 'God aid us', and the English 'Out'.[42]

Various later sources suggest that the Breton cavalry made up William's left wing, men from other parts of France the right wing, and the Conqueror himself commanded the Normans in the centre.

Poitiers mentions Norman infantry on the march but practically ignores them in the battle, his interest is all with the socially superior cavalry. But later sources do say that the first Norman attack was by infantry, which given the composition of the army and its order on the march, seems highly likely. Orderic, for example, describes the first move when 'the Norman infantry closed to attack the English'. The *Carmen* has the archers opening the battle, which is also likely, and says that the crossbowmen deliberately aimed at 'the faces of the English' to cause them to fall back. The writer adds that shields are no protection against crossbow bolts. The bolts 'destroyed the shields as if by a hailstorm'.[43]

The Tapestry beautifully depicts the cavalry riding casually and then moving to a charge, one with a sword, most with lances held overhead, some grasping them underarm and a few couched – including, perhaps significantly, the rider who first makes contact with the English shield-wall. The Tapestry also shows a group of four Norman archers aiming to shoot, one in a hauberk. One of the foremost pair seems to be standing on the far edge of a ditch, his left foot braced on the slope.[44]

The Battle

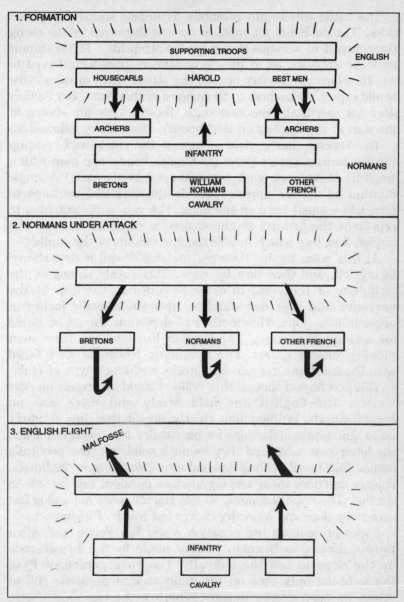

The main stages of the battle of Hastings: 1. the confrontation; 2. the English counter-attack; 3. the Norman breakthrough.
(Map: Mike Komarnyckyj)

The battle was begun promptly. Trumpets sounded on both sides. 'The duke and his men, in no way dismayed by the rising slope, began to advance slowly up the steep hill.' The Normans took the initiative, as in the circumstances they were forced to do. The Norman infantry opened the attack with 'missiles'. One would expect the archers to be engaged at this point, but Poitiers does not specifically mention them, though they are shown at the start of the fighting on the Tapestry. The cavalry followed in.

The Tapestry has a vivid picture of the shield-wall resisting the first impact, spears above the English heads, one man with a small hand axe, one with a two-handed battle axe.[45] A single diminutive archer appears beside the English, perhaps to represent a small force on the flank. The gap in the stitching to represent the ground might suggest a ditch in front of the English line, into which tumble the first victims of the conflict.

At this point in the Tapestry, the shield-wall is first shown facing left, and then directly right. This surely shows us the technique of the artist in order to continue the flow of the narrative and does not stand for two shield-walls facing in opposite directions. This method of depiction should be noted for a later discussion. The English hurled back their own missiles, chiefly spears. The advancing Normans were faced with the front-line axemen and others wielding a type of club.

This first impact showed that William could not expect an easy victory. The English line held firmly and there was no breakthrough. William had clearly hoped that this infantry onslaught would make gaps for his cavalry to exploit, but when the latter now advanced they found a solid line, the poetically named shield-wall, with spears and axes able to injure the horses. Poitiers describes them keeping in close position, side by side in the line. The slope was doing its job. Horses could not gallop fast up a steep slope and a cavalry charge lost much of its impact.

I was present on the occasion when Ian Peirce and Allen Brown, dressed in Norman armour made by the former, rode up the slope to test the difficulty. The back garden of Pyke House is the only area on the main section of Battle Hill to retain its open grassy nature. Whether the two riders were charging up the actual hill of 1066 we shall not reconsider. To charge up any similar steep slope would make the point.

The Battle

The experiment showed how well medieval cavalry needed to be trained. Professor Brown was almost pierced accidentally by his comrade's lance, and his horse bolted through the assembled 'Saxons' until, like Don Quixote, he was charging rather worryingly straight towards the brick walls of Pyke House. Later, his steed bolted down the hill, where Allen managed to guide it through a narrow gate which was an obstacle the Normans did not have to contend with. Ian and Allen's horses were not trained destriers, and although Allen had been in the cavalry, he had not ridden for some years. The experiment was therefore not totally authentic, but does not detract from its interest. The main lesson was how difficult it is on such a slope to gain much speed for a charge.

The Tapestry has vivid depictions of the action, axe against horse, falling men, bodies littering the lower margin, sometimes sliced off heads.[46] At one point, horses are shown at the foot of the hill, falling heavily into what appears to be water or possibly marsh. It is here that the supposed 'hillock' appears. Recalling a previous comment, this surely again is the artist simply showing the main hill of the battle in two views, as with the shield-wall, so that the action may continue. In which case, we do not need to search the ground for isolated hillocks.

The height of their position helped the English to deal out blows with an advantage as the enemy came within distance for close combat. 'The noise of the shouting from the Normans on one side and the barbarians on the other could barely be heard over the clash of weapons and the groans of the dying.' Poitiers says that the English with their weapons, presumably the axes in particular, were able to slice through shields and armour.

The English held off the Normans with swords; the first attack was halted and petered out. Poitiers says 'they began to drive them back', which surely implies some English movement forward. We should not view the shield-wall as an immobile force, as some historians have. It was quite capable of forward movement and advance; how otherwise could battles ever have been won, how was Stamford Bridge won?

Hastings was relatively static because the English knew that the height gave them advantage and the slope acted against cavalry, but they would look for a moment to advance to victory.

Clearly the English advanced a good distance, because Poitiers says that even the Norman spearmen, operating at a distance, now came under attack and were wounded. The result was a flight of the Norman infantry, and of the Bretons and other cavalry on the Norman left: 'Almost the whole of Duke William's battle line fell back.'

The first phase ended in English triumph. Not only had the infantry been driven back and some of the cavalry forced into flight, but there was now a rumour that Duke William had been killed. This does indeed suggest that the whole Norman line was in trouble. How otherwise could it be believed that William, in the centre of the line, had been brought down?

THE SECOND PHASE OF THE BATTLE

This was the crisis point for William. His troops were in disarray. The beginnings of a flight can very easily turn into broader panic. The rumour of his death could have been cause enough for a general flight.

The relative numbers of the armies have inspired thousands of words of print, mostly as we have suggested before, likely to be unprofitable in any except a very general sense. William of Poitiers, our best account, says that the English had a numerical advantage, but then he was biased. Again the unreliable Wace has a credible comment. He says that in his day many have explained the defeat by saying that Harold had a small force, but others say, 'and so do I, that he and the duke had man for man', and adds that William had more knights and more archers.[47]

I have been present at more than one reconstruction of the battle, again on the Battle site, of course. It does bring home something of the problem of deploying men and fighting over difficult, uneven and hilly ground. It also demonstrates the problem of fighting for long periods with heavy weapons and in armour. No medieval battle could have been fought hour after hour without lengthy breaks for the individual soldiers, and probably for the whole armies.

Almost the whole line of Duke William fell back . . . even the armies of glorious Rome, which won so many victories on land and sea, sometimes turned in flight, though supported by loyal troops, when they learned that their leader was killed, or thought that he was dead. The Normans believed that their duke had fallen.

The Normans were close to defeat. Even Poitiers admits to a flight. Only the commanders stood between them and the loss of the battle. William and his fellow leaders, Odo of Bayeux and Eustace of Boulogne among them, now showed their worth. No one man could have done it, the troops would simply have gone. Bishop Odo is shown on the Tapestry urging on his young men, waving his baton for attention rather than as a weapon.[48]

William tried to stand in the way but was failing. He had to rip off his helmet and show his face, the scene is vividly shown on the Bayeux Tapestry, right hand pushing the helmet back by its nasal, incidentally revealing that the headpiece of the hauberk covered the top of his head.[49] Like Odo, William is carrying a baton, a sign of command rather than a weapon. A rider next to him points at the duke, clearly saying that he is living. '"Look at me", he shouted. "I am still alive. With God's help I shall win. What madness makes you turn in flight? What retreat do you have if you flee? . . . if you keep going not a single one of you will escape."' In the *Carmen*, William's speech at this desperate moment went on for some nine lines of text.[50]

William himself rode forward, and it worked, they followed him, 'taking new courage from his words'. He raised his sword and charged into the enemy. They then turned on the men 'who had pursued them and wiped them out'. The chronicler says that the Conqueror 'led his forces with great skill, holding them when they turned in flight, giving them courage, sharing their danger. He was more often heard shouting to them to follow him than ordering them to go ahead of him.'

In the fighting which followed, the duke had three horses killed under him, each time finding a new mount and continuing to fight. Poitiers says that, each time, William killed the man who had brought down his horse, and showed his own physical strength, fighting with his sword and on occasion with his shield. Wace has an unverifiable incident with an English wrestler using an axe, who struck the duke 'on the head, and beat in his helmet, though without doing much injury'![51]

In the account of William of Poitiers, the first flight was a real one, but it was turned to advantage by the action of the Conqueror. This rings true. According to the chronicler, already by this point, the attack following on the reverse, the English line began to falter for the first time. This is important, because it explains Harold's failure or inability to counter-attack from here on. Poitiers says 'gaps began to appear in their ranks here and there, where the iron weapons of our brave soldiers were having their effect'. The chronicler records an individual act of valour at this point, when Robert fitz Roger de Beaumont led a battalion to the attack on the right wing. It was his first battle, and he 'laid about him with great courage'.

It was only now that William of Poitiers describes a feigned flight occurring. He says: 'they therefore withdrew, deliberately pretending to turn in flight. They were mindful of the fact that only a short time before their retreat had been turned into success.' The English saw victory in their grasp and, says Poitiers, a thousand of them pursued the retreating Normans. Then 'suddenly the Normans turned their horses, cut off the force which was pursuing them, made a complete circle around them, and massacred them to the last man'.

This tactic of the feigned flight has caused much debate. Many historians have believed it impossible. Lt.-Col.Lemmon wrote 'a "feigned retreat" was the recognised method by which chroniclers concealed the fact that the troops on their own side had run away', and thought the tactic 'impossible'.[52] But Poitiers does not disguise the first genuine flight, and does still describe feigned retreats.

The reasons of those who cannot accept the tactic have been those of 'common sense'. They contend that it was a tactic beyond the capabilities of eleventh-century cavalry. For some reason, most of them assume that the whole Norman line was supposed to have turned at once. It is true that Poitiers' account very much suggests that the first flight was genuine, and its outcome fortuitous, but he and others described feigned retreat tactics as well. It is also true that Poitiers says a thousand followed, but this is probably exaggeration unless it denoted not the single feigned flight but an English decision for a general advance. There is no reason to suppose that all the Norman cavalry used the tactic at once. We do not believe that they used a concerted charge with lances. They operated rather in smaller groups together. What one needs to see is a group of ten, twenty or fifty knights deciding on the manoeuvre.

We have pointed out in a previous chapter that feigned flights were a common ploy before 1066, and were used by the Normans on several occasions elsewhere. The historians who declare them impossible are flying in the face of the evidence; virtually all the chroniclers who go into detail include the tactic.[53] If we follow Poitiers, there seems no serious reason to discount the feigned flights. The first occasion was accidental, from then on they used the tactic once or twice deliberately and with some success. Some English were drawn off from the defensive position, and killed. If we consider this done by discrete sections of the Norman force, then obviously the English would lose men but not be annihilated, which is what happened.

One argument against the tactic is that it makes the fleeing force vulnerable, with backs to the enemy. The comment of the *Carmen* is interesting on this, suggesting a normal action in such a tactic. The writer says that, as they fled, 'shields covered their backs'; the straps of the shields of the mounted men would have allowed this.[54] The Normans had some success, there were gaps in the English line, but it still held as the rear ranks filled in for the dead and wounded. Poitiers says 'twice the Normans used this ruse with equal success', but the English line 'was still terrifying to behold', and the Normans 'had great difficulty in containing it'. This suggests that still there was that thin line between an English counter-attack and a deliberate drawing off by feigned flight. The feigned flights could very easily have turned into real ones.

William of Poitiers then describes a series of cavalry charges against the English line, which gradually wore down the English without breaking it. The English had by this time suffered heavy losses. There was another breathing space while each side licked its wounds. William, if not desperate, knew that daylight hours were running out. He needed a victory even more than Harold. He began to regroup for a final push.

The Battle of Hastings

Part of the fascination of the battle of Hastings is that it was such a close-fought thing. For all that the Normans had mounted cavalry and a stronger force of archers, for all that forces which relied on heavy infantry alone were to go out of fashion, these two very different armies had fought almost the whole day and the outcome was not by any means certain. The hill had blunted the impact of the cavalry and had made it more difficult for archers to shoot with effect. The shield-wall manned by heavy infantry, well armed and well disciplined, proved a match for the Norman cavalry as well as their infantry.

With hindsight we see the key moments. The repeated feigned flights had resulted in some deaths and gaps; the repeated cavalry attacks had gradually reduced the shield-wall. But now came the two killer punches. At some point, probably before Harold's death, his two younger brothers who had fought alongside him, Leofwin and Gyrth, were killed. William of Poitiers simply makes a statement that many English leaders were killed: 'their king was dead and his brothers with him'.

The death of the younger brothers is presented on the Tapestry at an early point in the battle, before William has shown his face: both killed by lances, Leofwin probably the figure wielding a battleaxe, Gyrth a spear.[55] Recently, it has been suggested that they may have fallen in an English advance. There very probably was such an attempt to win the battle, but there is no evidence of who was involved in it, or even what happened, except that clearly in the last resort it failed.[56] Again the elaboration by the *Carmen* does not carry conviction, with William killing Gyrth in hand-to-hand conflict while on foot.[57] No one else noticed that either.

The first killer punch was the death of Harold. The fact that his brothers had also been killed meant that the English lacked a commander. Before we look at the method of Harold's demise, let us briefly determine at what stage in the battle it occurred. All sources except one suggest or fit with a death towards the end of the battle, including our best source, Poitiers. The fly in the ointment is William of Jumièges, who states: 'Harold himself was slain, pierced with mortal wounds during the first assault.'[58]

There is no getting round the meaning of the words, but we cannot take this one comment against the weight of all the other evidence, though at least one later source does follow Jumièges. Suggestions have been made that the chronicler originally said something else, such as 'in the first rank', and there is a copyist's error, or that he meant 'the first attack in the final assault' – all the usual excuses when evidence does not fit. We can only say that Jumièges seems to have got this wrong, but his is a brief account, which goes straight on to the final stages of the fight and says that it was the death which led to the flight at nightfall.

William's last effort was an all-out one, involving every section of his force. We have seen that the Normans had both crossbowmen and archers with ordinary bows, and have argued elsewhere that the latter were in effect longbows. The events which now occurred help to support that argument, since the archery from some distance had the desired effect. William of Poitiers does not say much about this attack, just that 'the Normans shot arrows, hit and pierced the enemy'.[59] But the Tapestry at this point in the margin shows one archer after the other in a prolonged frieze aiming their weapons upwards: nineteen figures without a break, and then more a little further on.[60]

I have also argued elsewhere against the idea that the arrows were shot high up into the air to come down again on the English heads, largely because it would have been ineffective, the arrows would have lost their force. This does not mean that they would not adjust their shooting to cope with the higher position of the enemy.[61] Some of the English on the Tapestry catch the arrows in their shields, clearly shot with force since they become embedded. Harold was not the only one to suffer; a nameless Norman falls to the ground with an arrow in his head. For the first time the English line was seriously weakened, and some of the main front-line troops were killed, including Harold himself.

Some, generally more 'popular' works, still repeat the old chestnut that Harold was not killed by an arrow in the eye. This was an idea that stemmed from historians criticising the evidence. A number of late sources spoke of Harold being cut down with swords; the early works did not describe at all the manner of his death.[62] Our conclusions depend largely on how we interpret two sources in particular.

The first to consider is the *Carmen*. Those who accept its account have no arrow in the eye. But it is surely an incredible account, which none of the early sources confirm in any way. By it, the duke sees Harold fighting bravely. He summons to himself a little gang of three, like the magnificent seven: Eustace of Boulogne, whose actions are cowardly in other sources; Hugh the heir of Ponthieu, who is otherwise unknown and who did not succeed to Ponthieu; and 'Gilfardus', who is usually identified as Walter Giffard, he of the white hair and bald head according to Wace, another identification which has caused some problems.

The four, including the Conqueror, attack Harold: the first (none are named in this section of the poem) cleaves through his shield with a sword, drawing blood; the second smites off his head; the third pierces his belly with a lance; the fourth hacks off his leg and carries it away. There was then a 'rumour' that Harold was dead. Presumably after all that he was.

William of Malmesbury, possibly following the Tapestry, does have an unnamed knight maiming Harold *after* he was killed by an arrow; the knight in question is disgraced by the Conqueror for this deed, but this does not support the *Carmen* version in which William himself was one of the four attackers. This incident in the poem really does seem more incredible than any of its other incredible stories. Can one believe that William himself took part in the killing of Harold and no one else apart from the poet recorded the fact? Davis is surely right that this is a later legendary elaboration. It seems unlikely that the Conqueror took any part at all in Harold's killing. He could not even recognise him after the battle without help.[63]

The second and the most important source here is the Bayeux Tapestry.[64] The anti-arrow school argued that the figure dying with an arrow in the eye or head was not Harold. The following figure, under the words 'interfectus est' [was killed], is Harold, being hacked down by a rider with his sword. Again, this cannot be verified. But knowledge of the Tapestry's way of pointing out its facts would suggest that the lettering of the name 'Harold' above and around the first figure was meant to show that this was the king. A number of people have argued that *both* figures are Harold and it is a sort of cartoon strip representation of him being first hit by an arrow and secondly being finished off by a cavalryman.[65]

This view has been enhanced by the keen eye of a modern historian, David Bernstein. In a paper given to the Anglo-Norman Studies conference, he pointed out that if one looks carefully at the Tapestry, there are visible stitch marks by the head of the second figure; and the obvious interpretation is that they originally represented the shaft of an arrow in the eye of the second, falling figure too.[66]

This seems to settle the issue. In the view of the Tapestry at least, Harold Godwinson was hit by an arrow in the head, whether either or both of the figures were meant to be the king. The likely view is that both are Harold. Some later chroniclers give such an account: they may have followed the Tapestry, but even if their facts were not independent, at least they believed the Tapestry meant both figures to be Harold and that he was hit by an arrow.[67]

The archery had achieved the first major blow of the battle, and one that was fatal to English hopes as well as to their king. The loss of a commander in a medieval battle was very rarely followed by anything but defeat for the side which suffered the loss, and Hastings was no exception. If the English fought on it was from training and discipline, and because the best hope of survival was to slog out the final minutes of daylight and hope to retreat under cover of dark. They did not manage it.

Wace, for all our doubts, is a useful source for quotes, partly because his military knowledge was good even if his particular knowledge of Hastings was less so. He speaks of the lengthy battle, suggesting that the crisis came at about 3 p.m., after a long day when 'the battle was up and down, this way and that'.[68] William of Poitiers says that the remaining English were exhausted and at the end of their tether, which is not difficult to believe.

The Normans began to sense victory: 'the longer they fought the stronger they seemed to be; and their onslaught was even fiercer now than it had been at the beginning'. The duke fought in their midst, sparing none who crossed his path. In other words, after the infantry attack the cavalry made a final charge, and this time it worked. The shield-wall, which had withstood such a battering all day, finally broke and once that had happened there was no hope.

The English forces broke and fled. The Tapestry's final scene shows a miscellaneous band of Normans in pursuit, three wielding swords, one a spear and one carrying a bow ready to shoot.[69] A small and rather forlorn group of Englishmen are the last figures to survive on the Tapestry, some on horses, some on foot. One may have an arrow in his head, since the context does not seem to fit with him raising a spear. In the lower margin by this point the bodies have been stripped of their armour and lie naked, some without heads, one with a severed arm. The only hope of survival for those who remained was to reach the cover of the woods to the rear. Some ran on foot, some were able to ride. According to Poitiers this was on 'horses which they had seized' rather than their own, though there is no reason why others were not able to reclaim the mounts they had left behind earlier in the day. Poitiers says they went by roads and by places where there were none. Many, of course, were wounded and escape was difficult or impossible. 'Many died where they fell in the deep cover of the woods', others dropped exhausted along the way. There was a Norman pursuit. Some were cut down from behind, some were trampled under the horses' hoofs.

We shall again rely primarily on William of Poitiers for an account of the Malfosse incident. He does not give it a name or a clear location, though he describes the natural feature. In Poitiers, it clearly happens *after* the English had broken in flight.[70] He has no tale of a hillock in the middle of the battlefield. According to him, there was a last ditch defence made by a considerable force of English. They had taken up a good defensive position which the Normans approached during the pursuit.[71]

The reason this is called the Malfosse incident is that our old friend the Battle Abbey chronicler identified it as such. His modern editor queries what is meant, and suggests that it is possible that the name came later. Malfosse means 'evil ditch'. It could have been named for a variety of reasons: a description of its nature, a burial ditch. Everyone has assumed it was the site of this last resistance, and that is possible – but not certain.

Orderic Vitalis has two versions of the incident. The first is an interpolation in William of Jumièges. He also places the incident during the pursuit.[72] In this account, the event could have occurred anywhere as he speaks of a pursuit that continued into Sunday, and an incident that was on 'the following night' – though he probably means Saturday night. He wrote: 'for high grass concealed an ancient rampart' into which 'abyss of destruction' the Normans rode 'crushing each other to death'. He says 15,000 died here, a figure we need not take seriously. Orderic's second account, in *Ecclesiastical History*, is similar, though the feature becomes a 'broken rampart and labyrinth of ditches', and the victim Engenulf de Laigle is named. This revised account also makes it clear that he is speaking of Saturday night for the incident.[73]

The Battle Abbey chronicler gives more space to the Malfosse incident than to the rest of the battle, which is very odd and seems to require some explanation. It does not add to our confidence in him. He seems to have picked up some vivid tale, perhaps from local gossip, and tied it in with an account of the battle which is brief and largely uninformative. He says:

. . . a final disaster was revealed to all. Lamentable, just where the fighting was going on, and stretching for a considerable distance, an immense ditch yawned. It may have been a natural cleft in the earth or perhaps it had been hollowed out by storms. But in this waste ground it was overgrown with brambles and thistles, and could hardly be seen in time; and it swallowed great numbers, especially of Normans in pursuit of the English.

He says that they galloped unawares into the chasm and were killed: 'This deep pit has been named for the accident, and today it is called *Malfosse*.'[74] What we seem to have here is an original incident after the battle recorded by Poitiers, turned into something different in a rather confused manner by Orderic, and then a century after the event latched on to by the Battle Abbey chronicler for a local site, though he does not tell us where it is.

It seems ironic that the source which claims Battle Hill for the site of the battle is the one which also says the Malfosse was 'just where the battle was going on'. The Malfosse has been identified on the ground with reasonable certainty, and is just to the rear of Caldbec Hill, exactly where one might expect a last ditch resistance after the army had been forced to leave its first line of defence on the hill.[75] It is quite a way back from Battle Hill – though it could be a last ditch defence after flight from there.

The identification of the site depends primarily on a series of medieval records, including several thirteenth-century charters which refer clearly to the same name as 'Maufosse'. It is to be placed to the north of Caldbec Hill, behind Virgin's Lane and very close to the pool (which might be Senlac). Here, 600 yards north of Caldbec Hill, is to be found the natural feature known as Oakwood Gill, which is the natural feature most close to the chronicle descriptions: with a gully which Chevallier calls 'a deep ravine', with steep banks, brambles and undergrowth, a stream, just on the edge of Duniford Wood.[76]

The Conqueror was surprised to find this defended position, and wondered if these were reinforcements, which is possible. It may also have been a deliberate English plan to give some cover in the case of a retreat. At any rate, Poitiers says there were 'battalions' of men, making use of 'a deep gully and a series of ditches'. Eustace of Boulogne with fifty knights was intending to return, in Orderic it is in flight, preferring not to attack this tough position.[77] The Conqueror ordered him forward, but at that moment Eustace was hit between the shoulders, the blood spurted from nose and mouth. The Conqueror himself led an attack and the last resistance was crushed. William then returned to the battlefield. The day was his. One of the greatest battles in the history of England had come to its conclusion.

EIGHT

AFTERWARDS

William of Poitiers wrote: 'once he had completed his victory, the duke rode back to the battlefield to survey the dead. It was impossible to contemplate them without being moved to pity . . . the flower of English youth and nobility littered the ground far and wide.' As darkness drew on and night fell upon the battlefield, William could begin to appreciate what had happened on that day. The English king and two of his brothers had died. With Harold Hardrada killed at Stamford Bridge, the throne now awaited him.

William was a shrewd and generally cautious man and the invasion of England was the riskiest project he ever undertook. He knew that all was not over. The English had been beaten, but many had escaped. A lengthy pursuit was not wise, William needed his troops to stay close at hand, and he called them back. There were others of significance in the kingdom who had not been at Hastings, and whose attitude to him was not yet clear, including Edgar the Aetheling, who was the obvious figurehead for rebellion with the best claim to the throne by descent, and the northern earls, Edwin and Morcar. William of Poitiers says he proceeded with moderation.[1]

On first arriving, William had not rushed inland against a major town, and he was prepared to take his time again. His strategy soon emerged, with two main objectives: first, he wanted to secure his base on the coast; second, he wanted to take London. But before any of that, there was a certain amount of clearing up to be done. William camped for the night on the battlefield, the traditional manner of demonstrating victory. On the morrow, he returned to base at Hastings.

Scavengers and relatives came to search among the dead. No doubt some of the Normans joined in. The Tapestry shows men ripping off armour, which was clearly of tunic design rather than trousered, and good weapons would be searched for.[2] Relatives would seek the bodies of their loved ones for burial, though there must also have been a mass burial – possibly at the Malfosse. William arranged for the burial of his own dead, and left the English to see to theirs. Poitiers says their bodies were left to the vultures and the wolves, though William allowed the English to bury whom they wished.[3]

The main question for William in this was how to deal with the body of his rival. There is the story of identifying the body. It was said that Harold was so disfigured that he could not be recognised. Only by bringing his mistress, Edith, to the field, could the body be known. She identified him by certain hidden marks that only she (and perhaps his wife) could know. William of Poitiers gives some credence to this tale: 'Harold was recognised not by any insignia which he wore and certainly not from his features, but by certain distinguishing marks', but he says nothing of Edith Swanneck.[4]

We can assume from what we know that William had no wish to make much of Harold's burial or his burial-place, and that he feared some sort of cult in support. He refused Harold's family possession of the body, even when offered payment by the dead king's mother. This story may be accepted as it is in William of Poitiers. Orderic, who says she offered her son's body weight in gold for the corpse, bemoans that poor lady's position, with five of her seven sons now dead.[5]

It was said that William gave orders for Harold to be buried secretly by the shore. Poitiers tells us that William Malet was given the task to complete: 'and they said jokingly that his body should be placed there to guard the sea-shore and the sea, which in his fury he had formerly blockaded with arms'. We probably need not imagine him being buried on the beach, but at some point near to Hastings.[6]

Later, there grew up a tradition at Harold's own foundation of Waltham Abbey, that his body had been returned there for final interment, and possibly this occurred. It was a tradition recorded by a monk in 1177, based on hearsay from the 1120s.

Afterwards

But we may be more sceptical of the stories of Harold's survival after Hastings, like a second Arthur to fan the hopes of Old English recovery. One Waltham story was that Harold had been thrown to the ground among the dead, but was stunned and not killed. He was found, still breathing, by certain women, who bound his wounds and carried him off to a nearby cottage. He was taken to Winchester and hidden in a cellar for two years before recovering and going to Germany.[7]

THE CAMPAIGN AFTER HASTINGS

Again, we may best follow William of Poitiers for the Conqueror's movements in 1066 in the immediate aftermath of the battle. There is little reason to dispute them, and less reason to augment them than some historians have believed. Let us follow the verified movements first and then consider the unwarranted augmentations.

William placed Humphrey de Tilleul over the garrison which remained at Hastings, and set out eastwards to Romney, where a Norman advance guard had been attacked by the locals. Orderic says the Normans had landed there in error and were slaughtered. William showed the ruthless, merciless spirit with which his conquest would continue. The residents were punished harshly for their attack.

Then he marched on to Dover, often seen as the gateway to England. William had appreciated its significance before the invasion, as shown by his demands from Harold in Normandy. He showed his recognition of its importance now, by making it secure. There seems to have been some fortification on the site. Poitiers says that a crowd had collected but melted away at the Conqueror's approach. Orderic explains that local people had taken refuge there.

A fire was started by Normans seeking booty, but this may have been the town rather than the castle (if there was one), since the Conqueror agreed to pay for repairs and rebuilding of houses. Orderic's account sounds as if the Norman troops ignored offers to surrender before starting the fires.[8] Poitiers describes the fortress on its rock by the sea, which was now

157

enlarged and improved since, according to him, its defences were inadequate, and Dover Castle emerged as the great guardian of the south-east shore.

At this point, Poitiers says that the Normans suffered from dysentery, from eating freshly slaughtered meat and drinking the water, and that some died. Orderic says some suffered from the effects for the rest of their lives.[9] A number of the sick had to be left behind in the garrison at Dover as William progressed to Canterbury. This was the religious centre of England, and vital for him to hold. It would settle his grip on Kent and the south-east. The citizens of Canterbury were more ready to compromise and came out to meet him, swearing fidelity and giving hostages.

William made camp at what Poitiers calls the Broken Tower, whose identity is unknown.[10] Here the duke himself took ill, and his close attendants feared for his life. What would have happened had he died in 1066? The Norman Conquest, despite Hastings, was a frail thing still and would surely not have survived such a blow. But he was tough and refused even to give way to his illness.

Stigand, the controversially appointed Archbishop of Canterbury, no doubt fearing for his future under William, was involved in some attempt to form a party to oppose the victor. Others who toyed with opposition were the northern earls, Edwin and Morcar. Poitiers says that they held a meeting near London and proclaimed Edgar the Aetheling as their king.

London also at first took a hostile stance to the Conqueror. He sent a troop of 500 knights, according to Poitiers, and a force emerged from London to oppose them. The Normans beat them off, and the English retreated back inside the city walls. Orderic says there was mourning in the city for the many killed, as if the London force had been a large one.[11] The invaders set fire to the city on the southern side, and then withdrew. William himself moved on to the Thames, but not yet to London. He crossed by ford and bridge, coming to the borough of Wallingford. Archbishop Stigand thought better now of his opposition, probably hoping to make terms. He came to William at Wallingford and submitted, swearing fidelity and doing homage. He abandoned the cause of the Aetheling. Finally, William turned and headed for London.

Afterwards

Like Stigand, the citizens had been given time to consider their actions, and like the archbishop they moved from opposition to submission, coming out to meet William and handing over hostages. The writer of the D version of the *Anglo-Saxon Chronicle* thought 'it was a great piece of folly that they had not done it earlier'.[12] They met him at Berkhamsted, together with Archbishop Eadred of York and other bishops, with Edgar the Aetheling and the earls Edwin and Morcar.

Poitiers says that they asked William to take the crown and be their king. Edgar the Aetheling also submitted. According to Orderic: 'since he was a boy who was noble and honourable and a kinsman of the great King Edward, for he was his nephew's son, the duke received him with affection, and treated him as long as he lived like one of his own sons'.[13] Orderic does not say which son. Edgar did not remain unswervingly loyal to the Conqueror, but then neither did all of William's sons.

This then is the account of William's movements up to his coronation at Christmas 1066 in Westminster Abbey. It is time to deal with what was referred to above as an unwarranted account of William's movements in 1066 after the battle. Many historians have been involved in this process, so it seems unfair to light upon one in particular. However, to do so will make the point more firmly, so we shall use the account of this same period, from October to December 1066, as retailed by Beeler in *Warfare in England, 1066–1189*. It is the full-blown version of an idea first developed at the end of the nineteenth century.[14]

According to Beeler, William went to Romney and then 'via Burmarsh to Folkestone', and to Dover. He went on through Patrixbourne and Bekesbourne towards Canterbury. Meanwhile, raiding parties went via Littlebourne, Preston, Sturry and Chislet. The main army then concentrated at Lenham where forces reassembled from their trips to Ospringe, Eastling, Chilham, Brabourne, Stelling, Crundall, and Pluckley-cum-Pevington. From Lenham, the army moved on via Maidstone, Seal, Westerham, Limpsfield, Oxted, Tandridge and Godstone, where they halted a while.

The advance party which had gone on to London had been despatched from Seal, and went via Cudham, Chelsfield, Orpington, Eltham and Lewisham to Southwark. After burning the suburbs, they retired via Battersea, Tooting and Merton to Godstone. William then marched the whole army south of London via Ewell, Ashstead, Leatherhead, Guildford, Compton, Wanborough, Basing, Micheldever, Sutton Scotney and Hurstbourne.

Meanwhile, reinforcements came to William from Chichester or Portsmouth (Beeler is not certain which), via Fareham, Wickham, Bishop's Waltham, Droxford, Exton, Wanford, West and East Meon and Alresford. There they were met by 'a detachment from the main army' that came via Farnham, Hartley Maudit and Farringdon. The army in two columns then moved northwards to the Thames.

Then the left wing of the army moved west from Alresford to Lambourne; the right from Hurstbourne to Highclere, where it divided into two. One part went to Wantage and Wallingford, the other from Highclere to East Isley and Wallingford. Meanwhile, the left wing went through Farringdon, Sutton Courtney to Whittenham and Wallingford. Then from Wallingford the main army went along the Icknield Way to Risborough and Wendover.

Meanwhile, 'a flanking column' moved along to the north to Buckingham. From Risborough the army continued in three columns: the left to Aylesbury and Luton; the centre along the Icknield Way; the right through the valleys of Bulbourne and Gade. The left went via Aylesbury to rejoin the centre at Luton; the centre went on to Hertford; the right to Langford. A 'detachment' took Hitchin and then went on to a rendezvous at Hertford. The left went from Luton to Bedford and Hertford, and another 'detachment' to Cambridge, going south via Potton. Eventually, all joined forces at Hertford. The army was at last ready to deal with London.

You might consider the earlier account of the expedition, based chiefly on William of Poitiers, rather bare bones in comparison to this enviably detailed description of the route. One little question raises its ugly head. How did Beeler and those he was following gain their information? The answer is from Domesday Book. Now there, you would think, is a very solid source of information, more reliable than those biased chroniclers. Domesday is, of course, a magnificent source, but not, one would suggest, for the route of the army in 1066.

Afterwards

The whole thing stems from an interesting idea proposed by F.H. Baring in his article on 'The Conqueror's Footprints in Domesday' in 1898, and modified in his *Domesday Tables* in 1909.[15] The basic idea was that the amount of waste recorded in Domesday Book might relate to the degree of damage done by the invading army in 1066. Baring's suggested route was somewhat less detailed than the one above.

Some historians were immediately enraptured: A.M. Davies thought that Baring was the 'good fairy' who had waved his magic wand and put the whole march into order. It has since been often elaborated upon, for example, by Fowler, Butler and Beeler, but in many other works too. They also considered that the greater the waste, the greater the force, so that one could identify routes for the whole army, parts of the army and small groups. The route deduced in this way has got further and further away from any sort of reality.

The problem is that the question-marks against such a deduction are very considerable, enough to undermine any trust in it. Firstly, we do not know exactly what Domesday waste represents. Sometimes it appears not to mean actual waste at all, but some privileged assessment for the landholder concerned. Even if we have actual waste, Domesday rarely gives evidence of its cause, even less does it suggest when the waste occurred. Only in one instance does Domesday say that waste was caused by an army.[16] Then again, Domesday was drawn up twenty years after 1066. The waste it records might have resulted from events before 1066, when there had been a good deal of disturbance, say, the ravaging of 986, 1006 and 1041, or from any of the post-1066 rebellions and disorders. It is not at all certain anyway that a passing army would leave enduring damage of the kind envisaged; it would not compare with damage from a war fought over a region or even from lengthy sieges.

There is simply no way of distinguishing waste caused by the army in 1066 and waste caused by any other means at all – which might include all sorts of man-made or heaven-sent disasters. Therefore, to draw up a map marking all the manors where waste was heaviest is a very unreliable means of tracing the route of the army. When it was done, it did not seem to trace a route at all. However, those sold on the idea did not abandon it, far from it. They began to invent all sorts of divisions of the army to cover several routes and make use of all the scattered manors noted for waste, and even special detachments to go to isolated examples of waste which would not fit even with their multiplied routes.

The thing has become an enormous farce. So far as I know, although some have questioned aspects of it, the thesis has not been entirely rejected. It therefore seems worthwhile to have spent some space on it. In conclusion, we may say that the waste scheme may give a little assistance in confirming the chroniclers' evidence for William's route, but it is pointless to expect any detailed information from it. You will forgive me, I hope, if for the rest of the Conqueror's marches in 1066 and afterwards, I concentrate on what the chronicle evidence tells us.

William of Poitiers describes the coronation in London. According to him, William had refused to be consecrated by Stigand, and the Archbishop of York addressed the English people and asked them if they consented to William receiving the crown, to which they gave their assent 'joyfully, without hesitation'. Then the Bishop of Coutances addressed the Normans, and they expressed the same opinion. According to the *Anglo-Saxon Chronicle*, William had to promise 'that he would rule all this people as well as the best of kings before him, if they would be loyal to him', before Eadred would crown him. Poitiers continues: 'he [the Archbishop of York] put on the royal diadem and placed him on the royal throne in the presence and with the assent of numerous bishops and abbots in the basilica of St Peter'.[17] During the ceremony it was said that the Conqueror trembled, but from anxiety and humility rather than from fear.[18]

Poitiers' version of the disturbances which accompanied the coronation was that the mounted Norman guards, patrolling outside the abbey, heard the shouting in English and feared the worst. They then set fire to the suburbs. If true, it does not say much for the discipline of those guards. Others have thought that the chronicler was covering up some genuine opposition and rioting against William, with which the guards had to deal. As Orderic points out, the guards had been placed there for fear of such disturbance. He confirms that the Norman guards themselves started a fire, and this caused some inside the church to rush out in panic.[19]

The disturbances rather marred the occasion, but the coronation was accomplished with sufficient legality to satisfy the Church. Poitiers claimed that it was by hereditary right, but we know it was a claim which could not stand much investigation. Poitiers asserted that it was with the assent of the English people, but the noises outside the church were enough to remind William of what remained to be achieved before he could rule England in fact as well as in name. It was by force that William had taken the throne, and by force he would have to retain it. The Norman Conquest was not yet over, but a major success had been achieved and William, duke of Normandy, had become king of England.

THE COMPLETION OF THE CONQUEST

In the following years William had little time for rest. In effect, by Christmas 1066 he held the south-east of England. He must now turn his mind to the other regions. But he had also to keep a watchful eye on affairs in his duchy. Normandy could not be abandoned for long. So began that tedious business for the king-dukes of moving backwards and forwards between kingdom and duchy. Medieval government was always achieved on the move. William's conquest meant that his movements would from then on have to be much greater and involve frequent crossings of the Channel.

William made immediate efforts to reward those who had helped him. He gave vacated lands to his followers, he sent back gifts to the churches in Normandy, he sent gold and silver to Rome as well as Harold's banner of the Fighting Man. His abbey at Caen received various gifts of great value. Poitiers says that they celebrated his memory in a thousand French churches. Towns, castles, villages, monasteries congratulated him on his victory.

He took stock of the situation, and while in London began to make arrangements for the city and for his new kingdom: 'he took wise, just and merciful decisions'.[20] Poitiers says he forbade his men to drink in taverns in order to prevent the kind of disorders that would follow. He ordered them to keep within the law and to refrain from killing and rape, and set up severe punishments for those who disobeyed.

He left London and stayed a few days at Barking, while fortifications were erected within the city 'against the numerous and hostile inhabitants'.[21] After the disturbances during the coronation he wanted to be sure of security in London. The northern earls, Edwin and Morcar, made their peace with William, seeking his pardon. Other nobles did the same. He confirmed in their lands those who submitted, and treated them with honour.

The castle of Dover was put in the hands of his half-brother, Odo of Bayeux, who was made earl of Kent. With its proximity to the continent the Conqueror saw this as a vital region. William himself returned to Pevensey and prepared to cross to Normandy. He gave rewards to those men who had fought for him and were now departing with him for the continent. According to Orderic, they included men whose wives were misbehaving, 'consumed by fierce lust' and threatening to take other men if their husbands did not return. The chronicler laments: 'what could honourable men do if their lascivious wives polluted their beds with adultery?'.[22]

The Conqueror had other reasons. Leaving England in the hands of trusted lieutenants, he had to risk a return to the duchy while much of his new realm lay in uncertain subjection. The completion of the Conquest must be delayed while he made sure of the duchy. He took with him various hostages and important persons in order to guarantee peace in England, including Stigand, Edgar the Aetheling, the northern earls Edwin and Morcar, Earl Waltheof (son of the old earl of Northumbria, Siward), and many others to 'ensure that they would cause no disturbances during his absence'.[23] William crossed the Channel to Normandy in March 1067.

Poitiers says that the locals in the towns he passed through came out to greet him, even the humblest. As he approached Rouen the citizens, old, young, women, all came out to meet him, to see the hero, to acclaim and applaud. He celebrated his return at Easter 1067 in the church of Ste-Trinité at Fécamp, to which came a crowd of clergy, people and knights. Ralph de

Valois, father-in-law of the French king, came to offer congratulations, and William made show of various trophies brought back with him. Among the churches to receive gifts were those at Dives and Jumièges.

According to Baudri de Bourgueil, William's wife Matilda had a series of tapestries dealing with four subjects, and which she herself had made, displayed round her chamber. One of the set dealt with the conquest of England. Whether this is Baudri's imagination or not, who can tell, but it reflects an interest in the event and a pride in the achievement. The Bayeux Tapestry itself demonstrates the same attitude, as do the poems and chronicles which record it.[24]

William returned to England on 6 December 1067. Now he must proceed with the conquest. England had been left in the care of Odo of Bayeux, who held Dover and Kent, and of William fitz Osbern, who had been given command of Winchester and made deputy to the king in the south.[25] They were two of the Conqueror's closest associates. Poitiers says that the English did not dare to rebel openly, but that they conspired in secret, and sent frequent requests for aid to Denmark and elsewhere.[26]

William's first serious problem with the new kingdom came not from the English but from his ally, Eustace of Boulogne. The uncertainty of his loyalty is shown by the fact that William, before the invasion, kept Eustace's son at court 'as a guarantee of his faith'. Eustace conspired with men in Kent, who, says Poitiers, were easily moved by their hatred of the Normans, to attack the castle at Dover.[27]

Dover was the shared responsibility of Odo of Bayeux and Hugh de Montfort. At the time, they were in action to the north of the Thames. Eustace, informed by the locals who offered aid, came at night by sea to try and take Dover by surprise. A force of Kentishmen was in arms prepared to assist him, but the garrison was ready and did not succumb. Eustace was beaten off after a fight of several hours, 'shamefully defeated', and his nephew taken prisoner. Eustace retreated to his fleet on horseback and at once weighed anchor and escaped. The garrison made a sortie during this retreat, and savaged Eustace's rearguard, some of whom fell over the cliffs to their death, some committed suicide, some drowned. Later, Eustace made his peace with William.[28]

There was already trouble at the other extremity of the kingdom. William had made an appointment which might be open to criticism in selecting Copsi to be earl of Northumbria. Copsi had been Tostig's main lieutenant in the north, so perhaps this was a nod to the semi-alliance that Tostig had made with the duke, to be seen as a deliberate reminder that Tostig had been badly treated by his own brother. It was also a reward for embracing the Conqueror's cause, and Poitiers praises his personal ability.[29] Perhaps also it was an intended snub to Edwin and Morcar, whose allegiance was uncertain and whose family, from the Conqueror's viewpoint, might look too powerful.

But Copsi was not a good solution to the problems of Northumbria, where all southern appointments were viewed with scorn. Copsi barely had time to savour his appointment before he had been ambushed and murdered in March 1067. His assassin was the dispossessed descendant of the former earls of Bernicia, Oswulf. This is one of the last events recorded in William of Poitiers. The end of his chronicle has not been preserved, but it is thought that Orderic Vitalis continued to use it, giving his work an added value for these vital years of the completion of the Conquest.[30]

There were serious rebellions against William in England, but they lacked any unified control or even purpose. Although not always confined to regional personnel, they tended to be regional in their extent. Apart from problems on the border, William faced serious opposition in the north, at Exeter and in East Anglia. We cannot go into detail over his campaigns in these and other areas. But we may praise the consistency of his effort and success, even when we are horrified at the manner of its accomplishment.

The last few years of the 1060s was the period during which the conquest of the rest of England was achieved. Most of the great lords submitted, but it was soon obvious that many harboured resentments or rebellious inclinations. William of Jumièges wrote that William 'found many Englishmen whose fickle minds had turned away from loyalty'.[31] Ambushes of Norman soldiers were set up in various places. In 1067 there were rebellions in Hereford and Kent. The years 1068 to 1070 have recently been labelled the time of 'the English revolt', which broke out in various places but especially in the north.[32]

In 1068 Exeter, where Harold's mother resided, opposed the new king. The city sent messages to try and stir up support. The citizens manned the gates and the walls. William had already taken hostages, and one of these was blinded before the watching citizens. He surrounded the city and attempted to storm it, and then commenced mining operations.[33] The siege lasted eighteen days and ended in a surrender on terms. At once, William set about building a castle within the walls.

In 1068 William moved north in force and Mercia submitted to his presence. He captured York and fortified it. Norman control of the area only really began with this move, and was still a tender plant. York and the north was the most severe test of William's authority. The city 'was seething with discontent', and was not prepared to be swayed by its archbishop's attempts to persuade it to accept the changes.[34] The peace made with William was uneasy.

The year 1069 saw a concerted effort of those willing to oppose him in the north, including Earl Waltheof, Edgar the Aetheling and forces from Denmark and Scotland. It was the most important combination of enemies to oppose William as king. Sweyn Estrithsson sent a large fleet of 240 ships to England, and later came himself. The Danish fleet made several attempts at landing, but England's improved defences operated well and the Danes were forced to move on each time. They finally linked up with the English rebels when many rode and marched to meet them, 'rejoicing exceedingly'.[35]

Edgar the Aetheling spent much of the period of William's early reign in Scotland, and his sister Margaret married Malcolm III Canmore, the king of Scots (1058–93). Part of the Conqueror's relative tolerance of Edgar, despite the considerable threat from his birth and position, no doubt stemmed from William's desire to make peace with the Scots. Thus Edgar was to survive the reign and even go on the First Crusade.

The northern rebels and invaders concentrated at York. They included Earl Waltheof, Edgar the Aetheling, Earl Gospatric (a relative of Edgar's), the sons of Karli of the house of Bamburgh, Sweyn Estrithsson and Malcolm, king of Scots. Virtually all the powers of the north, past and present, English, Scottish and Danish, had combined against the Norman interlopers. It became 'a general rising of the north'.[36]

Trouble began on 28 January 1069 with an attack on a Norman expeditionary force which had advanced to Durham. The Durham chronicler says the Normans provoked the people by their aggression, which included killing men of the Church. The Northumbrians then caught the Normans by surprise early in the morning, and among those killed was Robert de Commines, the newly appointed earl of Northumbria. Then the gathering rebels focused their attention on York. A Norman force at York under Robert fitz Richard, the castellan of Clifford's Tower, chose to make a rash sortie against the rebels in 1069, and was massacred: 'many hundreds of Frenchmen' were killed.[37]

William Malet, who had survived by staying within the castle at York apparently with his wife and two children – a perilous place for them to be – sent to William for aid.[38] The king returned from Normandy and marched north again without hesitation. He was delayed at Pontefract but eventually Lisois de Moutiers found a ford. The rebels decided to get away and William recovered York; he 'spared no man', and built a second castle (the Old Baile), which was entrusted to William fitz Osbern.[39] Even after this there was an attack on both Norman castles, but fitz Osbern held them off. The Danish fleet, paid to withdraw by William after the defeat of the rebels, finally returned home in a sad state according to Orderic Vitalis.[40]

William punished the region with the most harsh of all his harsh measures in England, the harrying of the north. Harrying as a punishment was not new in England, but William's was so severe as to be long recalled. Symeon of Durham wrote that, as a result: 'there was no village inhabited between York and Durham'.[41] The harrying was condemned even by normally favourable chroniclers. Orderic wrote:

> nowhere else had William shown such cruelty. Shamefully he succumbed to this vice, for he made no effort to restrain his fury and punished the innocent with the guilty . . . My narrative has frequently had occasion to praise William, but for this act which condemned the innocent and guilty

alike to die by slow starvation I cannot commend him . . . I would rather lament the griefs and sufferings of the wretched people than make a vain attempt to flatter the perpetrator of such infamy.[42]

The Conqueror sought out any rebel, and any who got in the way. His troops spread over a great distance, combing woodland and remote areas, leaving no hiding place unsearched. He wanted the whole region north of the Humber to be deprived of food. Houses and crops were destroyed, any living creature that crossed the path of William's troops was slaughtered till a great band of ashes and waste spread over Yorkshire.

The Conqueror also dealt with the Scottish involvement. In 1072 William led an expedition into the northern realm. King Malcolm Canmore was forced to submit and do homage. The deal probably included the submission also of Edgar the Aetheling, who had frequently taken refuge north of the border and was the Scottish king's brother-in-law. He was forced to leave Scotland for Flanders, but within a couple of years Edgar had submitted, and was even able to appear at William's court.

In the meantime, there had also been problems in the west. Just as Scottish encouragement aided the northern rebels, so were the Welsh involved along the western borders. A Welsh rebellion was beaten down in 1069 and in the following year William took over Chester in person and sent an expedition into North Wales. There had been further disturbances in the south-west. Twice the surviving sons of Harold Godwinson brought a force from Ireland.

Three sons of Harold are named altogether: Godwin, Edmund and Magnus. They came first in 1068, and then again in the summer of 1069. On the first occasion they raided into the Avon and attacked Bristol, which fought them off, and then raided in Somerset. They brought sixty-four ships on the second occasion, landing in the mouth of the Taw.[43] They came to Exeter and caused devastation around the city. Count Brian for the Conqueror led out a force against them and there were two clashes which together destroyed the raiders, who went away in but two small ships. Harold's sons returned to Ireland. William of Jumièges thought that 1,700 had been killed in their venture.[44]

The failure of her grandsons was sufficient to cause Harold's mother, Gytha, to leave Exeter and go into exile abroad, where she died.[45]

There were widespread outbreaks of opposition, but all were crushed: at Chester, Shrewsbury, Stafford, Montacute, Exeter and elsewhere. Sometimes William dealt with it in person, sometimes men acted for him. The reliability of these troops under such leaders as Count Brian, William fitz Osbern and Robert of Mortain goes far to explain the success of the prolonged period of fighting which brought about the completion of the Conquest.

The final serious thrust of opposition broke out in East Anglia. This will always be associated in our minds with the half legendary personage of Hereward the Wake, identified as a thegn (perhaps a king's thegn) from Lincolnshire who had held three manors, and who was said to have been outlawed for an earlier attack on a Norman lord. One suggestion is that he had been involved in the northern revolt of 1069.[46]

Detail can be added to the bones of this story of Hereward only from the twelfth-century poem about his exploits, the *Gesta Herewardi* (Deeds of Hereward), and in this there is difficulty divorcing reliable material from legend. The fact that it was written does suggest a surviving anti-Norman attitude in England. We can say little about Hereward for sure. The rebellion of which he was part was a last throw by the combined surviving English nobles prepared to take up arms against the Normans. It finally broke the northern earls. The Conqueror had offered Edwin marriage to his own daughter. When this had been advised against by some of his courtiers, he had changed his mind, which had brought Edwin to the point of rebellion, with English and Welsh support.

Now Morcar joined the rebellion in Ely in 1071. The rebels had taken to this isolated and difficult area. Ely was then truly an island, surrounded by waters and treacherous marshland. But William approached in force, probably entered the island at Aldreth, and caused the rebels to flee. Morcar submitted, and Hereward escaped.[47] The real Hereward disappeared into obscurity - we know nothing more of him at all – but the legendary Hereward grew in stature as the years passed. Morcar

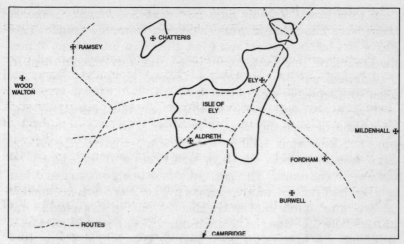

Ely in the eleventh century, when it was an island surrounded by water and marshes. (Map: Mike Komarnyckyj)

was thrown into prison under the guard of Robert de Beaumont, and stayed there for the rest of his life. Orderic says that in trying to raise help to get his brother released, Earl Edwin was killed after being betrayed by his own servants.[48]

As for Waltheof, son of Siward, he had been given Northamptonshire by the Conqueror, and also William's niece Judith in marriage in 1070. Orderic says he was handsome and of fine physique. He had no apparent reason to oppose William, having suffered more disappointment before the Conquest than after. Yet he conspired against William in 1075 with two of the newly appointed earls, Roger Montgomery of Hereford and Ralph the Breton of Norwich. Orderic says they spread the message that 'the man who now calls himself king is unworthy, since he is a bastard . . . He unjustly invaded the fair kingdom of England and unjustly slew its true heirs . . . all men hate him and his death would cause great rejoicing.'

The chronicler records that these two approached Waltheof, who was reluctant to join them and refused to take part in rebellion. The earls sought aid from Denmark, rebelled in 1075 and were beaten in battle. Later, Ralph fled to Denmark and then to Brittany. But his men in Norwich suffered: 'Some of them were blinded/And some banished from the land.'[49] Earl Roger was taken prisoner and tried, then cast into prison. When the Conqueror sent him gifts in prison the earl ordered them to be burned, causing William to swear he would never be released. Earl Roger died in fetters.[50]

If we may trust Orderic, Waltheof was not guilty. Lanfranc later also expressed the view of Waltheof's innocence. But it did not save him from William's vengeance against the rebels. According to Orderic, Waltheof was accused of conspiracy by his own wife, Judith. The earl admitted being approached but said he had refused to give support. The *Anglo-Saxon Chronicle* on the other hand implies Waltheof's guilt in conspiring, and rather oddly says that 'he accused himself' and sought pardon.[51] Waltheof was imprisoned for a year at Winchester. There were some at court ready to advise that he should be executed. The probable guilt of Waltheof was in failing to reveal the conspiracy of which he was aware.[52]

For fear of repercussions in Winchester, Earl Waltheof was taken from his prison early in the morning of 31 May 1076. The executioners allowed him to say the Lord's Prayer, but when he broke into tears before its completion, they would wait no longer and hacked off his head with a sword. According to Orderic, the severed head continued 'but deliver us from evil. Amen.'[53] The body was later exhumed and taken to Crowland for burial.

More trouble for William later in his reign came from his own half-brother, Odo of Bayeux, in whom 'vices were mingled with virtues' and who was also brought down for his opposition to the king.[54] It was said that Odo sought the papacy for himself, expecting help from the Normans in Sicily and planning to lead a band of knights from England. William scotched the scheme and arrested Odo probably in 1083. One assumes that William's complaint was that Odo was deserting his duties, but the whole tale has a fishy ring about it, and one suspects some other plotting of Odo's had come to the Conqueror's attention. Odo was imprisoned till the end of the reign. He would cause a similar stir after his release against the new king.

William's reign was hardly a happy one. At no time was he

free from cares. His quarrels with his own son, Robert Curthose, were perhaps as hurtful as any of the rebellions listed above. But William had won a throne, and his family retained it. The rebellions were all crushed, the opposition virtually annihilated. The Norman Conquest of England was one of the most complete and efficient conquests in history.

THE CONSEQUENCES OF THE CONQUEST

There were immediate effects of the Conquest in England: a new king, a new nobility and ruling class, a rash of castle building, changes in the Church. William began with words of tolerance, and permitted those English who submitted before his coronation to retain their positions and at least some of their lands. But within a decade he had obliterated the higher echelons of the Old English nobility. By the time of the Conqueror's death, the greater nobility in England was of continental extraction, though English blood often survived through marriage.

The success of the Conquest also fuelled an attitude of the Normans to their own warlike qualities, almost their invincibility. Such views had been growing already, a somewhat distorted idea of a Norman past leading to the present triumph, an idea of themselves as a distinct people rather glossing over the true history of their development, contributing to what has been seen by Ralph Davis as a Norman 'myth'.[55]

How far social structure altered after the Conquest is a matter of much controversy, and will always be so. We can but sketch a part of the discussion here. There has been debate over the nature of the settlement which followed the Conquest. Norman and French nobles took over much of the land. Others came in the wake of the Conquest seeking profits, some of whom settled in towns. Differentiating between Normans and English in the documents is a very difficult business, so analysis of the settlement is bound to be imprecise. The general conclusion must be that Normans and other French did come, nobles and their households, soldiers, townsmen, clergy and others, but that the numbers were not enormous. If William intended integration with the native population, a 'multi-racial settlement' as one historian has expressed it, then he was to a degree disappointed. Integration followed eventually, but during William's reign much tension remained between conquered and conquerors.[56]

The matter of social effects of the Conquest has usually been framed in terms relating to feudalism. We have already hinted that there were similarities in the society of the two regions. Recent historical research tends to emphasise the similarities rather than the differences. Feudalism, as we have said, is a construct of historians rather than a fact of medieval life, and they have made of it rather what they choose: one one thing, one another.

If we ask rather how did society in England change because of the Conquest, we may get a more satisfactory answer than by seeking to know if the Normans introduced feudalism to England. Certainly they did not transplant whole some living organism of society into a land whose old society died out. What occurred was much more of a merging, a new development in itself, fed from both sources.

Knight-service and castles, symptoms of what is generally seen as feudalism, were relatively recent developments in Normandy itself, and much less systematic than once thought. In England already there was a nobility which provided the élite of the military forces and which held land. In Normandy and England there was some land to which military service was attached, and other land to which it was not.

The circumstances of the Conquest, rather than any seeking after social change, provided the main impact. Invasion, conquest, rebellion: it was a time of crisis and insecurity. The Normans inevitably built fortifications quickly and in the style just becoming fashionable at home. That is, they built castles, and in the circumstances mostly cheap and quick ones made of earth and timber. One thing which did change was the function of the fighting men which military service produced. No longer would the English have entirely infantry forces, from now on the élite troops would be cavalry – though like the Normans they would balance the cavalry with good infantry.

The intention was not social change, but sometimes that was

the effect. The new lords of the land resided in their new fortifications. In such circumstances military force was required, and often quickly or even permanently for garrisons. The English system was not abandoned, but new elements entered into it. Here and there, quotas of military service were demanded, service in return for the land held, service in garrisons as well as in the field.

It was no more a system in England than it had been or was in Normandy, but it became more systematic in the course of time: arrangements for military service were regulated for peacetime needs as well as for the crisis years after 1066. So that England did become a society where the lords were also the military leadership, and where land-holding entailed providing forces for the king more or less commensurate with the land held – though never in a precise calculation. English society and its military arrangements had been heading in a similar direction, but the changes were more sudden than would otherwise have been the case.

It has not usually been easy to make comment on the fate of the ordinary English subject population. However, recent work has assisted in this matter, and we can see that changes were not always as drastic in all levels of society as might be thought, and that much of the Old English society survived. It has been suggested that the Normans 'introduced no new systems of agricultural exploitation or estate management'.[57]

The continuity in the lower ranks of society is much as one might have suspected, but can now be given some satisfactory basis in evidence. It supports the knowledge of continuity in some areas, not least in the retention of English as a language, and at least some aspects of Old English culture. This is not to say that some depression in social terms did not result from the changes. Domesday Book makes clear that many English peasants had to surrender something of their freedom as an accommodation with their new lords. Domesday does not have the whole story and rather minimises English survival, leaving out 'a whole stratum of free men'.[58] Many middling rank families are shown to have survived and even to have done well in the new conditions. The lower levels of royal service were also filled by Englishmen.[59]

But it is surely also true that, for many, the Conquest was a disaster. A recent article has stressed the 'catastrophic impact' upon the minds of the English that must have resulted.[60] A very high proportion of the nobility had been killed in the fighting of 1066, perhaps a half, with all the grief which that left behind for families and friends. Some of the women were pushed into unwelcome marriages, some took refuge in nunneries to escape such matches.

The destruction of property and houses for war was considerable. In many towns, such as Cambridge or Exeter, the Normans destroyed entire quarters in order to build new castles. The strength of the new monarchy was demonstrated by the level of taxation which could be enforced. The enforcers were often highly unpopular. We do not need to wait for Robin Hood to find hated sheriffs. It was written of one, Picot, that he was 'a hungry lion, a ravening wolf, a cunning fox, a dirty pig, an impudent dog'.[61]

The D chronicler wrote that the Normans 'built castles far and wide throughout this country, and distressed the wretched folk, and always after that it grew much worse'.[62] The harrying of the north brought misery to hundreds who could no longer survive in the devastated region. The Durham chronicler wrote: 'so great a famine prevailed that men, compelled by hunger, devoured human flesh, that of horses, dogs and cats, and whatever custom abhors . . . It was horrific to behold human corpses decaying in the houses, the streets and the roads.'[63]

The chroniclers do not often pass comment on the distress they describe, though giving enough evidence of suffering. However, Orderic Vitalis, who had lived his early boyhood in England and was half-English, thought that the English aided Eustace of Boulogne in rebellion because they were 'goaded by Norman oppression'. He says that 'England was exhausted with tribulation after tribulation . . . fire, rapine, and daily slaughter brought destruction and disaster on the wretched people and utterly laid waste the land'. Of the harrying of the north, he wrote: 'in consequence so serious a scarcity was felt in England, and so terrible a famine fell upon the humble and defenceless population, that more than 100,000 Christian folk . . . perished of hunger'.[64]

The change in the Church, if not so drastic as the changes in the nobility in terms of method, was as complete in terms of effect for the greater prelates. In the words of Barlow, 'the English Church had come under new management'. English bishops were allowed to continue, but on their deaths were replaced by a continental group. By 1073 the bishops included eight Normans, four Lotharingians, one Italian and only two Englishmen; by 1087 there were eleven Normans and one Englishman. The change in the abbeys was not quite so drastic, but a similar process was observed in most of the greater houses, continental abbots replacing English predecessors.

Stigand was permitted to hang on until 1070, partly because of his submission. But in 1070 he was removed and replaced by Lanfranc as Archbishop of Canterbury. Lanfranc was not Norman, but he had received preferment in the Norman Church before the Conquest. He was a leading figure in the Church, a thinker, writer, teacher and reformer and a great Archbishop of Canterbury. But he was a whole-hearted supporter of the Conqueror's regime.

Lanfranc also introduced Church reforms, with which he was already associated on the continent, into England. Such changes would no doubt have come into England without the Conquest in time, and we need not disparage the state of the Old English church. But as events turned, a number of significant reforms were introduced through the new episcopate and under the aegis of the new king.

It was also an age of great church building, and somewhat accidental that hundreds of the new stone churches either replaced older English buildings, or survived better than they did. There was also a centralising policy for episcopal sees. Where existing centres were in small and remote places they were often moved to a more urban and central position: Elmham to Thetford, Selsey to Chichester, Lichfield to Chester. This was a trend which had begun before the Conquest.

Leading churchmen played a major role in the Conqueror's administration, and it is not surprising that they should keep their continental ways. This must be one reason that the documentation of government, in particular the charters, reverted to Latin from Old English. Again, one need not attack the state of English government, it is simply that the Conquest brought certain changes with it. Both England and Normandy had reasonable systems before 1066, and both contributed something to the Anglo-Norman state which emerged. But one cannot deny that the Conquest brought change which would not otherwise have occurred in the form it did.

Thus shires and hundreds and many other English institutions survived, but would there, for example, ever have been a Domesday Book had there not been a Norman Conquest? The answer is surely no. The English system could have produced such a work, and its contents owed a great deal to existing English practice and methods, but there would have been no need for quite such a document without the Conquest and no driving force behind it without the Conqueror. Thus we possess one of the great records from the eleventh century, an absolute godsend to historians, a fund of all sorts of information.

In conclusion, we may ask what were the main political effects of the Conquest? They are mostly obvious but this does not make them any the less important. For a start, there was a new king and this would soon be seen as the beginning of a new dynasty – to such an extent that a thirteenth-century king would be known as Edward I, disregarding the rule of the Old English monarchs of that name. The Conqueror made some claims about his right by descent, but it was right by force which everyone recognised.

The Conquest had brought a new line to the throne. And for centuries, in some ways even till now, that has meant a king (or queen) of England who would not have been on the throne but for the events of 1066. More immediately, William's reign in England was followed by that of his two sons, William II Rufus (1087–1100) and Henry I (1100–35); then by his grandson, Stephen (1135–54) and his great-grandson, Henry II (1154–89). For all the changes and problems of succession which the period 1066 to 1189 covered, it is still true that William's line ruled in England, and of course would continue so to do.

The imposition of a French nobility also had its effects. The new lords of England belonged to families which mainly held considerable lands across the sea. For some time, this would cause a new situation in English politics, and obviously affected

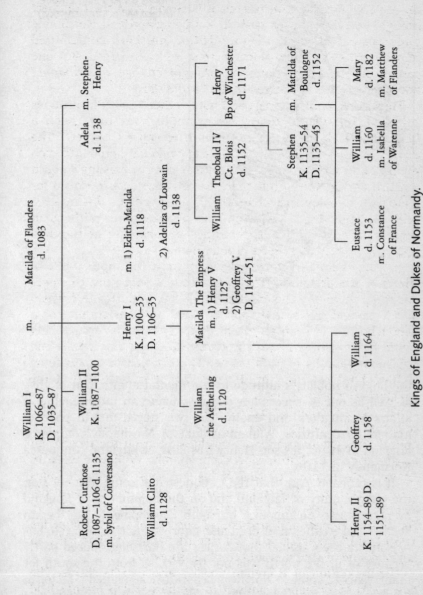

Kings of England and Dukes of Normandy.

Henry II's Angevin Empire.
(Map: Mike Komarnyckyj)

the English nobility's attitude to continental affairs. Out of this, as well as out of succession disputes, came an interweaving of affairs in kingdom and duchy. The two stayed tied in political matters for centuries. William as duke of Normandy conquered England in 1066; his son Henry I as king of England conquered Normandy in 1106.

It is probably true that the Conquest had some influence on the greater unity of England and on the dominance of England over its British neighbours. But both developments had begun before, and neither had dramatic improvement at once. It has reasonably been argued that despite the harrying, indeed partly because of it, the north was not truly ruled from the south for many years to come.[65] Northern separatism remained a factor in English politics long after William's death. But it is probably true that the English magnates lost something of their powers relative to the king. No Anglo-Norman earl would quite equate in status to, say, Godwin of Wessex. The powers of earls diminished somewhat and the powers of royal authority within the earldoms increased.

The link between England and Normandy brought even more dramatic enlargement to the rulers of England in time. Henry of Anjou, son of the Empress Matilda, inherited Anjou from his father; Normandy from his mother, but made possible by his father's conquest of it; and soon England. By various means he became lord of all western France, and what we know as the Angevin Empire was born. Out of that came inevitable conflict with the Capetian kings of France: the losses under King John, the revival in the later Middle Ages in the first stages of the Hundred Years' War. Not until the fifteenth century was this conflict truly determined, so that France as we know it would emerge, and the English crown would be shorn of nearly all its hold on continental lands.

In some sense, all of this came about because of Hastings and the Norman Conquest. Indeed, it would not be untrue to suggest that English history from 1066 until now is a consequence of the battle of Hastings. It would not otherwise have been as it has been. It truly was a great and significant battle: it changed a crown, it changed a nation, and it deserves its reputation as one of the few occasions and dates which everyone remembers. If I decided the dates of national holidays, 14 October would be one of them.

NOTES

Abbreviations Used

ANS	*Anglo-Norman Studies*
Bayeux Tapestry	*The Bayeux Tapestry*, ed. D.M. Wilson, London, 1985
BL	British Library
BM	British Museum
CG	*Château-Gaillard, Études de Castellologie Medievale*
CHF	Classiques de l'Histoire de France
EHR	*English Historical Review*
IPMK	*The Ideal and Practice of Medieval Knighthood*
JMH	*Journal of Medieval History*
MGH	*Monumenta Germaniae Historica*
PBA	*Proceedings of the British Academy*
RAB	*Studies in Medieval History presented to R. Allen Brown*, eds C. Harper-Bill, C. Holdsworth. J.L. Nelson, Woodbridge, 1989
RS	Rolls Series
ser.	series
Stevenson	*The Church Historians of England*, ed. J. Stevenson, 5 vols, London, 1853–8

Chapter One

1. William of Poitiers, *Histoire de Guillaume le Conquérant*, ed. R. Foreville, CHF, Paris, 1952, p. 206.
2. D.C. Douglas, *William the Conqueror*, London, 1964, p. 181 and n. 1; R.A. Brown, *The Normans and the Norman Conquest*, 2nd edn, Woodbridge, 1985, p. 122; Orderic Vitalis, *The Ecclesiastical History*, ed. M. Chibnall, 6 vols, Oxford, 1968–80, ii, p. 134 and n. 2; C. Morton and H. Muntz (eds), *Carmen de Hastingae Proelio*, Oxford, 1972, p. 10, ll. 125–6.
3. D. Whitelock, D.C. Douglas and S.I. Tucker (eds), *The Anglo-Saxon Chronicle*, London, 1961, 1012, pp. 91–2; G.P. Cubbin (ed.), *The Anglo-Saxon Chronicle*, vi, Cambridge, 1996, p. 57.

Notes

4. Asser, 'Life of King Alfred' in S. Keynes and M. Lapidge (eds), *Alfred the Great*, Harmondsworth, 1983, p. 98; compare John of Worcester, *Chronicle*, eds R.R. Darlington and P. McGurk, ii, Oxford, 1995 (only this vol published to date), p. 324.
5. John of Worcester, eds Darlington and McGurk, pp. 354, 378.
6. John of Worcester, eds Darlington and McGurk, p. 412.
7. E. John, chaps. 7–9, pp. 160–239 in James Campbell (ed.), *The Anglo-Saxons*, London, 1982, pp. 160, 172.
8. John of Worcester, eds Darlington and McGurk, p. 428, Whitelock *et al.* (eds), *Anglo-Saxon Chronicle*, p. 79.
9. John in Campbell (ed.), *Anglo-Saxons*, p. 192.
10. S. Keynes, *The Diplomas of King Aethelred 'the Unready'*, Cambridge, 1980, p. 158.
11. John of Worcester, eds Darlington and McGurk, pp. 430, 436; John in Campbell (ed.), *Anglo-Saxons*, p. 193; F. Barlow, *Edward the Confessor*, London, 1970, p. 3; Whitelock *et al.* (eds), *Anglo-Saxon Chronicle*, 986, 1005, 1014, pp. 81, 87, 93.
12. Barlow, *Edward*, p. 4.
13. Whitelock *et al.* (eds), *Anglo-Saxon Chronicle*, 991, p. 82; John of Worcester, eds Darlington and McGurk, p. 452.
14. Barlow, *Edward*, p. 11; John in Campbell (ed.), *Anglo-Saxons*, p. 198.
15. Whitelock *et al.* (eds), *Anglo-Saxon Chronicle*, 999, p. 85.
16. M.K. Lawson, *Cnut*, Harlow, 1993, p. 43.
17. Barlow, *Edward*, p. 15; Lawson, *Cnut*, p. 17.
18. Whitelock *et al.* (eds), *Anglo-Saxon Chronicle*, 1002, p. 86; Keynes, *Diplomas*, pp. 203–5; Cubbins (ed.), *Anglo-Saxon Chronicle*, p. 51.
19. John of Worcester, eds Darlington and McGurk, pp. 456, 470: '*perfidus dux*'.
20. Whitelock *et al.* (eds), *Anglo-Saxon Chronicle*, p. 92; Cubbins (ed.), *Anglo-Saxon Chronicle*, p. 58.
21. Whitelock *et al.* (eds), *Anglo-Saxon Chronicle*, 1014, p. 93; Cubbins (ed.), *Anglo-Saxon Chronicle*, p. 59.
22. W.E. Kapelle, *The Norman Conquest of the North*, London, 1979, e.g. p. 26.
23. Whitelock *et al.* (eds), *Anglo-Saxon Chronicle*, 1016, p. 95.
24. Lawson, *Cnut*, p. 38.
25. Whitelock *et al.* (eds), *Anglo-Saxon Chronicle*, 1017, p. 97.
26. John in Campbell, *Anglo-Saxons*, p. 216.
27. Barlow, *Edward*, p. 44; John of Worcester, eds Darlington and McGurk, p. 520.
28. Barlow, *Edward*, p. 48; Whitelock *et al.* (eds), *Anglo-Saxon Chronicle*, C and D, 1041, p. 106.
29. Whitelock *et al.* (eds), *Anglo-Saxon Chronicle*, 1042, p. 106; Cubbins (ed.), *Anglo-Saxon Chronicle*, p. 66

Chapter Two

1. F. Barlow (ed.), *Vita Aedwardi Regis*, 2nd edn, Oxford, 1992, p. 19.
2. Barlow, *Edward*, pp. 70–1; Barlow (ed.), *Vita*, p. 42.
3. John in Campbell (ed.), *Anglo-Saxons*, p. 221, from F. Maitland.
4. Barlow, *Edward*, p. 74.
5. Barlow, *Edward*, p. 39.
6. Barlow (ed.), *Vita*, p. 8.
7. Barlow (ed.), *Vita*, p. 44.
8. Barlow, *Edward*, pp. 81–4, 130; Barlow (ed.), *Vita*, pp. 14, 24, 90, 92.
9. Whitelock *et al.* (eds), *Anglo-Saxon Chronicle*, 1043, p. 107; Cubbins (ed.), *Anglo-Saxon Chronicle*, p. 67.
10. Barlow (ed.), *Vita*, pp. 28–30.
11. Barlow, *Edward*, p. 97: Edward 'provoked Godwin beyond endurance'.
12. Whitelock *et al.* (eds), *Anglo-Saxon Chronicle*, 1051, pp. 117, 118.
13. Barlow (ed.), *Vita*, p. 32.
14. Barlow (ed.), *Vita*, p. 36.
15. John of Worcester, eds Darlington and McGurk, p. 576: '*timidus dux Rauulfus*'.
16. Whitelock *et al.* (eds), *Anglo-Saxon Chronicle*, p. 124; Cubbins (ed.), *Anglo-Saxon Chronicle*, p. 73.
17. John of Worcester, eds Darlington and McGurk, p. 572.
18. Barlow (ed.), *Vita*, p. 44.
19. Barlow (ed.), *Vita*, p. 46; John of Worcester, eds Darlington and McGurk, p. 572.
20. Barlow, *Edward*, p. 208; John of Worcester, eds Darlington and McGurk, p. 578.
21. John of Worcester, eds Darlington and McGurk, p. 592.
22. John of Worcester, eds Darlington and McGurk, p. 596.
23. Whitelock *et al.* (eds), *Anglo-Saxon Chronicle*, 1065, p. 138; Barlow (ed.), *Vita*, p. 76; John of Worcester, eds Darlington and McGurk, p. 598.
24. John of Worcester, eds Darlington and McGurk, p. 598.
25. Barlow (ed.), *Vita*, p. 78.
26. Barlow (ed.), *Vita*, p. 48.
27. Barlow, *Edward*, pp. 195, 198; *Vita*, pp. 48–50, 58.
28. Barlow, *Edward*, p. 235.
29. Barlow, *Edward*, p. 239, Barlow (ed.), *Vita*, p. 78.
30. Barlow, *Edward*, p. 298.

Chapter Three

1. H.H. Howorth, 'A criticism of the life of Rollo as told by Dudo of St-Quentin', *Archaeologia*, xlv, 1880, pp. 235–50, p. 250.

Notes

2. Dudo of St-Quentin, *De Moribus et Actibus Primorum Ducum Normanniae*, ed. J. Lair, Caen, 1865, p. 159.

3. William of Jumièges (and Orderic Vitalis and Robert of Torigni), *Gesta Normannorum Ducum*, ed. E.M.C. van Houts, 2 vols, Oxford, 1992, 1995, ii, p. 76.

4. William of Poitiers, ed. Foreville, p. 31.

5. 'Rollo of Normandy' in D.C. Douglas, *Time and the Hour*, London, 1977. pp. 121–40, pp. 121–4. Rolf or Rorik, or Hrolfr, seems a likely original for Rollo or Rou, which are clearly Latin and French versions of the name. However, to accept the evidence of Snorri Sturlusson, writing in the thirteenth century, for Rolf and with Norse origins is even more perilous than accepting Dudo of St-Quentin's apparent belief in Danish origins. A lost charter of 913, in M. Fauroux (ed.), *Recueil des Actes des Ducs de Normandie de 911 à 1066*, Caen, 1961, pp. 19–20, and n. 4, suggests that Rolf was also christened Robert, which explains the popularity of that name among his descendants: p. 19: '*Igitur Rollo, qui et Robertus nomine sacri baptismatis*'. See E. Searle, *Predatory Kinship and the Creation of Norman Power, 840–1066*, Berkeley Ca, 1988, on 'counts'.

6. E. Privat (ed.), *Documents de l'Histoire de la Normandie*, Toulouse, 1972, p. 70, from Adelhelm, Bishop of Sées.

7. E. James, *The Origins of France*, London, 1982, p. 181. The quote is from the *Chronicle of St Benignus of Dijon*.

8. Douglas, 'Rollo', p. 126.

9. 'The rise of Normandy' in Douglas, *Time and the Hour*, pp. 95–119; see also in the same volume, 'Rollo', pp. 121–40, p. 127; and D. Bates, *Normandy Before the Norman Conquest*, Harlow, 1982.

10. R. McKitterick, *The Frankish Kingdoms under the Carolingians, 751–987*, Harlow, 1983, p. 237; Dudo, ed. Lair, pp. 168–9: p. 168: '*locum qui dicitur ad Sanctum Clerum*'. Douglas, 'Rollo', p. 129, discusses the possibility that Dudo invented the occasion using a meeting between Duke Richard I and Lothar at St-Clair as his inspiration.

11. Dudo, ed. Lair, pp. 168–9; reprinted in Privat (ed.), *Normandie*, with French translation, pp. 74–5; compare William of Jumièges, ed. van Houts, i, pp. 64–6, who closely follows Dudo. Dudo, ed. Lair, p. 168: '*ipsam terram ab Eptae fluviolo ad mare usque, quasi fundum et alodum, in sempiternum*'; '*Tunc Flandrensem terram, ut ex ea viveret, voluit rex ei dare*'; '*ei Britanniam dare, quae erat in confinio promissae terrae*'; p. 169: '*manus suas misit inter manus regis*'; '*Dedit itaque rex filiam suam, Gislam nomine, uxorem illi duci, terramque determinatam in alodo et in fundo, a flumine Eptae usque ad mare, totam Britanniam de qua posset vivere*'; '*Rolloni pedem regis nolenti osculari . . . jussit cuidam militi pedem regis osculari*'.

12. P. Lauer (ed.), *Recueil des Actes de Charles III le Simple, roi de France, 893–923*, Paris, 1940, i, no. 92, p. 209–12, p. 209: *'pro tutela regni'*; Privat (ed.), *Normandie*, p. 75.

13. Douglas, *William*, p. 129; *MGH Script*, xiii, p. 577.

14. Dudo, ed. Lair, p. 170: baptised *'comites suos et milites omnemque manum exercitus sui'*.

15. Douglas, 'Rollo', p. 133; Bates, *Normandy*, pp. 8,13; Dudo gives 'Gisla' or Gisela as the wife's name. The name Popa is suspiciously similar to Papia, wife of Richard II.

16. Privat (ed.), *Normandie*, p. 72.

17. Bates, *Normandy*, p. 9.

18. Bates, *Normandy*, p. 13.

19. William of Jumièges, ed. van Houts, i, p. 132.

20. Bates, *Normandy*, p. 14.

21. Searle, *Predatory Kinship*, e.g. pp. 131–42.

22. William of Jumièges, ed. van Houts, ii, p. 8.

23. William of Jumièges, ed. van Houts, ii, p. 6; Bates, *Normandy*, p. 73.

24. William of Jumièges, ed. van Houts, ii, p. 28.

25. Douglas.

26. William of Jumièges, ed. van Houts, ii, p. 30.

27. Bates, *Normandy*, p. 113.

28. K. Thompson, 'The Norman aristocracy before 1066: the example of the Montgomerys', *Historical Research*, lx, 1987, pp. 251–63, pp. 251–2, 255: Roger II Montgomery called himself *'ex northmannis northmannus'*.

29. William of Jumièges, ed. van Houts, ii, p. 46.

30. William of Jumièges, ed. van Houts, ii, pp. 48, 60, 82.

31. Douglas, *William*, p. 379. His mother's relatives are referred to as 'pollinctores' which means embalmers: Orderic Vitalis in William of Jumièges, ed. van Houts, p. 124.

32. William of Malmesbury, *Chronicle of the Kings of England*, ed. J.A. Giles, London, 1895, p. 259.

33. William of Jumièges, ed. van Houts, ii, p. 92; compare William of Poitiers, ed. Foreville, p. 22: castles built in 'seditious zeal'.

34. William of Jumièges, ed. van Houts, ii, p. 96.

35. William of Jumièges, ed. van Houts, ii, p. 92.

36. Douglas, *William*, p. 50; William of Poitiers, ed. Foreville, pp. 12–18; Wace, *Le Roman de Rou*, ed. A.J. Holden, 3 vols, Paris, 1971; for a translation see E. Taylor (ed.), *Master Wace, his Chronicle of the Norman Conquest from the Roman de Rou*, London, 1837: pp. 18–27; William of Poitiers, ed. Foreville, p. 19.

Notes

37. Bates, *Normandy*, p. 74.
38. William of Jumièges, ed. van Houts, ii, p. 104.
39. William of Poitiers, ed. Foreville, pp. 73–5.
40. Wace, ed. Holden, ii, p. 80, l. 5205–6: '*de lances fierent chevaliers/e od les ars traient archiers*'; Wace, ed. Taylor, p. 60.
41. William of Jumièges, ed. van Houts, ii, p. 150; William of Poitiers, ed. Foreville, p. 99.
42. Symeon of Durham, 'History of the Kings' in Stevenson, viii, pt II, 1855, p. 547.
43. L. Thorpe (ed.), *The Bayeux Tapestry and the Norman Invasion*, London, 1973, p. 46.
44. J.B. McNulty, 'The Lady Aelfgyva in the Bayeux Tapestry', *Speculum*, lv, 1980, pp. 659–68; M.W. Campbell, 'Aelfgyva: the mysterious lady of the Bayeux Tapestry', *Annales de Normandie*, xxxiv, 1984, pp. 127–45; *Bayeux Tapestry*, pl. 17, 18.
45. *Bayeux Tapestry*, pl. 19–21; Bates, *Normandy*, p. 83.
46. *Bayeux Tapestry*, pl. 25–6.
47. William of Jumièges, ed. van Houts, ii, p. 160; William of Poitiers, ed. Foreville, p. 103.
48. Barlow (ed.), *Vita*, p. 53.
49. Bates, *Normandy*, 241–3.
50. Bates, *Normandy*, p. 57.
51. K. Thompson, 'Family and influence to the south of Normandy in the eleventh century: the lordship of Bellême', *JMH*, xi, 1985, pp. 215–26; Bates, *Normandy*, p. 152.
52. William of Jumièges, ed. van Houts, ii, p. 128; Douglas, *William*, pp. 369–70: her remains were re-examined in 1961, but had previously been disturbed, so that there must remain a doubt about the bones being hers.
53. This granting of the banner has been questioned, e.g. by Bates, *Normandy*, p. 189, but it is difficult to see why William of Poitiers, ed. Foreville, p. 155, should not be accepted on this.

Chapter Four

1. *Carmen*, eds Morton and Muntz, p. 29. This work has been the subject of much debate over its dating: R.H.C. Davis, 'The Carmen de Hastingae Proelio', *EHR*, xciii, 1978, pp. 241–61, proposing a later date than had previously been accepted; and historians taking sides over the issue since. In the present writer's view Davis was probably correct to consider there was a problem, and the work may date from about 1100. It would still have interest as a source on armies of the eleventh century.

2. John of Worcester, eds Darlington and McGurk, p. 480.
3. R.P. Abels, *Lordship and Military Obligation in Anglo-Saxon England*, London, 1988, is an excellent recent work which reinforces this modern trend in thinking about the composition of English forces. See e.g. p. 37: the army was 'aristocratic in its basis'; also pp. 32, 160, 168, 175. The key work on housecarls is N. Hooper, 'The housecarls in England in the eleventh century', *ANS*, vii, 1985, pp. 161–76, which should be taken with the additional thoughts in N. Hooper, 'Military developments in the reign of Cnut' in A. Humble (ed.), *The Reign of Cnut*, London, 1994, pp. 89–100.
4. S. Pollington, *The English Warrior from Earliest Times to 1066*, Hockwold-cum-Wilton, 1996, p. 144: the Benty Grange helmet.
5. Pollington, *English Warrior*, p. 145: the Coppergate helmet.
6. William of Jumièges, ed. van Houts, ii, p. 24.
7. William of Poitiers, ed. Foreville, p. 185.
8. William of Poitiers, ed. Foreville, p. 169. The author, like many others, has been allowed to don a hauberk made by the historian of arms and armour, Ian Peirce.
9. *Bayeux Tapestry*, pl. 69; William of Poitiers, ed. Foreville, p. 183.
10. Pollington, *English Warrior*, p. 136.
11. William of Poitiers, ed. Foreville, p. 207.
12. Pollington, *English Warrior*, pp. 83, 97, 125, 244. The poem about Maldon is useful, but was probably written about thirty years after the event.
13. M. Strickland, paper to Battle Conference, to be published in *ANS*, xix. See N. Higham, *The Kingdom of Northumbria*, Stroud, 1993.
14. John of Worcester, eds Darlington and McGurk, p. 486.
15. Pollington, *English Warrior*, p. 127.
16. Henry of Huntingdon, *Historia Anglorum*, ed. T. Arnold, RS no. 74, London, 1965, p. 200.
17. J. Bradbury, *The Medieval Archer*, Woodbridge, 1985, pp. 22–40.
18. Anna Comnena, *The Alexiad*, Harmondsworth, 1969, pp. 163–5, 416.
19. *Bayeux Tapestry*, pl. 40–4; *Carmen*, eds Morton and Muntz, p. 8.
20. Anna Comnena, pp. 56–7; R. Glover, 'English warfare in 1066', *EHR*, xvii, 1952, pp. 1–18, p. 14.
21. See Hooper, 'Military developments'.
22. Abels, *Lordship*, pp. 115: '*caballum in exercitu*'; 110. John of Worcester, eds Darlington and McGurk, pp. 389, 934: '*equestri exercitu non modico*'.
23. Abels, *Lordship*, p. 13.
24. Abels, *Lordship*, p. 45; A. Williams, *The English and the Norman Conquest*, Woodbridge, 1995, pp. 191–2.

Notes

25. Abels, *Lordship*, p. 146.
26. *Carmen*, eds Morton and Muntz, p. 17.
27. William of Poitiers, ed. Foreville, p. 37.
28. Whitelock *et al.* (eds), *Anglo-Saxon Chronicle*, p. 142.
29. *Bayeux Tapestry*, pl. 36–9; William of Poitiers, ed. Foreville, p. 151.
30. John of Worcester, eds Darlington and McGurk, pp. 460–2.
31. Barlow (ed.), *Vita*, p. 20.
32. John of Worcester, eds Darlington and McGurk, p. 530.
33. Pollington, *English Warrior*, p. 151.
34. John of Worcester, eds Darlington and McGurk, p. 356; Pollington, *English Warrior*, pp. 236, 242; 244, ll. 267–71; '*bogan waeron bysige*'.
35. Bradbury, *Medieval Archer*, pp. 17–22; I. Gollancz (ed.), *The Exeter Book*, 2 vols, London, 1895, 1934; ii, p. 112, no. 23: '*Agof is min noma*'; Aldhelm, *Prose Works*, eds M. Lapidge and M. Herren, Cambridge, 1979, p. 163; Aldhelm, *Opera*, ed. R. Ehwald, *MGH Auctorum Antiquissimorum*, xv, Berlin, 1919, p. 230.
36. Snorri Sturlusson, *King Harald's Saga*, eds M. Magnusson and H. Palsson, Harmondsworth, 1966, p. 152.
37. Pollington, *English Warrior*, p. 155; Whitelock *et al.* (eds), *Anglo-Saxon Chronicle*, p. 145.
38. *Carmen*, (eds) Monroe and Muntz, p. 25.
39. Pollington, *English Warrior*, p. 152.
40. John of Worcester, eds Darlington and McGurk, p. 481: '*cum multo equitatu*'.
41. John of Worcester, eds Darlington and McGurk, p. 592: '*equitatu*', '*equestri . . . exercitu*'; a saying quoted by Pollington, *English Warrior*, p. 188: '*eorl sceal on eos boge*'; Williams, *Norman Conquest*, pp. 196–7.
42. Pollington, *English Warrior*, pp. 236, 242, 244; *Carmen*, eds Morton and Muntz, p. 25; John of Worcester, eds Darlington and McGurk, p. 487; William of Poitiers, ed. Foreville, p. 187, he also has the English abandoning the use of horses at this point.
43. Whitelock *et al.* (eds), *Anglo-Saxon Chronicle*, p. 130; John of Worcester, eds Darlington and McGurk, p. 576.
44. T. Cain. seminar paper at Institute of Historical Research, 1997, makes several interesting points about the early English use of cavalry at least in the north, as illustrated on northern carvings, though the evidence is rather of riding than fighting on horseback. I am grateful to Tom for passing me a copy of this paper more recently, entitled 'A hoary old question reconsidered: a case for Anglo-Saxon cavalry'.
45. *Bayeux Tapestry*, pl. 67; Abels, *Lordship*, p. 26; one notes that 'boys' (*pueri*) also appear in English households.
46. William of Poitiers, ed. Foreville, p. 109.

47. William of Jumièges, ed. van Houts, p. 120: '*impetus*' and '*concursu*' suggest charges, but is only cavalry by inference.
48. Wace, ed. Holden, ii, pp. 39–41, ll. 4091–156.
49. John of Worcester, eds Darlington and McGurk, p. 576: '*contra morem in equis pugnare*'.
50. William of Poitiers, ed. Foreville, p. 199.
51. William of Poitiers, ed. Foreville, p. 13.
52. William of Poitiers, ed. Foreville, pp. 25, 81–3.
53. William of Jumièges, ed. van Houts, p. 104; Giffard may be the 'Gilfardus' in *Carmen*, eds Morton and Muntz, p. 34, l. 539.
54. John of Worcester, eds Darlington and McGurk, p. 376, on Towcester, and Colchester which was repaired by Edward the Elder, who 'restored the wall'.
55. John of Worcester, eds Darlington and McGurk, e.g. about 885, p. 318, calls the fortification built against Rochester in the siege, therefore at least performing the function of a siege castle, a '*castellum*'; and p. 341 seems to distinguish smaller fortifications as 'castella' from towns.
56. Abels, *Lordship*, p. 92; G. Beresford, 'Goltho Manor, Lincolnshire: the buildings and their surrounding defences c.850–1150', *ANS*, iv, 1981, pp. 13–36, pp. 18, 31, 34.
57. Whitelock *et al.* (eds), *Anglo-Saxon Chronicle*, 1052, p. 125; 1055, p. 131.
58. William of Jumièges, ed. van Houts, pp. 102, 122, 124; William of Poitiers, ed. Foreville, pp. 19, 37, 43, 55.
59. J. Yver, 'Les châteux forts en Normandie jusqu'au milieu du XIIe siècle', *Bulletin de la Société des Antiquaires de Normandie*, liii, 1955–6, pp. 28–115, pp. 47, 49; William of Jumièges, ed. van Houts, p. 208; William of Poitiers, ed. Foreville, p. 106.

Chapter Five

1. Barlow, *Edward*, p. 213; Barlow (ed.), *Vita*, p. 6.
2. Barlow, *Edward*, p. 300.
3. Barlow (ed.), *Vita*, p. 112.
4. Barlow (ed.), *Vita*, p. 116.
5. Barlow (ed.), *Vita*, p. 122.
6. Barlow (ed.), *Vita*, pp. 80–2, 112, 118–20, 122–4; Barlow, *Edward*, pp. 249–52; Wace, ed. Taylor, p. 93; Wace, ed. Holden, ii, pp. 101–2, ll. 5809–10. On the latter see M. Bennett, 'Wace and warfare', *ANS*, xi, 1988, pp. 37–58; *Bayeux Tapestry*, pl. 30.
7. John of Worcester, eds Darlington and McGurk, p. 598.
8. Barlow (ed.), *Vita*, pp. 151–3; Barlow, *Edward*, pp. 269, 282.

Notes

9. *Bayeux Tapestry*, pl. 29–30.
10. John of Worcester, eds Darlington and McGurk, p. 601; Whitelock *et al.* (eds), *Anglo-Saxon Chronicle*, p. 140; *Bayeux Tapestry*, pl. 31.
11. *Bayeux Tapestry*, pl. 31.
12. Douglas, *William*, pp. 181–2; William of Poitiers, ed. Foreville, p. 146; John of Worcester, eds Darlington and McGurk, pp. 590–2, 600; Whitelock *et al.* (eds), *Anglo-Saxon Chronicle*, p. 140; Cubbins (ed.), *Anglo-Saxon Chronicle*, p. 79.
13. Barlow (ed.), *Vita*, p. 48.
14. John of Worcester, eds Darlington and McGurk, p. 602: '*pedestrem exercitum locis opportunis circa ripas maris locabat*'.
15. M. Swanton, *The Lives of the Last Englishmen*, x, ser. B, New York, 1984: from BL Harleian MS 3776, dated about 1205; the story sounds suspiciously like confusion with Godwin.
16. Whitelock *et al.* (eds), *Anglo-Saxon Chronicle*, p. 140; Cubbins (ed.), *Anglo-Saxon Chronicle*, p. 79.
17. John of Worcester, eds Darlington and McGurk, p. 602.
18. Whitelock *et al.* (eds), *Anglo-Saxon Chronicle*, p. 140, and n. 8; John of Worcester, eds Darlington and McGurk, p. 598; F.M. Stenton, *Anglo-Saxon England*, 2nd edn, Oxford, 1947, p. 578–9.
19. Whitelock *et al.* (eds), *Anglo-Saxon Chronicle*, p. 141; Cubbins (ed.), *Anglo-Saxon Chronicle*, p. 79.
20. W.M. Aird, 'St Cuthbert, the Scots and the Normans', *ANS*, xvi, 1993, pp. 2–3, 7.
21. Sturlusson, *King Harald's Saga*: the following account of Hardrada's early career uses the saga, which is chronological: quoted and significant passages are on pp. 30–1, 45, 61, 64, 90, 93, 109, 113, 128, 136, 138, 144, 152.
22. This is probably Jaroslav I of Kiev (1018–55).
23. Ulf was brother of Gytha, wife of Earl Godwin of Wessex.
24. Whitelock *et al.* (eds), *Anglo-Saxon Chronicle*, p. 141.
25. John of Worcester, eds Darlington and McGurk, p. 602.
26. John of Worcester, eds Darlington and McGurk, p. 602: he disbanded the fleet and the infantry forces.
27. John of Worcester, eds Darlington and McGurk, p. 602; Geoffrey Gaimar, 'The History of the English', in Stevenson, ii, pt II, 1854, p. 793.
28. John of Worcester, eds Darlington and McGurk, p. 602; Whitelock *et al.* (eds), *Anglo-Saxon Chronicle*, p. 143; F.W. Brooks, *The Battle of Stamford Bridge*, East Yorkshire Local History Society series, no. 6, 1963, p. 12. Brooks is presumably thinking as others have that, like the march south, it was an infantry march, but there is no reason to believe this was any more true of the march north than of the march south.

29. A.H. Burne, *More Battlefields of England*, London, 1952, p. 92, suggested a different position for the early bridge, P. Warner, *British Battle Fields, the North*, London, 1975, p. 21, and W. Seymour, *Battles in Britain*, i, London, 1975, p. 9, both agree with Burne; but the argument is not convincing. Brooks, *Stamford Bridge*, p. 19, disagrees with Burne.

30. D. Howarth, *The Year of the Conquest*, London, 1977, p. 106, reports on small horse-shoes being found in the locality in the nineteenth century, but gives no reference. In any case: 1) it is difficult to give credence to Sturlusson's cavalry; 2) even if relating to transport horses, it still seems unlikely to have any connection with the battle (lots of killed and abandoned horses from the winning side?).

31. Whitelock *et al.* (eds), *Anglo-Saxon Chronicle*, p. 144–5.

32. Whitelock *et al.* (eds), *Anglo-Saxon Chronicle*, p. 144.

33. Sturlusson, *King Harald's Saga*, p. 151–3; Whitelock *et al.* (eds), *Anglo-Saxon Chronicle*, p. 142; John of Worcester, eds Darlington and McGurk, p. 604.

34. Sturlusson, *King Harald's Saga*, pp. 154–5; Whitelock *et al.* (eds), *Anglo-Saxon Chronicle*, p. 142.

35. Whitelock *et al.* (eds), *Anglo-Saxon Chronicle*, p. 144. John of Worcester, eds Darlington and McGurk, pp. 602–4, has 500, with twenty ships for the return; Gaimar in Stevenson, p. 793, also has twenty.

36. Brooks, *Stamford Bridge*, p. 21; Orderic Vitalis, ed. Chibnall, ii, p. 168.

37. William of Poitiers, ed. Foreville, p. 154.

38. Wace, ed. Taylor, pp. 97–107; Wace, ed. Holden, ii, pp. 107–15, the quote is l. 6048; has William fitz Osbern in favour of going, and William taking counsel.

39. For example, Wace, ed. Taylor, p. 98: 'he perjured himself for a kingdom'; Wace, ed. Holden, ii, p. 106, l. 5947.

40. William of Poitiers, ed. Foreville, p. 151; Orderic Vitalis, ed. Chibnall, ii, p. 144.

41. Wace, ed. Taylor, p. 120: 'I remember it well, although I was but a lad, that there were 700 ships less four'; Wace, ed. Holden, ii, p. 123, ll. 6424–5: '*bien m'en sovient, mais vaslet ere –/que set cenz nes, quatre meins, furent*'.

42. C.H. Lemmon, 'The campaign of 1066' in *The Norman Conquest its Setting and Impact*, London, 1966, p. 85 gives some previous estimates (varying from 10,000 to 60,000) and adds his own; P.P. Wright, *Hastings*, Moreton-in-Marsh, 1996, estimates 7,500 including combatants. C.M. Gillmor, 'The naval logistics of the cross-Channel operation, 1066', *ANS*, vii, 1984, pp. 105–31, has some interesting speculation, but vainly attempts to estimate the size of the fleet with

Notes

precision, and even the number of workmen and trees felled; see also B. Bachrach, 'The military administration of the Norman Conquest', *ANS*, viii, 1986, pp. 1–25.

43. M. Bennett, 'Norman naval activity in the Mediterranean c. 1060–c. 1108', *ANS*, xv, 1992, pp. 41–58.
44. Wace, ed. Taylor, p. 117; Wace, ed. Holden, ii, p. 120.
45. *Bayeux Tapestry*, pl. 35–6.
46. Foreville (ed.), *Gesta Gulielmi Ducis Normannorum et Regis Anglorum*. The introduction includes an excellent account of the chronicler's career. Key information in the following section to the landing in England comes from pp. 12, 30, 42, 100, 104, 146, 150–62.
47. Wace, ed. Taylor, p. 76; Wace, ed. Holden, ii, p. 94. Wace is interesting at this point, telling us that he is using more than one source: one which has the forbidding, and one which says it was to promise the crown: 'how the matter really was I never knew', and nor do we.
48. William of Poitiers, ed. Foreville, p. 152, translation from R.A. Brown, *The Normans and the Norman Conquest*, 2nd edn, Woodbridge, 1985, p. 132.
49. *Carmen*, eds Morton and Muntz, p. 4, ll. 40–4.
50. See D. Bates, *William the Conqueror*, London, 1983, p. 65, where he accepts the banner story; Orderic Vitalis, ed. Chibnall, ii, p. 170.
51. *Carmen*, eds Morton and Muntz, p. 6, ll. 53, 59, 63–4.
52. C. and G. Grainge, 'The Pevensey expedition: brilliantly executed plan or near disaster?', *Mariner's Mirror*, 1993, pp. 261–73.
53. Gillmor, 'Naval logistics', p. 124; J. Gillingham, 'William the Bastard at war', reprinted in S. Morillo, *The Battle of Hastings*, Woodbridge, 1996, pp. 96–112, p. 109.
54. *Carmen*, eds Morton and Muntz, p. 6.
55. Wace, ed. Holden, ii, p. 124, ll. 6453–5.
56. Lemmon, 'Campaign', p. 89; Wright, *Hastings*, p. 52 quotes E.A. Freeman, *The History of the Norman Conquest in England*, 6 vols, Oxford, 1867–79, iii, p. 410. Wace, ed. Holden, ii, pp. 124–5; William of Poitiers, ed. Foreville, p. 164.

Chapter Six

1. A useful general guide is A. Gransden, *Historical Writing in England* c. *550 to* c. *1307*, London, 1974.
2. William of Poitiers, ed. Foreville. Translations of part of the work with the battle may be found in D.C. Douglas and G.W. Greenaway (eds), *English Historical Documents*, ii, 1042–1189, 2nd edn, London, 1981; and Brown (ed.), *The Norman Conquest*, London, 1984 – both of these have a good selection of sources of the Conquest.

193

3. William of Jumièges, ed. van Houts.
4. Whitelock *et al.* (eds), *Anglo-Saxon Chronicle*. The 'Collaborative Edition' (eds D. Dumville and S. Keynes) is at present incomplete, but will become the foremost academic edition of the *Anglo-Saxon Chronicle* with the text in Old English. Of the volumes published to date, vol. vi (ed. G.P. Cubbins) of the D manuscript is the most valuable for events of the Conquest.
5. John of Worcester, eds Darlington and McGurk.
6. See *Bayeux Tapestry* which has excellent colour photos. See also F.M. Stenton (ed.), *The Bayeux Tapestry*, 2nd edn, London, 1965; Thorpe (ed.), *The Bayeux Tapestry*, which also has a translation of part of William of Poitiers. N.P. Brooks and H.E. Walker, 'The authority and interpretation of the Bayeux Tapestry', *ANS*, iii, 1980, pp. 1–21.
7. *Carmen*, eds Morton and Muntz; Davis, 'Carmen', pp. 241–61.
8. Wace, ed. Holden; Wace, ed. Taylor; Bennett, 'Wace and warfare'.
9. William of Malmesbury, *De Gestis Regum Anglorum*, ed. W. Stubbs, RS no. 90, 2 vols, London, 1887–9; William of Malmesbury, ed. Giles.
10. Orderic Vitalis, ed. Chibnall; M. Chibnall, *The World of Orderic Vitalis*, Oxford, 1984.
11. Henry of Huntingdon, *Historia Anglorum*, ed. D. Greenway, Oxford, 1996; Henry of Huntingdon, ed. Arnold; Henry of Huntingdon, *Chronicle*, ed. T. Forester, London, 1853; N.F. Partner, *Serious Entertainments*, Chicago, 1977.
12. E. Searle (ed.), *The Chronicle of Battle Abbey*, Oxford, 1980.

Chapter Seven

1. William of Malmesbury, ed. Stubbs, ii, p. 300; translation from William of Malmesbury, ed. Giles, p. 274; Wace, ed. Holden, ii, p. 128, ll. 6573–90; Brown, *The Normans and the Norman Conquest*, p. 133 and n. 61.
2. Bennett, 'Wace and warfare', pp. 238–9; Wace, ed. Holden, ii, ll. 6483–8: '*saillir fors e nes deschargier,/ ancres jeter, cordes sachier,/ escuz e seles fors porter,/ destriers e palefreiz tirer./ Li archier sunt primes issu,/ al terrain sunt primes venu*'.
3. A. Williams, 'Land and power in the eleventh century: the estates of Harold Godwineson', *ANS*, iii, 1981.
4. *Bayeux Tapestry*, pl. 49–50.
5. *Bayeux Tapestry*, pl. 43–8.
6. J. Gillingham, 'William the Bastard at war' in *RAB*, pp. 141–58, reprinted in Strickland (ed.), *Anglo-Norman Warfare*, pp. 143–60,

Notes

especially pp. 146–7, points out that there were long periods when William avoided battles; pp. 157–58 on the Breton campaign.

7. *Bayeux Tapestry*, pl. 50; Thorpe (ed.), *The Bayeux Tapestry*, p. 47; William of Poitiers, ed. Foreville, p. 180.

8. *Bayeux Tapestry*, pl. 50.

9. John of Worcester, eds Darlington and McGurk, p. 604; Wace, ed. Taylor, p. 173; Wace, ed. Holden, ii, p. 173, ll. 7743–4: *'Daneis les orent damagiez/ e Tosti les out empeiriez'*.

10. William of Poitiers, ed. Foreville, p. 186.

11. Orderic Vitalis, cd. Chibnall, ii, p. 172.

12. *Bayeux Tapestry*, pl. 61–2.

13. William of Jumièges, ed. van Houts, ii, p. 168.

14. J. Bradbury, 'Battles in England and Normandy, 1066–1154', *ANS*, vi, 1983, pp. 1–12, p. 4.

15. Wace, ed. Taylor, p. 255, at least has the goodness to admit: 'I was not there to see'; Wace, ed. Holden, ii, p. 215, ll. 8851–2.

16. R.A. Brown, 'The Battle of Hastings', *ANS*, iii, 1980, pp. 1–21; reprinted in M. Strickland (ed.), *Anglo-Norman Warfare*, Woodbridge, 1992, pp. 161–81, p. 163

17. *Chronicle of Battle Abbey*, ed. Searle, pp. 4–5, where the editor shows that early claims for the abbey depend partly on forged charters, pp. 15–16, that the Malfosse information is not solid, and, pp. 17–23, that the vow to build the abbey is dubious.

18. *Chronicle of Battle Abbey*, ed. Searle, pp. 42–6.

19. Some later ones did, notably Wace, ed. Taylor, p. 143: Harold erected his gonfanon 'where the abbey of the battle is now built', but also adds that he had it surrounded by a ditch with an entrance on three sides; Wace, ed. Holden, ii, p. 142, ll. 6964–6: *ou l'abeïe/ de la Bataille est establie'*.

20. C. Plummer (ed.), *Two of the Saxon Chronicles Parallel*, 2 vols, Oxford, 1892, i., p. 199; Whitelock *et al.* (eds), *Anglo-Saxon Chronicle*, D, p. 143; cf. G.P. Cubbin (ed.), *The Anglo-Saxon Chronicle*, vi, Cambridge, 1996, p. 80: and *'com him togenes æt ¬ære haran apuldran'*.

21. I am aware that R.A. Brown thought otherwise, 'Hastings' in Strickland (ed.), *Anglo-Norman Warfare*, p. 169: 'Harold cannot possibly have selected the place of battle well in advance'. One is hesitant to quote Wace, ed. Taylor, p. 174, in support of anything, but his comment is interesting: Harold placing his men where he knew the Normans 'would come and attack him'; Wace, ed. Holden, ii, p. 173, ll. 7745–6.

22. *Carmen*, eds Morton and Muntz, p. 24.

23. Orderic Vitalis, ed. Chibnall, ii, p. 172: *'ad locum qui Senlac antiquitus*

uocabatur'. Freeman chose to call it the battle of Senlac because it was not actually fought at Hastings, which J.H. Round rubbished, *Feudal England*, London, 1895, reset reprint 1964, pp. 259–63.

24. *Bayeux Tapestry*, pl. 52.
25. *Bayeux Tapestry*, pl. 66–7.
26. On the Malfosse see C.T. Chevallier, 'Where was the Malfosse? the end of the battle of Hastings', *SAC*, 101, 1963, pp. 1–13, which outlines earlier ideas too.
27. Ian Peirce tells a good tale that his father found some buried remains which turned to dust, but agrees this is somewhat uncertain evidence, though I am sure he would dispute changing the location.
28. Round, *Feudal England*, p. 261, points out that Domesday Book refers to the abbey as 'de loco belli'; it is also in Domesday called the abbey of 'Labatailge'.
29. *Bayeux Tapestry*, pl. 71; William of Poitiers, ed. Foreville, p. 224; William of Malmesbury, ed. Stubbs, ii, p. 302.
30. Wace, ed. Holden, ii, p. 175, ll. 7793–800; Wace, ed. Taylor, p. 176. Freeman, *History of the Norman Conquest*, 1873, iii, p. 443; Round, *Feudal England*, pp. 258–305, esp. pp. 264–73; 307–8. Wace has a ditch around the position of the standard at the assembly point: a great fosse with three entrances, and on the morning of battle he has Harold and Gyrth on warhorses emerging from entrenchments, Wace, ed. Taylor, p. 143; Wace, ed. Holden, ii, p. 143, ll. 6969–72. There is often a suspicion of muddle between chronicle references to ramparts and some more solid construction in the minds of historians. As recently as 1996, Wright, *Hastings*, seems still to accept the palisade, though wondering about the length of time for construction, p. 78; Bradbury, *Medieval Archer*, p. 28.
31. Wace, ed. Taylor, p. 175; Wace, ed. Holden, ii, pp. 173–4, ll. 7767–8.
32. The quotations use either my own translations, or that from Thorpe (ed.), *The Bayeux Tapestry*, pp. 32–55. William of Poitiers, ed. Foreville, the battle account is pp. 186–204, only key quotations will be footnoted separately.
33. John of Worcester, eds Darlington and McGurk, p. 604, though trust is destroyed by the fact that he gets the date wrong.
34. Orderic Vitalis, ed. Chibnall, ii, p. 172.
35. William of Malmesbury, ed. Giles, p. 276; William of Malmesbury, ed. Stubbs, ii, p. 302; Wace, ed. Taylor, pp. 155–6; Wace, ed. Holden, ii, pp. 156–7, with slight variant spellings, e.g. 'drincheheil'. This passage could illustrate Round's contention that Wace borrowed information on Hastings from Malmesbury.
36. William of Jumièges, ed. van Houts, p. 168.

37. William of Malmesbury, ed. Giles, p. 277; William of Malmesbury, ed. Stubbs, ii, p. 302.

38. William of Poitiers, ed. Foreville, p. 184; *Carmen*, eds Morton and Muntz, has crossbowmen too. John of Worcester, eds Darlington and McGurk, p. 604, adds slingers to the Norman infantry.

39. Whitelock *et al.* (eds), *Anglo-Saxon Chronicle*, D, p. 143; Cubbins (ed.), *Anglo-Saxon Chronicle*, p. 80: '*Wyllelm him com ongean on unwear, ær his folc gefylced wære*'.

40. Whitelock *et al.* (eds), *Anglo-Saxon Chronicle*, D, p. 143; Cubbin (ed.), *Anglo-Saxon Chronicle*, p. 80; John of Worcester, eds Darlington and McGurk, p. 604: many left the battle line and the few with constant hearts stayed.

41. *Carmen*, eds Morton and Muntz, p. 24; *Chronicle of Battle Abbey*, ed. Searle, p. 38: the English 'on foot'; William of Malmesbury, ed. Giles, p. 276: 'all were on foot'; William of Malmesbury, ed. Stubbs, ii, p. 302; Wace, ed. Taylor, p. 238: 'the English knew not how to joust nor bear arms on horseback'; Wace, ed. Holden, ii, p. 206, ll. 8603–4: '*Engleis ne saveient joster/ ne a cheval armes porter*'.

42. Wace, ed. Taylor, p. 183, his brother Gyrth answers: 'he is a fool who believes in luck'; p. 191, the battle cries: '*Dex aie*' and '*Ut*'; Wace, ed. Holden, ii, p. 179, l. 7923: '"*Fols est*", dist Guert, "*qui en sort creit*"'; p. 184, ll. 8057–8: '*Normant escrient "Deus aïe!"/La gent englesche "Ut!" escrie*'; William of Jumièges, ed. van Houts, p. 168.

43. Orderic Vitalis, ed. Chibnall, ii, p. 174; *Carmen*, eds Morton and Muntz, pp. 22–6. Baudri de Bourgueil, *Oeuvres Poétiques*, ed. P. Abrahams, Paris, 1926, p. 197, l. 409, also has crossbows: '*atque balistis*'.

44. *Bayeux Tapestry*, pl. 57–61,

45. *Bayeux Tapestry*, pl. 61–2.

46. *Bayeux Tapestry*, pl. 64–7.

47. Wacc, ed. Taylor, pp. 175–6; Wace, ed. Holden, ii, p. 174, ll. 7784–5.

48. *Bayeux Tapestry*, pl. 67.

49. *Bayeux Tapestry*, pl. 68.

50. *Carmen*, eds Morton and Muntz, p. 30.

51. Wace, ed. Taylor, p. 249; Wace, ed. Holden, ii, p. 210, ll. 8717–26.

52. Lemmon, ' Campaign', p. 109; others to doubt the flight include Glover, 'English warfare', p. 12; Wright, *Hastings*, p. 93: 'extremely unlikely'.

53. Apart from Poitiers, the feigned flight appears in Orderic Vitalis, ed. Chibnall, ii, p. 174, who recognises it as a 'hazardous stratagem'; *Carmen*, eds Morton and Muntz, p. 28; *Chronicle of Battle Abbey*, ed. Scarle, p. 38; William of Malmesbury, ed. Giles, pp. 276–7; William of Malmesbury, ed. Stubbs, ii, p. 303; Baudri de Bourgueil, ed. Abrahams, p. 208; Wace, ed. Taylor, pp. 198–200: the Normans call '*Dex aie*' as the signal to stop and

turn, and 'like fools they broke their line'; Wace, ed. Holden, ii, pp. 189–92. See also B. Bachrach, 'The feigned retreat at Hastings', *Medieval Studies*, xxxiii, pp. 344–7.

54. *Carmen*, eds Morton and Muntz, p. 28.

55. *Bayeux Tapestry*, pl. 64.

56. S. Morillo, 'Hastings: an unusual battle', in S. Morillo (ed.), *The Battle of Hastings, Sources and Interpretations*, Woodbridge, 1996, pp. 220–30, p. 224.

57. *Carmen*, eds Morton and Muntz, p. 30.

58. William of Jumièges, ed. van Houts, p. 168: '*Heroldus etiam ipse in primo militum congressu occubuit uulneribus letaliter confossus*'; is followed by Orderic Vitalis, ed. Chibnall, ii, p. 176; F.H. Baring, *Domesday Tables for the Counties of Surrey, Berkshire, Middlesex, Hertford, Buckingham and Bedford and the New Forest*, London, 1909, p. 220, suggests *progressu* for *congressu*, but this is speculation.

59. William of Poitiers, ed. Foreville, p. 194.

60. *Bayeux Tapestry*, pl. 68–70.

61. Bradbury, *Medieval Archer*, p. 26. The idea of shooting high comes from later sources: Henry of Huntingdon, ed. Greenway, p. 394, and Wace, ed. Holden, ii, pp. 188–9, ll. 8145–59, 8161–4; Wace, ed. Taylor, p. 197: they 'shot their arrows upwards into the air', and is still accepted by Wright, *Hastings*, p. 97.

62. *Chronicle of Battle Abbey*, ed. Searle, p. 38: 'their king was laid low by a chance blow'.

63. *Carmen*, eds Morton and Muntz, pp. 34–6,116–20, appendix D, where the identification of the four is discussed. The editors' belief that the heir of Ponthieu in the source is called Hugh is accepted, though others have differed. William of Malmesbury, ed. Stubbs, ii, p. 303; Wace, ed. Taylor, p. 169; Wace, ed. Holden, ii, p. 167, l. 7605: '*Veez mon chief blanc e chanu*'.

64. *Bayeux Tapestry*, pl. 71.

65. *Bayeux Tapestry*; Wace, ed. Taylor, p. 198; Wace, ed. Holden, ii, p. 189, ll. 8161–8, is one source who follows this: an arrow 'struck Harold above his right eye, and put it out', though he survived to pull it out. He says that 'an arrow was well shot' became a saying among the English to the French; and ed. Taylor, pp. 252–4; ed. Holden, pp. 213–14: 'sorely wounded in his eye by the arrow', after which an armed man beat him down and cut through his thigh. He also says the duke struck him, but that he may already have been dead: 'I know not who it was who slew him'. A strong point which Brooks and Walker, 'Authority and interpretation', p. 32, make is that the standard bearer is also shown twice: standing and falling.

66. D. Bernstein, 'The blinding of Harold and the meaning of the Bayeux Tapestry', *ANS*, v, 1982, pp. 40–64.
67. William of Malmesbury, ed. Giles, p. 277: Harold 'fell from having his brain pierced by an arrow'; William of Malmesbury, ed. Stubbs, ii, p. 303; Baudri de Bourgueil, ed. Abrahams, p. 209, l. 463, an arrow from the sky: '*perforat Hairaldum*'.
68. Wace, ed. Taylor, p. 197; Wace, ed. Holden, ii, p. 187, l. 8132: '*fu si deça, fu si dela*'.
69. *Bayeux Tapestry*, pl. 72–3.
70. William of Malmesbury, ed. Giles, p. 277; William of Malmesbury, ed. Stubbs, ii, p. 303, has the incident in the middle of the battle, but his account is dependent on other sources and this seems to be an error; Wace, ed. Taylor, pp. 193–4; Wace, ed. Holden, ii, pp. 185–6, who may have been following Malmesbury, speaks of a fosse in the middle of the battlefield, which the Normans crossed and then fell back into; he also, ed. Taylor, p. 255, ed. Holden, pp. 215–16, has English during flight falling into water when a bridge breaks, but this seems to be when entering London.
71. R.A. Brown, 'Hastings' in Strickland (ed.), *Anglo-Norman Warfare*, p. 180, suggests that the Malfosse legend may have grown from an incident during the battle, associated with the 'hillock' on the Tapestry, possibly as a result of the feigned flights. We have preferred to stick with Poitiers, but do not discount the possibility of the legend growing by misuse of the earlier sources. Incidentally, the mid-battle incident, with a site of ditches and so on, would fit better with Caldbec than Battle.
72. William of Jumièges, ed. van Houts, pp. 168–70: '*sequenti nocti*'.
73. Orderic Vitalis, ed. Chibnall, ii, pp. 176–8; William of Malmesbury, ed. Giles, p. 277; William of Malmesbury, ed. Stubbs, ii, p. 303, has a deep ditch and a short passage, possibly meaning a causeway over the ditch.
74. *Chronicle of Battle Abbey*, ed. Searle, pp. 38, 15–16.
75. Lemmon, 'Campaign', p. 97; Chevallier, 'Malfosse', p. 3.
76. Chevallier, 'Malfosse'; Lemmon, 'Campaign', pp. 111–12.
77. Orderic Vitalis, ed. Chibnall, ii, p. 178.

Chapter Eight

1. William of Poitiers, ed. Foreville, p. 210; N. Hooper, 'Edgar the Aetheling: Anglo-Saxon prince, rebel and crusader', *Anglo-Saxon England*, xiv, 1985, pp. 197–214.
2. *Bayeux Tapestry*, pl. 71–2.
3. William of Poitiers, ed. Foreville, p. 210.

4. Thorpe (ed.), *The Bayeux Tapestry*, p. 54.
5. Orderic Vitalis, ed. Chibnall, ii, p. 178.
6. William of Poitiers, ed. Foreville, p. 204; Thorpe (ed.), *The Bayeux Tapestry*, p. 54.
7. Swanton, *Three Lives of the Last Englishmen*, p. 13.
8. Orderic Vitalis, ed. Chibnall, ii, p. 180.
9. Orderic Vitalis, ed. Chibnall, ii, p. 180.
10. William of Poitiers, ed. Foreville, p. 212: 'ad Fractam Turrim'.
11. Orderic Vitalis, ed. Chibnall, ii, p. 180.
12. Whitelock *et al.* (eds), *Anglo-Saxon Chronicle*, p. 144; Cubbins (ed.), *Anglo-Saxon Chronicle*, p. 80.
13. Orderic Vitalis, ed. Chibnall, ii, p. 182.
14. J. Beeler, *Warfare in England, 1066–1189*, New York, 1966, pp. 25–33.
15. F.H. Baring, 'The Conqueror's footprints in Domesday', *EHR*, xiii, 1898, pp. 17–25; Baring, *Domesday Tables*; G.H. Fowler, 'The devastation of Bedfordshire and the neighbouring counties in 1065 and 1066', *Archaeologia*, lxxii, 1922, pp. 41–50; D. Butler, *1066: the Story of a Year*, London, 1966; A.M. Davies, 'Eleventh century Buckinghamshire', *Records of Buckinghamshire*, x, 1916, pp. 69–74; and J. Bradbury, 'An introduction to the Buckinghamshire Domesday', in A. Williams and R.W.H. Erskine (eds), *The Buckinghamshire Domesday*, London, 1988, p. 32. The idea goes back beyond Baring in origin, see J.J.N. Palmer, 'The Conqueror's footprints'. Palmer puts damaging questions against the Baring thesis, but does not draw the full conclusions, and has missed my 1988 comments.
16. R. Welldon Finn, *The Norman Conquest and its Effects upon the Economy*, London, 1971, p. 19.
17. William of Poitiers, ed. Foreville, p. 220.
18. J. Nelson, 'The rites of the conqueror', *ANS*, 1981.
19. Orderic Vitalis, ed. Chibnall, ii, p. 182–4.
20. William of Poitiers, ed. Foreville, p. 230.
21. Orderic Vitalis, ed. Chibnall, ii, p. 194.
22. Orderic Vitalis, ed. Chibnall, ii, p. 218.
23. Orderic Vitalis, ed. Chibnall, ii, p. 196.
24. Baudri de Bourgueil, ed. Abrahams, p. 196.
25. Orderic Vitalis, ed. Chibnall, ii, p. 196.
26. William of Poitiers, ed. Foreville, p. 264.
27. William of Poitiers, ed. Foreville, p. 266.
28. Orderic Vitalis, ed. Chibnall, ii, p. 204–6.
29. William of Poitiers, ed. Foreville, pp. 268–70.
30. Orderic Vitalis, ed. Chibnall, ii, p. 208 has the last information clearly derived from Poitiers' surviving manuscript, from then on we may

Notes

expect material from Poitiers but only surviving in Orderic. This is made practically certain by Orderic's comment, p. 258: 'William of Poitiers has brought his history up to this point': i.e. Orderic, pp. 208–58, must make use of the lost end section of Poitiers.

31. William of Jumièges, ed. van Houts, ii, p. 178.
32. Williams, *The Norman Conquest*, p. 24.
33. Orderic Vitalis, ed. Chibnall, ii, p. 212.
34. Orderic Vitalis, ed. Chibnall, ii, p. 216.
35. Whitelock *et al.* (eds), *Anglo-Saxon Chronicle*, p. 150.
36. Kapelle, *The Norman Conquest*, p. 112.
37. Whitelock *et al.* (eds), *Anglo-Saxon Chronicle*, p. 150; Symeon of Durham in Stevenson, p. 550; Cubbins (ed.), *Anglo-Saxon Chronicle*, p. 84.
38. Symeon of Durham in Stevenson, p. 551.
39. Orderic Vitalis, ed. Chibnall, ii, pp. 222, 230.
40. Orderic Vitalis, ed. Chibnall, ii, p. 234.
41. Symeon of Durham in Stevenson, p. 551.
42. Orderic Vitalis, ed. Chibnall, ii, pp. 230–2.
43. Whitelock *et al.* (eds), *Anglo-Saxon Chronicle*, pp. 148–9, D and John of Worcester, eds Darlington amd McGurk, give sixty-four ships; Orderic Vitalis, ed. Chibnall, ii, p. 224 has sixty-six.
44. William of Jumièges, ed. van Houts, ii, p. 182.
45. It is not certain when she went, it may have been before the second raid, since John of Worcester has 1068. Orderic says she went to France, Worcester has Flanders – which seems more likely.
46. Williams, *The Norman Conquest*, pp. 35, 49–50 and n. 21.
47. Whitelock *et al.* (eds), *Anglo-Saxon Chronicle*, p. 154.
48. Orderic Vitalis, ed. Chibnall, ii, p. 258.
49. Whitelock *et al.* (eds), *Anglo-Saxon Chronicle*, p. 158.
50. Orderic Vitalis, ed. Chibnall, ii, p. 318.
51. Whitelock *et al.* (eds), *Anglo-Saxon Chronicle*, p. 157; Cubbins (ed.), *Anglo-Saxon Chronicle*, p. 87: 'wreide hine sylfne, 7 bæd forgyfenysse, 7 bead gærsuman'.
52. William of Malmesbury, ed. Stubbs, ii, pp. 313–14.
53. Orderic Vitalis, ed. Chibnall, ii, p. 322; Symeon of Durham in Stevenson, p. 563, has an axe.
54. Orderic Vitalis, ed. Chibnall, ii, p. 266.
55. R.H.C. Davis, *The Normans and their Myth*, London, 1976; G. Loud, 'The *Gens Normannorum* – myth or reality', *PBA*, iv, 1981, pp. 104–16; M. Bennett, 'Stereotype Normans in Old French vernacular literature', *ANS*, ix, 1986, pp. 25–42. Searle, *Predatory Kinship*, suggests there was some reality to the ideas of a Scandinavian inheritance.

56. D.J.A. Matthew, *The Norman Conquest*, London, 1966, p. 97.
57. Williams, *The Norman Conquest*, p. 3.
58. Williams, *The Norman Conquest*, p. 85.
59. Williams, *The Norman Conquest*, pp. 3, 103.
60. E. van Houts, 'The trauma of 1066', *History Today*, 46, 1996, pp. 9–15, p. 9.
61. Williams, *The Norman Conquest*, p. 88; E.O. Blake (ed.), *Liber Eliensis*, Camden 3rd ser, xcii, London, 1962, p. 211.
62. Whitelock *et al.* (eds), *Anglo-Saxon Chronicle*, p. 145; Cubbins (ed.), *Anglo-Saxon Chronicle*, p. 81: '7 warhton castelas wide geond ¬as eode, 7 ¬earn folc swencte, 7 aððan hit yflade swiðe'.
63. Symeon of Durham in Stevenson, p. 551.
64. Orderic Vitalis, ed. Chibnall, ii, pp. 204, 220, 232.
65. Kapelle, *The Norman Conquest*, e.g. p. 233.

BIBLIOGRAPHY

PRIMARY SOURCES

Aldhelm, *Opera*, ed. R. Ehwald, *MGH Auctorum Antiquissimorum*, xv, Berlin, 1919

Aldhelm, *Prose Works*, eds M. Lapidge and M. Herren, Cambridge, 1979

Anglo-Saxon Chronicle, The, eds D. Whitelock, D.C. Douglas and S.I. Tucker, London, 1961

Anglo-Saxon Chronicle, The, in C. Plummer and J. Earle (eds), *Two of the Saxon Chronicles Parallel*, 2 vols, Oxford, 1892

Anglo-Saxon Chronicle, The, ed. G.P. Cubbin, vi, Cambridge, 1996

Asser, 'Life of King Alfred', in S. Keynes and M. Lapidge (eds), *Alfred the Great*, Harmondsworth, 1983, pp. 67–110

Battle Abbey, The Chronicle of, ed. E. Searle, Oxford, 1980

Baudri de Bourgueil, *Oeuvres Poétiques*, ed. P. Abrahams, Paris, 1926

Bayeux Tapestry, The, ed. D.M. Wilson, London, 1985

Bayeux Tapestry, The, ed. F.M. Stenton, 2nd edn, London, 1965

Bayeux Tapestry and the Norman Invasion, The, ed. L. Thorpe, London, 1973

Carmen de Hastingae Proelio, eds C. Morton and H. Muntz, Oxford, 1972

Comnena, Anna, *The Alexiad*, Harmondsworth, 1969

Dudo of St-Quentin, *De Moribus et Actibus Primorum Ducum Normanniae*, ed. J. Lair, Caen, 1865

Encomium Emmae Reginae, RHS, Camden 3rd ser., lxxii, London, 1949

English Historical Documents, ii, 1042–1189, eds D.C. Douglas and G.W. Greenaway, 2nd edn, London, 1981

Exeter Book, The, ed. I. Gollancz, 2 vols, London, 1895, 1934

Fauroux, M., ed., *Recueil des Actes des Ducs de Normandie de 911 à 1066*, Caen, 1961

Gaimar, Geoffrey, *L'Estoire des Engles*, eds T.D. Hardy and C.T. Martin, RS no. 91, 2 vols. London, 1888–9

Gaimar, Geoffrey, 'The History of the English', in Stevenson, ii, pt. II, pp. 727–809

Huntingdon, Henry of, *Historia Anglorum*, ed. D. Greenway, Oxford, 1996

Huntingdon, Henry of, *Historia Anglorum*, ed. T. Arnold, RS no. 74, London, 1965

Huntingdon, Henry of, *Chronicle*, ed. T. Forester, London, 1853

Jumièges,William of, (and Orderic Vitalis and Robert of Torigni), *Gesta Normannorum Ducum*, ed. E.M.C. van Houts, 2 vols, Oxford, 1992–5

Keynes, S., (ed.). *The Diplomas of King Aethelred 'the Unready'*, Cambridge, 1980

Lauer, P., ed., *Recueil des Actes de Charles III le Simple, roi de France, 893–923*, Paris, 1940–9

Liber Eliensis, ed. E.O. Blake, Camden 3rd ser., xcii, London, 1962

Malmesbury, William of, *De Gestis Regum Anglorum*, ed. W. Stubbs, RS no. 90, 2 vols, London, 1887–9

Malmesbury, William of, *Chronicle of the Kings of England*, ed. J.A. Giles, London, 1895

Norman Conquest, The, ed. R.A. Brown, London, 1984

Poitiers, William of, *Histoire de Guillaume le Conquérant*, ed. R. Foreville, CHF, Paris, 1952

Privat, E., (ed.). *Documents de l'Histoire de la Normandie*, Toulouse, 1972

Stevenson, J. *The Church Historians of England*, 5 vols, London, 1853–8 (a number of the chronicles in Stevenson have been reprinted separately by Llanerch Enterprises

Sturlusson, Snorri, *King Harald's Saga*, ed. M. Magnusson and H. Palsson, Harmondsworth, 1966

Symeon of Durham, *Opera*, ed. T. Arnold, 2 vols, RS no. 75, London, 1882–85

Vita Aedwardi Regis, ed. F. Barlow, 2nd edn, Oxford, 1992

Vitalis, Orderic, *The Ecclesiastical History*, ed. M. Chibnall, 6 vols, Oxford, 1968–80

Wace, *Le Roman de Rou*, ed. A.J. Holden, 3 vols, Paris, 1970–3

Wace, *Master Wace, His Chronicle of the Norman Conquest from the Roman de Rou*, ed. E. Taylor, London, 1837

Worcester, John of, *Chronicle*, eds R.R. Darlington and P. McGurk, ii, Oxford, 1995

SECONDARY SOURCES

Aird, W.M. 'St Cuthbert, the Scots and the Normans', *ANS*, xvi, 1993, pp. 1–20

Abels, R.P. *Lordship and Military Obligation in Anglo-Saxon England*, London, 1988

Bachrach, B. 'Some observations on the military administration of the Norman Conquest', *ANS*, viii, 1985, pp. 1–25

——. 'The feigned retreat at Hastings', *Medieval Studies*, xxxiii, 1971, pp. 344–7

Bibliography

Baring, F.H. *Domesday Tables for the Counties of Surrey, Berkshire, Middlesex, Hertford, Buckingham and Bedford and the New Forest*, London, 1909

——. 'The Conqueror's footprints in Domesday', *EHR*, xii, 1898, pp. 17–25

Barlow, F. *Edward the Confessor*, London, 1970

——. *The Feudal Kingdom of England, 1042–1216*, London, 1955

Bates, D. *Normandy Before the Norman Conquest*, Harlow, 1982

——. 'The rise and fall of Normandy, *c.* 911–1204', in D. Bates and A. Curry (eds), *England and Normandy in the Middle Ages*, London, 1994, pp. 19–35

——. *William the Conqueror*, London, 1983

Beeler, J. *Warfare in England, 1066–1189*, New York, 1966

Bennett, M. 'Norman naval activity in the Mediterranean *c.* 1060–*c.* 1108', *ANS*, xv, 1992, pp. 41–58

——. 'Poetry as history? the *Roman de Rou* of Wace as a source for the Norman Conquest', *ANS*, v, 1982, pp. 21–39

——. 'Stereotype Normans in Old French vernacular literature', *ANS*, ix, 1986, pp. 25–42

——. 'Wace and warfare', *ANS*, xi, 1988, pp. 37–58

Beresford, G. 'Goltho Manor, Lincolnshire: the buildings and their surrounding defences *c.* 850–1150', *ANS*, iv, 1981, pp. 13–36

Bernstein, D.J. 'The blinding of Harold and the meaning of the Bayeux Tapestry', *ANS*, v, 1982, pp. 40–64

——. *The Mystery of the Bayeux Tapestry*, London, 1986

Bradbury, J. 'An introduction to the Buckinghamshire Domesday', in A. Williams and R.W.H. Erskine (eds), *The Buckinghamshire Domesday*, London, 1988

——. 'Battles in England and Normandy, 1066–1154', *ANS*, vi, 1983, pp. 1–12

——. *The Medieval Archer*, Woodbridge, 1985

Brooks, F.W. *The Battle of Stamford Bridge*, East Yorkshire Local History Society series, no. 6, 1963

Brooks, N.P., and Walker, H.E. 'The authority and interpretation of the Bayeux Tapestry', *ANS*, i, 1978, pp. 1–34

Brown, E.A.R. 'The tyranny of a construct: feudalism and historians', *American Historical Review*, lxxix, 1974, pp. 1,063–88

Brown, R.A. 'The battle of Hastings', *ANS*, iii, 1980, pp. 1–21

——. *The Normans and the Norman Conquest*, 2nd edn, Woodbridge, 1985

Burne, A.H. *More Battlefields of England*, London, 1952

Butler, D. *1066, the Story of a Year*, London, 1966

Campbell, J., (ed.). *The Anglo-Saxons*, London, 1982

Campbell, M.W. 'Aelfgyva: the mysterious lady of the Bayeux Tapestry', *Annales de Normandie*, xxxiv, 1984, pp. 127–45

Chevallier, C.T. 'Where was the Malfosse? the end of the battle of Hastings', *SAC*, 101, 1963, pp. 1–13

Chibnall, M. *The World of Orderic Vitalis*, Oxford, 1984

Cutler, K.E. 'Edith, queen of England, 1045–66', *Mediaeval Studies*, xxxv, 1973, pp. 222–31

Davies, A.M. 'Eleventh century Buckinghamshire', *Records of Buckinghamshire*, x, 1916, pp. 69–74

Davis, R.H.C. 'The Carmen de Hastingae Proelio', *EHR*, xciii, 1978, pp. 241–61

——. *The Normans and their Myth*, London, 1976

Delbrück, H. *History of the Art of War*, iii, trans. W.J. Renfroe Jr., Westport Connecticut, 1982

Douglas, D.C. 'Companions of the Conqueror', *History*, xxviii, 1943, pp. 129–47

——. *The Norman Achievement, 1050–1100*, London, 1969

——. 'The rise of Normandy', *PBA*, xxxiii, 1947

——. *Time and the Hour*, London, 1977

——. *William the Conqueror*, London, 1964

Finn, R.W. *The Norman Conquest and its Effects upon the Economy*, London, 1971

Fowler, G.H. 'The devastation of Bedfordshire and the neighbouring counties in 1065 and 1066', *Archaeologia*, lxxii, 1922, pp. 41–51

Freeman, E.A. *The History of the Norman Conquest in England*, 6 vols, Oxford, 1867–79

——. *William the Conqueror*, London, 1888

Gillingham, J. 'William the Bastard at war', *RAB*, pp. 141–58

Gillmor, C.M. 'The naval logistics of the cross-Channel operation, 1066', *ANS*, vii, 1984, pp. 105–31

Glover, R. 'English warfare in 1066', *EHR*, xvii, 1952, pp. 1–18

Grainge, C.and G. 'The Pevensey expedition: brilliantly executed plan or near disaster?', *Mariner's Mirror*, 1993, pp. 261–73

Gransden, A. *Historical Writing in England c. 550 to c. 1307*, London, 1974

Higham, N. *The Kingdom of Northumbria, AD 350–1100*, Stroud, 1993

Hollister, C.W. *Anglo-Saxon Military Institutions on the Eve of the Norman Conquest*, Oxford, 1962

——. *The Military Organisation of Norman England*, Oxford, 1965

Hooper, N. 'Edgar the Aetheling: Anglo-Saxon prince, rebel and crusader', *Anglo-Saxon England*, xiv, 1985, pp. 197–214

——. 'Some observations on the navy in late Anglo-Saxon England', *RAB*, pp. 203–13

——. 'The housecarls in England in the eleventh century', *ANS*, vii, 1985, pp. 161–76

Bibliography

Houts, E.M.C. van. 'The trauma of 1066', *History Today*, 46, 1996, pp. 9–15

Howarth, D. *The Year of the Conquest*, London, 1977

Howorth, H.H. 'A criticism of the life of Rollo as told by Dudo of St-Quentin', *Archaeologia*, xlv, 1880, pp. 235–50

James, E. *The Origins of France*, London, 1982

Jones, G. *A History of the Vikings*, London, 1968

Kapelle, W.E. *The Norman Conquest of the North*, London, 1979

Kiff, J. 'Images of war: illustrations of warfare in early eleventh-century England', *ANS*, vii, 1984, pp. 177–94

Lawson, M.K. *Cnut*, Harlow, 1993

Lemmon, C.H. 'The campaign of 1066', in *The Norman Conquest its Setting and Impact*, London, 1966

Le Patourel, J. *The Norman Empire*, Oxford, 1976

Lloyd, A. *The Year of the Conqueror*, London, 1966

Loud, G. 'The Gens Normannorum – myth or reality', *PBA*, iv, 1981, pp. 104–16

Loyn, H.R. *Anglo-Saxon England and the Norman Conquest*, London, 1962

——. *The Governance of Anglo-Saxon England, 500–1087*, London, 1984

——. *The Making of the English Nation, from the Anglo-Saxons to Edward I*, London, 1991

——. *The Norman Conquest*, 3rd edn, London, 1982

Matthew, D.J.A. *The Norman Conquest*, London, 1966

McKitterick, R. *The Frankish Kingdoms under the Carolingians, 751–987*, Harlow, 1983

McNulty, J.B. 'The Lady Aelfgyva in the Bayeux Tapestry', *Speculum*, lv, 1980, pp. 659–68

Morillo, S., (ed.). *The Battle of Hastings, Sources and Interpretations*, Woodbridge, 1996

——. *Warfare under the Anglo-Norman Kings, 1066–1135*, Woodbridge, 1994

Nelson, J. 'The rites of the Conqueror', *ANS*, 1981

Nicholas, D. *Medieval Flanders*, Harlow, 1992

Palmer, J.J.N. 'The Conqueror's footprints in Domesday Book' in A. Ayton and T.L. Price (eds), *The Medieval Military Revolution*, London, 1995, pp. 23–44

Partner, N.F. *Serious Entertainments*, Chicago, 1977

Peirce, I. 'Arms, armour and warfare in the eleventh century', *ANS*, x, 1987, pp. 237–57

——. 'The development of the medieval sword c. 850–1300', *IPMK*, iii, 1988, pp. 139–58

——. 'The knight, his arms and armour in the eleventh and twelfth centuries', *IPMK*, i, 1986, pp. 152–64

Pollington, S. *The English Warrior from Earliest Times to 1066*, Hockwold-cum-Wilton, 1996

Reynolds, S. *Fiefs and Vassals*, Oxford, 1994

Round, J.H. *Feudal England*, London, 1895, reset reprint, 1964

Rumble, A., (ed.). *The Reign of Cnut*, London, 1994

Sawyer, P.H. *From Roman Britain to Norman England*, London, 1978

———. *The Age of the Vikings*, 2nd edn, London, 1971

Searle, E. *Predatory Kinship and the Creation of Norman Power, 840–1066*, Berkeley Ca, 1988

Seymour, W. *Battles in Britain*, i, London, 1975

Stenton, D.M. *William the Conqueror*, London, 1927

Stenton, F.M. *Anglo-Saxon England*, 2nd edn, Oxford, 1947

Strickland, M., (ed.). *Anglo-Norman Warfare*, Woodbridge, 1992

Swanton, M. *The Lives of the Last Englishmen*, x, ser. B, New York, 1984

Tetlow, E. *The Enigma of Hastings*, London, 1974

Thompson, K., 'Family and influence to the south of Normandy in the eleventh century: the lordship of Bellême', *JMH*, xi, 1985, pp. 215–26

———. 'The Norman aristocracy before 1066: the example of the Montgomerys', *Historical Research*, lx, 1987, pp. 251–63

Warner, P. *British Battle Fields, the North*, London, 1975

Williams, A. 'Land and power in the eleventh century: the estates of Harold Godwineson', *ANS*, iii, 1981

———. *The English and the Norman Conquest*, Woodbridge, 1995

Wright, P.P. *Hastings*, Moreton-in-Marsh, 1996

Yver, J. 'Les châteaux forts en Normandie jusqu'au milieu du XIIe siècle', *Bulletin de la Société des Antiquaires de Normandie*, liii, 1955–6, pp. 28–115

INDEX

m = map: t = family tree

Aberlemno stone 68
Adela, daughter of Fulk III 52t
Adela, daughter of Robert I, The Frisian 53t
Adela, daughter of Robert the Pious 44t
Adelaide, daughter of Robert I 35t
Adelaide of Poitou 44t
Aelfgar, son of Leofric 27
Aelfgifu of Northampton 13t, 14, 16, 89t
Aelfgifu of Northumbria 5, 11, 89t
Aelfgyva 55
Aelfheah, Archbishop of Canterbury 4
Aelfhere 6
Aelric 25
Aescferth 78
Aethelred II (978–1016) 5, 7–9, 10–11, 12, 13, 34, 35t, 76, 88, 89t, 106
Aethelstan, King (925–39) 5t, 6, 72
Aethelwold 6
Aethelwulf 4
Agatha, wife of Edward the Exile 13
Aldhelm 78
Alençon 86, 106
Alexander II, pope 108
Alfred, son of Aethelred II (d. 1036) 5t, 11, 13, 17, 21, 26, 34, 89t
Alfred the Great (871–99) 3, 4–6
Alice, daughter of Richard II of Normandy 35t
Angevin Empire 180m, 181
Anglo-Saxon Chronicle 7, 78, 95, 113, 120, 172
    Aethelred 9, 10, 12
    Edward the Confessor 24, 91, 93
    Stamford Bridge 78, 102
    Battle of Hastings 132, 138
    William takes the crown 159, 162
Anjou 33m, 50, 51, 52
Anjou, Counts of 52t

Anna Comnena 70, 71
archers 62, 69, 70, 142
    English 77–9, 128–9
    Norman 77, 79–80, 140, 149, 151
    see also arms
armies 60–2, 71–87
    see also English Army; military tactics; Norman Army
armour 63, 156
    hauberks 63–4, 69, 138, 145
    helmets 63, 69, 145
    shields 65–6
    spurs 71
    see also cavalry; infantry
arms 60–71, 79
    axes 67, 68–9, 142, 143
    crossbows 80–1, 140
    lances 68, 70
    spears 67–8
    swords 67, 70, 143
    see also archers; cavalry; infantry
Arnulf III (1070–1) 53t
Arques 86
Asmund, nephew of Hardrada 98
Assandun, battle of 12

Baldwin II, count of Hainault 53t
Baldwin IV (988–1035), count of Flanders 53t
Baldwin V (1035–67), count of Flanders 25, 27, 53t, 58, 95–6
Baldwin VI (1067–70), count of Flanders 53t
Baring, F H 161
Battle Abbey 130m, 131, 195
    Chronicle of Battle Abbey 119–20, 129–31, 153
Battle Hill 133, 134–5, 139m, 142, 153
Baudri de Bourgueil 165

Bayeux 87
Bayeux Cathedral 114, 117
Bayeux Tapestry 1, 82, 87, 120, 114–5, 165
  arms and armour 60, 62, 64–5, 66, 67, 68, 70, 77, 80, 81, 149
  Harold's time in Normandy 54–5, 56
  death of Edward and coronation of Harold 91, 92, 93
  William's preparations 76, 106
  William waiting for Harold's arrival 123–4, 125
  Battle of Hastings 134, 140–2, 143, 145, 150–2
  events after the battle 156
Beatrice, daughter of Hugh Capet 44t
Beaumont, Roger de 51
Beaumont family 83
Beaurain 87
Bede 73
Beeler, J 159–60
Benedict X, pope (1058–9) 93
Benoît, A 115
Beorn, son of Harold Fairhair 24–5, 99t
Bernard the Philosopher 79–80
Blackhorse Hill 138, 139m
Blois 33m
Bonneville-sur-Touques 55
Bosham 81
Brentford 12
Breton Campaign 52, 54–5, 124
Bretons 85, 144
Brian, Count 169, 170
Brionne 86–7
Brittany 33m, 38, 39, 41, 51, 52, 54–5, 76, 87
Brown, Allen 129, 142–3
Brunanburgh, battle of (937) 6
burghal system 6
Burgundy 38m
Byrhtnoth, Ealdorman 6, 9, 68, 82
Byzantine Varangian Guard 84

Caen 59
Caen Abbey 163
Caldbec Hill 132–5, 139m, 153, 154
Cambridge 176
Canterbury 158, 159
Capetian Kings of France 37, 44t
Caradoc 28
Carmen de Hastingae Proelio 115–6, 120,

132–3, 138, 140, 147, 148, 150, 187
Carolingian Empire 37–8, 39m, 83
castles 85–6
cavalry 62
  arms and armour 64, 65–6, 68, 69–71
  English 81, 82
  Norman 69–70, 77, 81
Charles III of West Francia (898–922) (Charles the Simple) 38–42
Chartres, battle of 39
Chester 7
Christianity 4, 15, 42, 45
  Christian Church 73, 177
Christina, daughter of Edward the Exile 89t
Civitate, battle of (1053) 85
Cnut the Great, king of Denmark (1016–35) 4, 9, 11, 12–16, 34, 35t, 61, 81, 89t, 94, 98, 99t
  empire of 14m, 14–15
  family of 13t
coinage 7, 16
Conan II, count of Brittany 55
Conrad II, German Emperor 15
conroys 85
Copsi, Earl 96, 166
Corfe 7
Cotton, Sir John 112
Coutances 43
Coutances, Bishop of 162
Crispin, Robert 57

danegeld 10
Danes 3, 6, 10, 167, 168
Davies, A M 161
Davis, R H C 116–7, 150, 173
Dee, River 7
Delyan, Peter 97
Denmark 16, 20
Denmark, kings of 99t
Dinan 87
Dives 165
Dol 87
Domesday Book 61, 73, 81, 133, 160–1, 175, 178
Domfront 86
Dover 26, 56, 86, 157–8, 159, 165, 127m
  Dover Castle 158, 164

Index

Dreux, battle of (1014) 63
Drogo, count of Mantes 88–9, 89t
Dudo of St Quentin 34, 40, 112, 185
Dunnere, ceorl 68
Dunstan, Archbishop of Canterbury 7
Durham 168

Eadgifu, abbess of Leominster 24
Eadred (946–55), son of Edward the
    Elder 5tr
Eadred, Archbishop of York 93, 159,
    162
Eadred, Bishop of Worcester 25
Eadric Streona of Mercia 11, 12, 15
Eadwig (955–9) 5
earldoms, system of 15
Easige, Archbishop of Canterbury 25
East Anglia 3–4, 6, 15, 22m, 27, 170
Edgar (959–75), father of Aethelred II
    5t, 7
Edgar the Aetheling (d.1125) 5t, 54,
    89–90, 89t, 92, 93–4, 155,
    158, 159, 164, 167, 169
Edington, battle of (878) 4
Edith, wife of Edward the Confessor 18,
    27, 23–4, 30, 57, 89t, 90, 91
Edith, wife of Harold, formerly wife of
    Gruffydd 94
Edith-Matilda, wife of Henry I 89t
Edith Swanneck 95, 156
Edmund (939–46) 5t, 6
Edmund, son of Edmund Ironside 13,
    89t,
Edmund, son of Harold 169
Edmund Ironside (1016) 5t, 12, 14, 16,
    28, 88, 89t
Edward I (1239–1307) 178
Edward the Confessor (1042–66) 5t, 11,
    13, 17, 18–19, 34, 76, 81,
    84
    genealogy 35t, 89t
    reign of 20–31
    death 31, 90–2
    succession 30–1, 52–4, 56–7,
        88–90, 105, 106
Edward the Exile (d.1057) 6, 13, 28, 31,
    56, 88, 89, 91
    genealogy 5t, 89t
Edward the Martyr (975–9) 5t, 7
Edwin, earl of Mercia 94, 96, 100–1,
    155, 158, 159, 164, 170
Einar, spokesman 98

Eleanor, daughter of Richard II of
    Normandy 35t
Elizabeth, wife of Harold Hardrada 98
Ely 170, 171m
Emma, daughter of Hugh the Great 45
Emma of Normandy, wife of Aethelred
    II and Cnut (d. 1052) 5, 11,
    13, 14, 16, 17–19, 24, 34,
    35t, 57, 89t
Engenulf de Laigle 153
England 2, 173–6
English army 60–2, 71–2, 74, 75, 81,
    125, 126
    cavalry 81, 82–4, 103, 138–40,
        174, 187
    defeat 151–2
    infantry 65, 67, 138–40, 174
    naval fleet 71, 76–7, 109, 137
Eric, earl of Northumbria 12, 15
Eric Bloodaxe 7
Ermengarde, daughter of Fulk III 52t
Essex 6
Estrith, daughter of Cnut 98
Estrith, sister of Cnut 13, 99t
Eustace II, count of Boulogne 25–6, 116,
    145, 150, 154, 165, 176
Exeter 167, 169, 176
Exeter Book 78
Eystein Orri 103

Falaise 48
Fécamp 34, 164
feudalism 174
fiefdoms 73
Flanders 2–3, 25, 33m, 41, 58, 76
Flanders, counts of 53t
Flodoard 42
Florence of Worcester *see* John of
    Worcester
Forest of Dean 79
France 2
Francia 37, 38m
Franco, Archbishop 40–1
Frank's Casket 78
French Revolution 115
Fulk III Nerra of Anjou (987–1040) 52t
Fulk IV le Réchin of Anjou
    (1067–1109) 52, 52t, 85

Gaimar 101
Gate Fulford, battle of (1066) 79, 101,
    127m

Geoffrey, Count Gâtinais 52t
Geoffrey III Martel of Anjou (1040–60) 51, 52, 52t
Geoffrey IV the bearded of Anjou (1060–7 d.1096) 52, 52t
Geoffrey de Mayenne 52
Gerald of Wales 79
Gertrude, daughter of Robert I, The Frisian 53t
Giffard, Walter 85, 116, 150
Gilbert de Brionne 49
Gisela, daughter of Hugh Capet 44t
Gisela (Popa), daughter of Charles III 41, 42, 186
Godgifu, wife of Drogo 21, 26, 88, 89t
Godwin, Earl of Wessex (d.1053) 15, 17, 18, 18t, 21, 23, 24, 25, 26–7, 181
Godwin, son of Harold 169
Godwin family 18t, 22m, 23, 24, 27–8, 54
Goltho, Lincolnshire 85
Gospatric, Earl 167
Gruffydd 28, 94
Guiscard, Robert 71
Gunnhild, daughter of Cnut 13t
Gunnhild, daugher of Godwin 18t
Gunnor, wife of Richard I of Normandy 44–5
Guthorm, nephew of Hardrada 98
Guthroth, father of Harold II, king of Norway 99t
Guy, Bishop of Amiens 116, 117
Guy de Brionne 49
Guy of Ponthieu, Count 25, 50–1, 54
Gwent 79
Gyrth, brother of Harold II 18, 22m, 66, 148
Gytha 18, 23, 156, 167, 169

Hadwise, offspring of Robert the Pious 44t
Hakon, Earl 54, 56, 98, 106
Hale-Bopp comet 1
Halley's comet 1–2, 95
Harald, son of Sweyn Forkbeard 11–12
Harold, Viking leader 44
Harold I, Harefoot (1035–40) 13, 16, 17–18, 89t
Harold II, king of Denmark (1014–18) 99t

Harold II, king of England (Harold Godwinson) 1–2, 22m, 25, 26, 27, 81, 85, 96
    arms and standards 66, 135, 163
    genealogy 18t, 89t
    military ability 76, 104, 121, 126, 127, 136–7
    relationship with Edward the Confessor 28–30
    visit to and imprisonment in Normandy 31, 52–6, 87, 91
    succession 88, 90, 91, 92–3, 107
    marriage 94–5
    Stamford Bridge, Battle of 100–4
    march to Hastings from Stamford Bridge 82, 129
    Hastings, Battle of 121–54, 130m
    death of 80, 116, 148–51, 156, 198
Harold II, king of Norway (963–78) 99t
Harold III, king of Norway see Harold Hardrada
Harold Bluetooth, king of Denmark (936–83) 99t
Harold Fairhair, King of Norway (900–33) 39, 99t
Harold Godwinson see Harold II
Harold Hardrada, King of Norway (1047–66) (Harold Sigurdsson, Harold III) 21, 88, 92, 94, 95, 96–100, 99t
Harthacnut (1040–2) 13, 16–17, 18–19, 77, 89t
Hastings 122, 123
    Hastings castle 87
Hastings, Battle of (1066) 77, 79, 80, 110–1, 121–54
    Malfosse incident 120, 133, 134, 141m, 152–4
    maps 127m, 130m, 139m, 141m
    site 129–34
Hedgland 120
Henry I, king of England (1100–35) 89t, 178, 180, 179t
Henry I, king of France (1031–60) 44t, 48, 49–50, 51, 52
Henry II, king of England (1154–89) 117, 178, 179t, 180m, 181
Henry II, German Emperor 13
Henry III, German Emperor 31
Henry III, Holy Roman Emperor 13t
Henry of Huntingdon 119, 120

Index

Hereford 86
Hereford, battle of (1055) 82
Hereward the Wake 170–1
Herlève 35t, 48, 51
Herluin de Conteville 35t
hidage assessment 73–4, 76
Hildegarde, daughter of Ermengarde 52t
Hugh, heir of Ponthieu 116, 150
Hugh, son of Henry I of France 44t
Hugh, son of Robert the Pious 44t
Hugh Capet (987–96), King of France 44t, 45
Hugh de Montfort 165
Hugh of Maine 63
Hugh the Great 45
Humphrey de Tilleul 157

industrial development 16
infantry
  arms and armour 64, 65–6
  English 65, 67, 138–40, 174
  Norman 140, 144, 151
Ireland 2, 6, 15
Isle of Man 15
Isle of Wight 77, 95
Italy 57
Ivry 87
Ivry, count of 45

Jaroslav, King 98
John, King of England 181
John of Worcester 77, 84, 92, 94, 95, 101, 113–4, 125, 136, 138
Judith, first wife of Richard II of Normandy 35t, 45, 47
Judith, wife of Tostig 27
Judith, wife of Waltheof 171, 172
Jumièges 43, 165

Karli, sons of 167
knighting ceremony 84, 106

Lanfranc, Archbishop of Canterbury 177
Leo IX, Pope (1048–54) 58
Leofric, earl of Mercia 15, 21, 24, 26, 27, 95
Leofwin Godwinson 18t, 22m, 26, 69, 148
Liégarde, wife of William Longsword 43

Lincoln, battle of 69
Lisois de Moutiers 168
London 11, 12, 16, 158–9
Lothar 45
Louis IV, King of France (936–54) 43, 44

Macbeth 96
Magnus, son of Harold 169
Magnus I, king of Norway (1035–47), king of Denmark (1042–7) (Magnus the Good) 18, 20–1, 99t
Magnus II, king of Norway (1066–9) 99t
Maine 51, 52, 76
Malcolm III Canmore, king of Scotland 28, 89t, 96, 169
Maldon, battle of (991) 9, 61, 68, 72, 78, 82
Malet, William 156, 168
Malfosse incident see Hastings, Battle of
Margaret, wife of Malcolm III 28, 89t, 167
Matilda, wife of William the Conqueror (d. 1083) 53t, 58, 108, 165, 179t
Matilda, Empress 179t, 181
Mauger, Archbishop of Rouen (d.1054) 35t, 47, 50
Mercia 3–4, 6–7, 11, 12, 15, 17, 22m, 28, 167
Messina, battle of (1060) 85
Michael IV the Paphlagonian, Emperor (1034–41) 97
Michael V, Emperor (1041–2) 97
military tactics 136–7, 149
  feigned flight 85, 146–7
  shield-wall 81–2, 135–6, 142, 148, 151, 196
Monfaucon 115
Monte Maggiore, battle of (1041) 84–5
Montgomery, Roger 51, 171–2
Montgomery family 46–7, 83
Mont–St–Michel 45
Morcar, Earl 29, 94, 95, 96, 100–1, 155, 158, 159, 164, 170–1
Mortemer, battle of 50–1
Muriel, daughter of Robert I 35t

Nissa, battle of (1062) 98
Norman Army 61–2, 71–2, 159–62

arms 80–1
cavalry 82–3, 84–5, 138, 147, 151
infantry 140, 144, 151
navy 76–7, 105–6
tactics 146–7
Norman settlement in England 173
Normandy 2–3, 13, 21, 32–42, 33m, 43, 47, 105–6, 180, 181
Normandy, Dukes of 35t
Northamptonshire 171
Northern England 180
Northern rising (1069) 167–9, 176
Northumberland 12
Northumbria 3–4, 7, 12, 15, 17, 22m, 29–30, 96
Norway 15, 16
Norway, kings of 99t

Odin 67
Odo, Bishop of Bayeux (d.1097), later Earl of Kent 35t, 51, 55, 82, 87, 114, 115, 123–4, 145, 164, 165, 172
Offa 3–4
Olaf, son of Harold Fairhair 99t
Olaf I Tryggvasson, king of Norway (995–1000) 9, 99t
Olaf III, king of Norway (1969–93) 99t, 104
Olaf, St (1016–28) 97, 98, 99t
Orderdic Vitalis 112, 113, 116, 118–9, 120, 166
    Battle of Stanford Bridge 104
    Battle of Hastings 105, 126, 133, 137, 140
    Malfosse incident 152–3, 154
    William's succession 159, 162
    Harold's burial 156
    after Battle of Hastings 157, 158, 164, 171, 172
    harrying of the north 168, 176
Orkney 95–6
Osbern, steward 49
Osbert of Clare 92
Oswulf 166

Papia, second wife of Richard II of Normandy 35t, 47, 186
Peace of God 58
Peirce, Ian 65, 142–3
Pentecost's Castle 86
Pertz, G H 116

Pevensey 87, 109, 121, 122–3, 127m
Philip I, king of France (1060–1108) 44t, 52
Picot, sheriff 176
Popa see Gisela, daughter of Charles III; Papia
Portskewet 28
Pucklechurch, Gloucs 6
Pyke House 134, 142, 143

Ralph de Valois 164–5
Ralph the Breton 171–2
Ralph the Timid, Earl of Hereford (d.1057), formerly Ralph of Mantes 23, 25, 26, 27, 82, 84, 88, 89t
Rennes 87
Richard I, duke of Normandy (942–96) 11, 34, 35t, 44–5
Richard II, duke of Normandy (996–1026) 11, 13, 34, 35t, 45, 46, 47, 80
Richard III, duke of Normandy (1026–7) 32, 35t, 47
Richard of Aversa 85
Richer of Reims 45–6
Robert, count of Mortain (d.1095) 35t, 51, 170
Robert, son of Robert the Pious 44t
Robert I, duke of Normandy (1027–35) 13–14, 17, 32, 35t, 47–8, 51
Robert I, The Frisian, count of Flanders (1071–93) 53t
Robert II, count of Flanders (1093–1111) 53t
Robert Curthose, duke of Normandy (1087–1106, d 1135) 173, 179t
Robert de Beaumont 171
Robert de Commines 168
Robert de Grandmesnil 82
Robert fitz Richard 168
Robert fitz Wimarc 90, 137
Robert of Jumièges 21, 25, 26, 27
Robert of Montgomery 118
Robert of Torigny 113
Robert the Pious (996–1031), King of France 44t
Robert the Strong, duke of France 40–1
Robert's Castle 86
Roger fitz Roger de Beaumont 146

Index

Rollo/Rolf of Normandy 34, 36m, 37, 38–43, 117, 185
Romney 157, 159
Rouen 39, 41, 42, 43, 87, 164
Round, J H 135–6

Saint Olaf's Saga 97
Scandinavian invasion 2, 3, 6, 9
    see also Vikings, Danes
Scandinavian settlement and integration 34, 46
Scotland 2, 7, 15, 167, 169
Senlac 133
Sherston, battle of (1016) 68, 81
Sherwood Forest 79
Sicily 57, 83, 85, 106
Sihtric, Norse King of York 6, 44
Siward, earl of Northumbria 15, 21, 24, 26, 28, 96, 164
Snorri Sturlusson 78, 83–4, 95, 96–8, 100
St-Aubin-sur-Scie, battle of (1053) 50, 85
St Brice's Day slaughter (1002) 10
St-Clair-Sur-Epte 40–1
St-James-de-Beuvron 87
St-Valery 108, 127m
Stamford Bridge, battle of (1066) 69, 78, 79, 83–4, 100–4, 102m, 125–6, 127m
Stephen, King of England (1135–54) 68–9, 178, 179t
Stephen Harding Bible 66
Stigand, Archbishop of Canterbury 24, 27, 90, 93, 158, 162, 164, 177
Stiklesdad, battle of (1030) 97
Styrkar, Hardrada's marshall 104
Sweden 15
Sweyn, King of Norway (d.1036) 13t, 16, 17
Sweyn II Erithsson, king of Denmark (1047–74) 20, 30, 93–4, 98, 99t, 100, 104, 167
Sweyn Forkbeard, king of Denmark (983–1014) 4, 9, 11, 12, 99t
Sweyn Godwinson 18, 22m, 24–5, 26, 27–8
Symeon of Durham 168

Taillefer 116
Telham Hill 120, 138, 139m

Tettenhall, battle of (910) 6
Thora, second wife of Harold Hardrada 98
Thorberg Arnason 98
Thorfinn, sons of 100
Thorkell the Tall, earl of East Anglia 11, 12, 15, 16
Tosny, Roger de 57
Tostig, son of Godwin 18, 22m, 27, 28, 29–30, 81, 94, 95–6, 100, 101, 104, 166
Towcester 85
tributes 9–10
Trondheim Church 4
Trygvi, father of Olaf I, king of Norway 99t
Turold 49

Uhtred, earl of Northumbria 12, 15
Ulf, Earl 95, 98
Ulfketel 15

Val-ès-Dunes, battle of (1047) 49, 83
Varaville, battle of (1057) 51, 80, 85
Vienna, Museum of Armour 63
Vikings 3–4, 6, 36, 63, 66–7, 82–3
Vita Aedwardi 20, 23, 24, 25, 26, 29, 30, 91, 92, 93

Wace 117–8, 120
    Val-ès-Dunes, battle of (1047) 49, 51, 68, 83, 85, 91, 125
    Willam's preparations for invasion 105, 106, 107, 108
    Battle of Hastings 135–6, 137, 140, 144, 146, 151
Wales 2, 4, 28, 79, 169
Wallingford 61, 158, 160
Waltham Abbey 95, 156
Waltheof, Earl 164, 167, 171, 172
Warenne, William de 51
Warenne family 83
Wedmore, peace treaty 4
Wessex 3, 4–6, 12, 15, 22m, 28
Wessex, kings of 5t
Westminster Abbey 90, 92, 93, 162
William, count of Arques (d.1053) 35t, 47, 50
William, son of Richard II of Normandy 35t
William I, duke of Normandy (William Longsword) (c.924–42) 36m, 43–4

William I, king of England (The
        Conqueror) (1035–87) 29,
        32, 64, 65, 76, 100, 164
    genealogy 35t, 37, 179t
    claim to English throne 30, 34–6,
        57, 88, 92, 106
    life before the invasion 21, 48–59,
        106
    marriage 58–9, 104
    knighting ceremony 84, 106
    Harold's visit to Normany and
        imprisonment 31, 52–6, 87,
        91
    Breton campaign 55, 124
    preparations for war 75, 76
    invasion 104–6, 107–9, 121
    Battle of Hastings 122–5, 130m,
        137–8, 140, 144, 145, 149,
        150, 154
    death of Harold 116–7, 150
    Hastings to London 155–61
    coronation 162–3
    rewarding of followers 163–4
    return to Normandy 164–5
    rebellions and uprisings 165–73
William II Rufus, king of England
        (1087–1100) 178, 179t
William fitz Osbern 51, 64, 165, 168,
        170
William of Jumièges 55, 79–80, 112–3,
        119, 120, 129, 137, 140,
        148–9, 152–3, 166, 169

William of Malmesbury 118, 120, 135,
        137, 138, 150
William of Poitiers 36, 64, 112, 120
    Normandy, history of 49, 50
    William's earlier life 104, 106, 108
    Harold 1–2, 53, 55, 91, 93, 107,
        156
    Battle of Hastings, start of battle
        124, 132, 137–8, 140, 142,
        143
    Battle of Hastings, second phase
        144, 145, 146–7, 148, 149,
        151, 152
    Malfosse incident 152, 154
    William's victory and coronation
        155, 156, 159, 162
    after the battle 157, 158, 163–4,
        165, 166
William of Volpiano 46
Winchester 16, 18, 25
Worcester 18
Wulfnoth of Sussex 11, 15
Wulfnoth, son of Godwin 18t, 54, 56,
        106
Wulfstan 10

York 6, 7, 12, 101, 103, 127m, 167,
        168
Yorkshire 12

Zoë, Empress 97–8